#1 *New York Times* Bestselling Author

MARK DRISCOLL

A CALL TO
RESURGENCE

WILL CHRISTIANITY HAVE A FUNERAL OR A FUTURE?

Tyndale House Publishers, Inc.
Carol Stream, Illinois

Praise for
A Call to Resurgence

Mark Driscoll and I minister in very different contexts. He is in the extremely secular Northwest, and I pastor a church in Dallas, Texas. Though we have different obstacles and challenges we face due to the contexts we minister to, we have in common the deep hope that the gospel of Jesus Christ boldly proclaimed from the Scriptures will transform lives and bring a church to life. This book is about hope. Despite all the naysayers about the future of the church in North America, I agree with Driscoll and this book that there is a real opportunity here to see the Church of Jesus Christ grow and make an impact in a growing hostile and secularized society. If you are fearful of the growing antagonism of the world and the marginalization of the church, then let this book encourage you.

MATT CHANDLER
Lead pastor of The Village Church, president of the Acts 29 church-planting network, and author of *The Explicit Gospel, Creature of the Word,* and *To Live is Christ, To Die is Gain*

This book is dedicated to the young men and women—who may be totally lost or may be new Christians—who will be filled with the Holy Spirit and raised up by God to lead a new movement of gospel-centered, missional ministry. I'm praying for you and excited to see who you are. May you labor to the glory of God and not merely the good of your tribe. While you are young, go ahead, take a risk, and make a difference.

If you love Jesus, do something. If you are not ready to do something, get ready and then do something. If you do something and God does not bless it, then do something else. Whatever you do, do it under the authority of a Bible-believing, Jesus-loving local church. Give your life to what Jesus gave his life for—the church.

Visit Tyndale online at www.tyndale.com.

A Call to Resurgence: Will Christianity Have a Funeral or a Future?

Designed by Jacqueline L. Nuñez

Published in association with Yates & Yates, LLP (www.yates2.com).

ISBN 978-1-4143-8362-0

ISBN 978-1-4143-8948-6 (International Trade Paper Edition)

Printed in the United States of America

19 18 17 16 15 14 13
7   6   5   4   3   2   1

TABLE OF CONTENTS

ACKNOWLEDGMENTS

I want to thank Dr. Justin Holcomb and the team at Docent Research Group for their help on parts of this project. I especially want to thank Pastor Dave, Pastor Sutton, and the people of Mars Hill Church, whom I love with a father's affection. Thank you for the honor it is to teach the Bible and lead the mission at our church.

Chapter 1

CHRISTENDOM IS DEAD
WELCOME TO THE UNITED STATES OF SEATTLE

I HAVE SPENT THE LAST twenty years of my life ministering in one of the least churched and most liberal cities in America.

In many ways, Seattle is not just post-Christian; it's pre-Christian. We never had a Christian heyday. The Puritans landed on the other side of the nation. The Great Awakenings did not touch my hibernating hometown. The evangelical church-planting movements, the denominations, the publishing companies, and the theological institutions spread to the South and Midwest but never to the Great North Left. The county I live in voted enthusiastically for gay marriage and marijuana, which means I can now smoke a joint while marrying a dude. The Netherlands decriminalized marijuana;

Jamaica overlooks it; we legalized it, so I guess we're to the left of Amsterdam and Kingston, if you can believe it.

When I first planted Mars Hill Church out of a college ministry in Seattle in 1996, we were a small group of broke, newly converted, single indie rockers trying to reach a city that was home to more dogs and cats than children or evangelicals. Today a growing majority in the United States, Canada, and Europe—especially young people and urbanites—think and act pretty much the same as the people I've been trying to reach. In the providence of God, I was granted, along with other ministers in cities like mine, the great honor to plow new ground and scatter gospel seed early—with all the birds, rocks, and thorns that Jesus promised.*

Of course, the rest of the country and the world are not destined to become just like Seattle. But I am convinced that what my church has seen become normative in our city will soon become normative elsewhere. The tsunami of cultural change hit our beach first, which puts us in a position to help others learn from our fruit and our failure. Maybe our little church plant was like Noah's dove, sent to explore the landscape of a new world.

I have been hated, protested, despised, lied about, threatened, and maligned so many times and in so many ways I could not even begin to recount them all. I have made mistakes, committed sins, failed, and said things in ways that should have slowed down the forward progress of the gospel. Yet while we started with about a dozen mainly broke, single,

---

* See Matthew 13:1-23.

arty people in the living room of our rental home with literally nothing but an open Bible and open hearts, we've seen God graciously build a church one changed life at a time. We've become one of our nation's largest and fastest-growing churches, based upon an hour-plus of Bible preaching every week. It truly makes no sense. But every time the media ask me what the secret is, I tell them the same thing: it does not matter what is against you if Jesus is with you.

Jesus said the fields are "ripe for harvest,"* and he was not exaggerating. For multiple years in a row we have baptized over a thousand new Christians. Many if not most of them are young, single, college educated, and not virgins, who have spent more time with porn than with Paul and who represent the first generation of faith in their families, breaking decades of unbelief, perversion, addiction, and folly. All of this is happening in what some affectionately call The People's Republic of Seattle. Our run won't last forever, and not every church will experience exactly what we have, but there are reasons for hope.

For those Christians concerned that culture is trending more hostile to the faith, I assure you after two decades on the front line that this is not a time of retreat but rather resurgence. This is not a time for compromise but rather courage. The fields are ripe. And as Jesus says, "the laborers are few"†—in part because the prophets of doom are many. I'm frankly sick of all the books and movies trying to predict

* John 4:35, NIV.
† Matthew 9:37.

when Jesus will return and we'll get to start our eternal vacation at his all-inclusive resort called heaven. I'm also sick of the nerd parade of books and conferences that approach the Bible like scholars whose mission is to get their master's rather than soldiers who are on mission with their Master.

We've got work to do. There are lost people to reach, churches to plant, and nations to evangelize. Hell is hot, forever is a long time, and it's our turn to stop making a dent and start making a difference. This is no time to trade in boots for flip-flops. The days are darker, which means our resolve must be stronger and our convictions clearer.

ONE NATION, UNDER GOD?

If you don't believe me that evangelical Christians' days are getting darker, consider the spirituality of our 2012 presidential candidates. Unlike in past elections, candidates proving themselves to be born-again Christians is no longer seen as helpful for campaigning. The loser's beliefs were clearly Mormon. The winner's beliefs were clearly unclear.

On January 21, 2013, Barack Obama placed his hand on a Bible he may not entirely believe to take an oath to a God he may not entirely know.[1] Jesus alone will judge his soul one day, but in the meantime we are free to be confused by a man who says he's a Christian while ending his speech to America's largest abortion provider with, "Thank you, Planned Parenthood. God bless you."[2] Anyway, with a hand on the Bible, he swore to faithfully execute the office of president of the United States, concluding with the words, "So help me God." He then made a speech that invoked God five times.[3] In a conspicuous display of religious pageantry, an array of leaders representing numerous faith traditions witnessed the event, each offering some nebulous greeting card statement from the Sky Fairy while wearing a robe or fancy hat, because the best way to keep up a farce is to *really* play along and pay attention to the details.

Barack Obama then took his place as the leader of a nation whose money says "In God We Trust" without even the courtesy of a punch line to let us know it's a joke. At the very least, the photos of the dead presidents on our currency should show them smirking to clue us in on the ruse.

One notable omission on the inauguration stage was Pastor Louie Giglio. He was dumped like a prom date with tuberculosis, although the official report was that he withdrew.[4] He had been invited to offer an opening prayer as the token evangelical. Louie is by all accounts a great, noncontroversial guy—unlike some of us—which is pretty much what you'd expect from a guy named Louie who wears scarves. He's known for leading the Passion Movement, which hosts conferences for upward of sixty thousand college students who flock to Atlanta every year to hear from God's Word and sing God's praises. He has given years of his life and raised millions of dollars to free people from human trafficking and the sex trade. He started a popular church in Atlanta, where he loves and serves people. It's no wonder the Obama administration took notice and invited Giglio to give the benediction at the second inaugural festivities.

The hose found the bees' nest when a website published excerpts from a sermon Louie had delivered almost two decades prior.[5] In that message this pastor had the audacity to point out that, according to the Bible, the homosexual lifestyle is unacceptable in God's eyes. The disclosure had its intended effect. Like-minded critics jumped on the story, and a guy who could have won "most huggable" in Bible college became Public Enemy Number One overnight—all because he was God's messenger instead of God's editor. Forty-eight hours after receiving the invitation to join President Obama onstage, Louie Giglio was scratched from the schedule. Clearly embarrassed by their original choice, the Presidential Inaugural Committee went into damage-control mode and issued a statement assuring the nation that "we were not aware of Pastor Giglio's past comments at the time of his selection and they don't reflect our desire to celebrate the strength and diversity of our country. . . . As we now work to select someone to deliver the benediction, we will ensure their beliefs reflect this administration's vision of inclusion and acceptance for all Americans."[6]

Like most hypocrisy, the irony was unintentional, I'm sure, as those who are most vocal about tolerance are often the most intolerant. While the nation celebrated tolerance, liberation, and homosexuality, the evangelical Christian was forced to get into the closet. When George W. Bush was in office, he personally addressed the annual meeting of the Southern Baptist Convention by either satellite or video at least four times in two terms and got a standing ovation from conservative evangelicals who were respected and influential at the highest levels of government. In President Obama's first term, the White House had invited Rick Warren to pray. This time around, however, one of the faith's most likable, well-meaning, accessible representatives was barred from participation. When evangelicals can't even land a token appearance at an event orchestrated to reflect the various facets of American society, it's clear that Christian clout has reached its expiration date and been pulled off the shelf.

The Inaugural Committee replaced Louie Giglio with a very nice, unquestionably pro-gay Episcopalian pastor in a bathrobe, brought in from central casting to lend an air of formal spirituality to the whole affair.[7] The prayer he offered was forgettable and diplomatic; he's about as likely to preach repentance as I am to get pregnant. The Associated Press reported on the significance of the whole ordeal: "There may be no clearer reflection of this moment in American religious life than the tensions surrounding prayers at President Barack Obama's inauguration."[8]

January 21, 2013, was more than Inauguration Day. It was also a funeral. The highest office in the land made it clear: "inclusion and acceptance for all Americans" no longer includes Bible-believing, evangelical Christians.

As far as Western civilization is concerned, Christendom is officially dead.

AN OBITUARY FOR CHRISTENDOM

Like many deaths, the final demise of Christendom occurred after a long, painful struggle that started in the 1960s and 1970s. Christendom took a serious beating during those years from the fatal five: gender confusion, sex, abortions, drugs, and Spiritless spirituality. Strength and vigor waned as Christendom grew old and tired in the 1980s and 1990s. By the turn of the millennium, it could no longer fight back. Finally, after more than a decade of labored breathing and a weakening heart, Christendom has gone the way of all flesh.

But before we move forward into a future without Christendom, it's important to look back to see where we've come from. What exactly *is* Christendom, how is it different from Christianity itself, and how does it relate to the church today?

The life of modern Christendom began about the time of the Reformation and lasted roughly five hundred years, depending on which historian you read. The United States of America was among the most adventurous experiments of Christendom. It was a nation established in large part by professing Christians motivated by Christian values to accomplish Christian purposes.

For many years Christendom shaped the development of

Western culture in general and American culture specifically. Judeo-Christian ethics provided a shared moral infrastructure, the church and its leaders were welcome participants in the fabric of society, a common vocabulary facilitated discussion regarding the public good, and religious organizations benefited from certain legal and financial advantages (for example, nonprofit designations for ministries and tax deductions for giving to the church).

Practically, this did not mean that everyone was born again, loved Jesus, hated sin, and believed the Bible. Devotion to a particular deity was not as important as being a moral person and good citizen. Even so, a common heritage of faith resulted in a general consensus on many social issues. For example, in the days of Christendom, couples were discouraged from living together before marriage. Conventional wisdom said that the best context for raising children was heterosexual marriage. Pornography, prostitution, and drugs were considered wrong. And at least until the 1990s, Christendom in America wielded great political and cultural power in the form of the Religious Right and the Moral Majority, a term that almost no one would use to describe Christians today, unless while scoffing.

In many ways, the world benefited greatly from the collective conscience instilled by Christendom. But the era came with plenty of disadvantages as well. Those representing majority values were often guilty of cruelty toward those in the minority. The wealthy and powerful could justify horrible atrocities with token references to out-of-context Scripture.

Christendom sometimes enabled rampant hypocrisy, undermining the credibility of Jesus, the gospel, and the Bible.

Christendom bears the fingerprints of our faith, but it is *not* Christianity. In fact, when a society favors Christians, people are incentivized to claim the faith whether they actually believe it or not. Publicly practicing some aspects of Christianity—baptizing a child, getting married in a church, giving money to a church, attending services on occasion—included enough perks to encourage people simply to go with the flow. Christendom may have created a favorable environment for Christians, but it often did so at the expense of true Christianity.

THE RISE OF CIVIL RELIGION

Now that Christendom is dead, don't be surprised if you see its corpse lurching around like a zombie, inhabited by an impostor wearing what's left of the body. As *New York Times* columnist Ross Douthat observes, "America's problem isn't too much religion, or too little of it. It's *bad* religion: the slow-motion collapse of traditional Christianity and the rise of a variety of destructive pseudo-Christianities in its place."[9] One of the most common "pseudo-Christianities" is a construct known since a landmark 1967 essay by sociologist Robert Bellah as "American civil religion." In this rival religion, who God is and how God is to be worshiped are secondary matters we can agree to disagree on so long as all theologies and houses of worship conform to a basic moral framework that serves the primary matter of making a great nation.[10]

American civil religion is not a recent phenomenon. In his farewell address President George Washington said, "Of all the dispositions and habits which lead to political prosperity, Religion and Morality are indispensable supports. . . . Reason and experience both forbid us to expect that National morality can prevail in exclusion of religious principle."[11]

Likewise, 150 years later, President-elect Dwight Eisenhower said, "Our form of government has no sense unless it is founded in a deeply-felt religious faith, and I don't care what it is."[12]

What has changed since the days of Washington and Eisenhower is that Christendom is no longer the legitimizing center of American civil religion. Instead, our nation has created its own religion that appropriates many of the symbols and narratives of Christendom but without the substance of Christianity. Think of American civil religion in biblical terms: America is Israel. The Revolution is our Exodus. The Declaration of Independence, Bill of Rights, and Constitution compose our canon of sacred scripture. Abraham Lincoln is our Moses. Independence Day is our Easter. Our national enemies are our Satan. Benedict Arnold is our Judas. The Founding Fathers are our apostles. Taxes are our tithes. Patriotic songs are our hymnal. The Pledge of Allegiance is our sinner's prayer. And the president is our preacher, which is why throughout the history of the office our leaders have referred to "God" without any definition or clarification, allowing people to privately import their own understanding of a higher power.

Due to the ongoing existence of American civil religion, many evangelicals are oblivious to the fact that Christendom is dead and real Christianity is in serious decline. Those in the United States may have a general sense that Christianity is struggling in Europe, but many remain fairly optimistic about our "one nation under God." As long as we see Christmas trees on government property, as long as *The Bible* miniseries gets good ratings, and as long as we hear public figures talk about "faith," many believers naively assume that real Christianity is alive and well and respected by the majority of our people.

Brace yourself. It's an illusion.

BRUTAL REALITY

If you're reading this book, most likely you're an evangelical Christian (or one of my critics looking for rocks to throw, which I have piled for your convenience). While many definitions of evangelicalism exist, this diverse and delightfully dysfunctional family of God is perhaps best identified by four distinguishing characteristics:

- **Bible.** The Bible is God's true Word.
- **Cross.** Jesus died on the cross for our sins.

- **Conversion.** Individuals need to be personally converted.
- **Activism.** Belief in the gospel needs to be expressed outwardly.[13]

Based on these criteria, what percentage of Americans could be classified as evangelical Christian? Take a guess.

The answer is around 8 percent. Yes, there are more left-handed people, more Texans, and more pet cats than evangelicals in America.

Common statistics estimate that evangelicals represent anywhere between 40 to 70 percent of the country's total population, or approximately 130 million people. However, more extensive research cited by John Dickerson in his book *The Great Evangelical Recession* indicates that the actual range is between 7 and 8.9 percent, somewhere between 22 and 28 million people.[14] Moreover, all studies indicate that younger people are less likely to be evangelical. According to a 2012 Gallup poll, about 6.4 percent of the US population ages eighteen to twenty-nine identify themselves as lesbian, gay, bisexual, or transgendered, which means in all likelihood there are as many young people with alternative sexual lifestyles as there are active young evangelicals in the United States.[15]

Why do we see such a great discrepancy between the true number of evangelicals and the number of evangelicals reported in popular statistics? Thorough research confirms the cultural trend evident around us: many of those presumed to be Christians do not possess true faith. Rather, in the world of post-Christendom, true Christian belief has been replaced with a borrowed faith, a lost faith, or no faith at all. Depending on your demographic (namely, where you live and how old you are), at least one of these three will probably sound painfully familiar.

Borrowed Faith

The world of Christendom permitted a superficial faith that could be outwardly practiced but not inwardly experienced. The result was numerous somewhat moral, churchgoing unbelievers who wrongly assumed they were believers and not merely traditionalists. They borrowed the faith of prior generations, especially that of their older family members, such as a devout grandmother.

Those with a borrowed faith feel some degree of affinity or obligation to the church or to the denomination to which their parents or grandparents were committed. Faith borrowers do not want to be socially ostracized for lack of a church connection, and they want the church to be there as needed for major life events like births, weddings, holidays, or funerals. For the faith borrowers, church is more of a hotel than a home. They do not give their lives to the church or love the church as Jesus did. They consider the church to be a civic organization available to meet public needs when deemed beneficial.

England's royal family is a classic case of borrowed faith. Queen Elizabeth II reportedly "is a devout Christian, with a deep sense of religious duty, who attends church on a weekly basis." Her grandson, however, is another story. Prince William was wed in a church at a ceremony officiated by a pastor. He will one day ascend the British throne as king of the realm, which means his official duties will include "Defender of the Faith and Supreme Governor of the Church of England." Yet the prince and his wife "rarely, if ever" attend regular services. They wrote a prayer for their wedding ceremony, and they give money to charity, but they go to church only for official ceremonies or special occasions. William was baptized in the church as a baby, confirmed in the church as a young man, and married in the church as an adult. One day he will be the most powerful leader of the national denomination, but if you have questions regarding the royal couple's view of sin, repentance, Jesus, or the Bible, you're not likely going to get an answer.[16]

The prince is certainly not alone in the cradle of Christendom. Prince William appears to be like other British men his age, barely 8 percent of whom attend church regularly. According to a survey by Christian charity Tearfund, the United Kingdom is "among Europe's four least [religiously] observant countries": "Two-thirds of those polled had not been to church in the past year, except for baptisms, weddings, or funerals," although 53 percent still "identified themselves as Christian."[17] Another study indicates that back on our side of the pond, more than 40 percent of professing US evangelicals do not attend church weekly, and more than 60 percent of professing American mainline Christians do not attend weekly.[18] One Christian leader concludes, "In short, millions who consider themselves Christians limit their church attendance largely to holidays, weddings, and funerals."[19]

For generations the countries of Christendom have operated on borrowed faith. Your options were to play along with the faith or be shunned from society. Nineteenth-century philosopher Søren Kierkegaard saw the storm clouds on the horizon sooner than most. He criticized state religion, particularly in his home country of Denmark, a "Christian nation" united under the official Church of Denmark. At the time, state churches issued baptisms for babies much like the United States doles out Social Security numbers. Everyone was a Christian, which made the label all but meaningless. Kierkegaard's lament echoes today: "Christendom has done away with Christianity without being quite aware of it."[20]

Lost Faith

The inevitable result of borrowed faith is lost faith. People born into a family anchored in Christendom tend to assume they're right with God, regardless of whether they personally turn from sin and trust in Jesus. In common conversation, when asked how they became Christians, those with lost faith (or borrowed faith teetering on the brink) will talk about being born into a Christian family or about how they've always been Christian.

With the death of Christendom, however, the cultural

advantages of Christianity have diminished, and many people have decided to drop the charade altogether. This shouldn't come as a surprise; without inward conversion there's no reason to expect outward devotion. Younger generations increasingly feel less obligated even to profess Christianity, and society increasingly provides less incentive to do so. The advent of mass media, digital communication, and global travel have made competing religions, spiritualities, and philosophies (including agnosticism and atheism) more acceptable and fashionable. In contrast, Christendom is the old way, led by old people for old people. It's no wonder young people stop attending church, stop giving to the church, and stop practicing faith through Bible reading, a lifestyle of repentance, and passion for Jesus Christ.

In many ways, this is my story. I was raised in an Irish Catholic home. My family is from County Cork in southern Ireland, and we have been devoutly Catholic for as far back as any history can be traced. (My father and I ventured to the homeland to investigate the Driscoll heritage for ourselves.) My paternal grandmother was a staunch Catholic who preferred Latin Mass and was not enthusiastic about the changes adopted at the Second Vatican Council in 1965. Despite her emphasis on tradition, it is my sincere belief that my grandmother did possess saving faith in Jesus and was born again by the Holy Spirit rather than being just born into the church. My mother was also born into a Catholic family, but she was born again during the Catholic Charismatic Renewal of the 1970s, when she started attending prayer meetings and Bible studies with evangelical charismatics.

So I was born into a Catholic family with a believing mother and grandmother. I was baptized as an infant, went to Catholic school for a few years, and served as an altar boy. By the time I was a teenager, however, I attended church only for holidays, weddings, and funerals, mainly because that's what my family did. I enjoyed traditions such as sitting under stained glass by candlelight during midnight Mass on Christmas Eve, but beyond the aesthetics I had no interest in church. I professed a faith that I most certainly did not possess and hardly ever practiced.

In my junior year of high school I met an evangelical pastor's daughter named Grace (who is now my wife, my best friend, and the mother of our five children). Smitten with her, I asked her out. She responded by asking me if I was a Christian, to which I replied with a confident yes. After dating me for a while, however, she began to have her suspicions. I had no innate zeal for Jesus or Scripture and showed no evidence of new life in Christ. She gave me a nice Bible as a gift, and by God's grace I was saved while reading it during my freshman year in college.

The "seeker sensitive" movement arose in the waning years of Christendom to reach moral pagans like me, who were occasionally in church but not in Christ. Christian leaders like Bill Hybels rightly surmised that evangelism needed to occur not only in the world but also in the church. Numerous people baptized as infants in a church, raised in a church, married in a church, and remembered at their funerals in a church were actually going to hell. Subsequently, an evangelistic effort began to reach lost "Christians" sitting in the pews week after week, people who were physically alive but spiritually dead.

Seeker churches often met in nontraditional buildings, removed decorative crosses, replaced stained glass with video screens, and sought to provide a different experience than the traditional church of Christendom in hopes of attracting and converting people from the appearance of Christianity to a legitimate relationship with Christ. Whether or not you agree with the principles and methods of seeker-sensitive ministry, the effort was designed to provide a solution to Christendom's epidemic problem: lost people like me who wrongly thought they were Christians.

Today the seeker-sensitive approach no longer yields many conversions, especially among younger people, because the culture has changed. Christian pretenders don't have to pretend anymore. In a demonstration of very humble honesty, Bill Hybels's Willow Creek Community Church—the epicenter of seeker-sensitive ministry—published the Reveal study in 2008. The report admitted that the church was having trouble sustaining effective evangelistic ministry according to their methods. I believe that the diminishing returns can be attributed in large part to the fact that the market has dried up. People used to attend church and write checks because they loved the moral values derived from the teachings of Moses and felt some sense of tradition, habit, or obligation. Now those with borrowed faith or lost faith are more commonly opting to join those with no faith at all.

No Faith

A study conducted by researchers from the University of California—Berkeley and Duke University reported in 2013 that "religious affiliation in the United States is at its lowest point since it began to be tracked in the 1930s." According to the study, "one in five Americans claimed they had no religious preference, more than double the number reported in 1990."[21]

Study after study confirms much of the same: when asked about their religious affiliation, a growing percentage of the population now respond "none."[22] In 2012, *Time* magazine listed "The Rise of the Nones" among the top ten trends changing American life. The article describes how more people are "turning away from organized religion and yet seeking rich if unorthodox ways to build spiritual lives."[23]

The "Nones" often describe themselves as "spiritual but not religious." Like one woman I met, they say things like, "My garden is my church." Another example is actress Jodie Foster, who said in an interview that she was an atheist and then added, "But I absolutely love religions and the rituals. Even though I don't believe in God. We celebrate pretty much every religion in our family with the kids."[24]

If they're interested in any organized religion at all (maybe for the sake of their kids), these kinds of Nones prefer a loose affiliation with a benign denomination of the Unitarian Universalists variety, where rough edges like sin, repentance, monotheism, and heaven and hell are sanded off to provide an affirming, inoffensive community without Christ. This allows some tradition without tenets and spirituality without the Spirit.

In early 2013, *Boston* magazine published an article by a mother who had long ago abandoned her Christian faith and is now wrestling with the practicalities of raising her children in a nonreligious home. In one notable passage, she describes the patchwork None culture:

> We Nones are atheists, agnostics, unchurched believers, "spiritual" types, lapsed Jews and Catholics, and people who just don't care. Religiosity often has a natural kind of life cycle, in which people move away from religion in their teens and twenties, and then come back around when they marry and have kids. That's not our story. We Nones move away but never come back.
>
> And our numbers are growing. Twenty percent of American adults now say that they believe in nothing in particular. Forty-six million adults identify themselves as religiously unaffiliated, and 88 percent of them say they have no interest in joining a religious institution. This is a seismic cultural shift with the potential to profoundly reshape our society—not to mention our families.[25]

The spiritual temperature has changed very suddenly in the United States. For many years, the None population was small—a mere 5 to 7 percent. Then it exploded quickly. This is very different from what happened in Europe. There, unbelief warmed up slowly, as if in a Crock-Pot. In the US, unbelief has warmed up as if in a microwave. While unbelief is heating up, belief is cooling down. The percentage of Christian converts is not keeping pace with our growing population as unbelief overtakes Christianity.[26]

For those sheltered in the culs-de-sac of Christendom, all of this may come as a surprise. But life among the Nones is already normative for those of us who have spent our lives in places like Seattle, where the end of Christendom is a non-event because there was never really a beginning. As early as 2004, the Pacific Northwest was dubbed "the None Zone" because the majority of the region's population had already begun to identify their religious preference as "none."[27] The death of Christendom is old news out here. The Bible Belt and other lingering pockets of cultural Christianity are simply catching up.

After the 2012 election, I was talking with a friend from the great nation of Texas. He was shocked that the rest of the nation was so vocally anti-Christian and pro-gay. He was unaware that things were unwell in the Lone Star State, where between 2000 and 2005, attendance in evangelical churches dropped by 2.6 percent, even as the overall population grew by about 2 percent.[28] I smirked and told him, "Welcome to the United States of Seattle."

WHEN "CHRISTIAN" NO LONGER MEANS CHRISTIAN

With the epic rise of borrowed faith, lost faith, and no faith, what's left of actual Christian faith? The present-day blend of beliefs, traditions, and spiritualities makes it difficult to identify a remnant, especially when all of the ingredients have been marinated in the brine of American civil religion and Judeo-Christian ethics. Everything comes out of the mix with a hint of Christianity and vice versa.

Spiritual leaders who find an audience among the borroweds, losts, and Nones often make the mistake of turning one attribute of God into the totality of God. For example, John's declaration that "God is love"* gets flipped so that "Love is God," and "love" means that God does not forbid anything or judge anyone. Never mind that the most commonly mentioned attribute of God in Scripture is holiness, that the Bible speaks of God's wrath over six hundred times with some twenty different words, or that Jesus speaks of hell more than anyone in the Bible. Love wins; God loses.

For evidence, look no further than the church. Our secular-but-spiritual therapeutic culture, combined with psychology and the professional counseling movement, has recast the church as a social service organization that exists to do kind things like feed people, provide aid to anyone outside of the church, and help hurting people within the church—all without judging or calling them to repentance of any sin in their lives. That's the approved, acceptable role

---

* 1 John 4:8.

23

of the church in the post-Christendom world. Lots of good works; little if any Good News. Lots of relationships; little if any repentance. Lots of talk about institutional sin; little if any talk about personal sin. Lots of concern about suffering; little if any concern about eternal suffering.

Many Christians of the borrowed or lost faith variety have gladly accepted society's new vision for the church. They may still gather in traditional buildings and conduct traditional liturgies, but the emphasis is on community service, social justice, and self-help sermons from pastors who are inoffensive and nice, providing care but not making converts. In many of these congregations, the church favors *showing* the gospel and abandons *speaking* the gospel altogether.

The problem is, the gospel cannot be shown; it *must* be spoken. Love, grace, mercy, justice, and the like can be shown with works. The gospel of Jesus Christ, however, must be spoken with words, because the gospel of Jesus Christ is not about *our* deeds but rather *Jesus'* deeds: his sinless life, substitutionary death, burial, and bodily resurrection for the salvation of sinners. And without the gospel of Jesus Christ, you may still have morality, spirituality, and charity, but what you don't have is Christianity. Real Christianity results in these things but cannot be replaced by them.

This is precisely what the apostle Paul says in what is perhaps the most succinct statement of the gospel in all of Scripture. He reminds us that the gospel is about our Savior and must be spoken ("preached"):

I would remind you, brothers, of the gospel I preached to you, which you received, in which you stand, and by which you are being saved, if you hold fast to the word I preached to you—unless you believed in vain. For I delivered to you as of first importance what I also received: that Christ died for our sins in accordance with the Scriptures, that he was buried, that he was raised on the third day in accordance with the Scriptures.*

The gospel—the Good News—is about what Jesus has done, and it must be spoken. Good deeds are about what Jesus wants us to do, and they must be shown. Good deeds can serve people, but only the Good News can save them. When good deeds are confused with the Good News, bad things happen. As Jesus said,

You will recognize [false prophets] by their fruits. Not everyone who says to me, "Lord, Lord," will enter the kingdom of heaven, but the one who does the will of my Father who is in heaven. On that day many will say to me, "Lord, Lord, did we not prophesy in your name, and cast out demons in your name, and do many mighty works in your name?" And then will I declare to them, "I never knew you; depart from me, you workers of lawlessness."†

---

* 1 Corinthians 15:1-4.
† Matthew 7:20-23.

According to Jesus, not everyone who talks like a Christian or acts like a Christian is actually a Christian. You can be born into a Christian family and not be a Christian. You can be baptized and not be a Christian. You can attend a Christian school and not be a Christian. You can pray every day and not be a Christian. You can be a ministry leader and not be a Christian. You can be a generous and helpful person and not be a Christian. You can believe in God and not be a Christian. You can swear an oath on two Bibles and not be a Christian. If the legacy of Judas has taught us anything, we should know that just because people identify themselves as followers of Jesus, it doesn't mean they actually believe. Rather, we see in this passage and elsewhere in Scripture that true Christianity is a faith that must be professed, practiced, and possessed:

- *To profess faith* means to confess Jesus Christ as Lord and proclaim this faith to others in hopes that they, too, will turn from sin and trust in Jesus alone for salvation.
- *To practice faith* means to live a new life of worship patterned after Jesus and to be empowered by the Holy Spirit to continually repent of sin, obey Scripture, fellowship with other believers, serve in love, and partake in the sacraments such as Communion and baptism.
- *To possess faith* means that God has implanted the life of Jesus in you. Once you were a sinner separated

from God, and now you are a child adopted by God, redeemed and forgiven by the Holy Spirit's power.

Only God knows the heart, but unless people demonstrate the "fruit" of all three aspects, we have no reason to believe that they actually are saved followers of Jesus. We can profess faith ("Lord, Lord") and practice faith ("mighty works") without actually possessing faith ("I never knew you").

American civil religion resembles Christianity because it appropriates the language of Scripture and uses the Judeo-Christian framework to control and unite the populace. Borrowed faith resembles Christianity because it promotes religious tradition and occasional church attendance. Lost faith resembles Christianity because it can often point to a heritage of faith. Even "None" faith can resemble Christianity by mimicking spiritual disciplines and promoting social justice.

Do not be deceived.

We can love, respect, and enjoy those who are not Christians, of course. But if people believe they're Christians and thus safe from hell and the wrath of God, when most likely they are not, it is absolutely unloving to allow them to proceed in their delusion. If we truly care about alleviating human suffering, then we must concern ourselves not only with practicing good deeds but also with preaching the Good News in hopes that people trust in Jesus and avoid eternal suffering—which is the worst suffering of all.

FUNERAL OR FUTURE?

This chapter contains more about politics than I've said in my entire preaching career. But this is not a political book. Politics do not lead culture so much as follow culture, contrary to what some believe. We elect our candidates to represent and realize the desires of a majority, not to force-feed policy on their constituency. My interests in politics are not political, but missiological: What do these events reveal about Western culture, and how does that affect our efforts to reach people with the Good News of Jesus Christ?

The role evangelical Christians are playing (or *not* playing) on the national stage today is a clear snapshot of how the spiritual landscape of Western civilization has changed, along with our place in it. The 2012 election season shocked a lot of evangelicals living in suburban, conservative contexts who wrongly believed we were still an influential and respected majority.

I'm not exactly mourning the loss of Christendom, a religious culture that at times bred hypocrisy, false assurance, and legalism. But Christian faith is not just losing its market share. Civil religion and borrowed faith have confused the substance of Christian faith to the point where it is losing its salvation message. I don't care about preserving Christendom. My concern is the gospel of Jesus Christ, humanity's one and only hope. To borrow the words of Jude, "I found it necessary to write appealing to you to contend for the faith that was once for all delivered to the saints."*

More and more, we have less and less clarity about what we believe. There are fewer and fewer people (including even so-called Christians) who care what we believe. Simply stated, today's evangelicals are not weighty, nor do they see clearly. The reality is obvious if you haven't chosen to close your eyes. We're approaching a cliff. The river of culture is surging headlong toward the brink—if it hasn't begun to tumble over already—and the waters are carrying away Christians by the millions. Many will cower, lose their grip, and fall over the edge.

For those ready to dig in and hang on, however, this book is an unflinching look at what we're up against and what it will take to not just survive but to thrive and accomplish the mission God has given us to extend a hand of rescue to those drowning all around us. It is a call not of retreat but of resurgence.

The death of Christendom means life just got a lot more difficult for anyone who really does want to be a Christian and follow Jesus. And we have every reason to believe that things are only going to get worse.

Jesus speaks to our present and future, saying, "Blessed are you when others revile you and persecute you and utter all kinds of evil against you falsely on my account. Rejoice and be glad, for your reward is great in heaven, for so they

---

* Jude 1:3.

persecuted the prophets who were before you."* We are going to be persecuted. And much of that will come not as much in the form of getting thrown to the lions as getting thrown to the critics. But we are to keep our wits and rejoice with gladness because this life is as close to hell as we will ever get. God will call some of us to endure overt persecution and die for the cause of Jesus. God will call all of us to endure covert persecution and live for the cause of Jesus. Both are forms of persecution, as some are called to die for Christ while others are called to live for Christ. Either way, the Christian life is hard, and the Bible does not sugarcoat this reality. In fact, if you never experience any sort of persecution, you probably need to consider whether you're truly following Jesus. The Bible says that "all who desire to live a godly life in Christ Jesus will be persecuted."†

Whatever we do, we must not lose our saltiness. Jesus says, "You are the salt of the earth, but if salt has lost its taste, how shall its saltiness be restored? It is no longer good for anything except to be thrown out and trampled under people's feet."‡ Salt preserves, flavors, and creates thirst. Salty believers are tempted to lose their saltiness by denying the hard truths and backing down on the tough issues to avoid persecution.

But God tells us, "Fear not." This is the most common commandment in the entire Bible, appearing roughly 150 times, because this is the most common problem for the

---

* Matthew 5:11-12.
† 2 Timothy 3:12.
‡ Matthew 5:13.

Christian. Who are you afraid of? What are you afraid of? That fear will paralyze you. It will cause you not to live courageously and boldly. Jesus knows that there are reasons for you to be afraid. And yet he says, "Fear not."

Nearly every time the Bible commands us to "fear not," it also tells us why. Not because we will see things turn around soon, or even ever. Not because it's going to be easy. And not because we will be vindicated in this life. Instead, when we are told, "Fear not," in some fashion God is telling us, "I am with you." Jesus, through the presence of the Holy Spirit, lives in us, works through us, goes with us, and will never leave us or forsake us, because he promised to be with us always, until the end of the age, as we limp toward home.

The Jesus who goes with you is a God who has experienced tribulation, poverty, slander, suffering, and death. He is always present to comfort you because he has walked the road that you are on and is waiting with nail-scarred hands to embrace you at its end. Since he has walked that road for you, his invitation to walk it with him is a great honor.

This is not a political book. This is not a reactionary book. This is a prophetic book.

Christendom is dead.

Jesus is alive.

Stay salty.

Fear not.

Chapter 2

STANDING KNOCKOUT
HOW WE GOT OUR BELL RUNG

GROWING UP, I didn't go to youth group or church camp.
I didn't know there was Christian music. The only Bible I
remember in our house was an enormous coffee table version you could stand under for safety during an earthquake.
I assumed the Religious Right was wrong simply because
it was led by old white guys in suits. And I thought chas-
tity pledges sounded like the stuff of superheroes—special
powers not held by mere mortals like me. Superman can fly.
Aquaman can breathe under water. And Celibacyman can
keep his hands to himself.

When I was a freshman in college, Jesus saved me, and
I knew I needed to find a church. Afraid of joining a cult,

I finally picked a church because the pastor seemed normal and taught from the Bible in plain English—unlike some other churches I visited, where the pastors kept referring to Greek words (it was *all* Greek to me). I didn't know it, but I had become an accidental evangelical.

Entering the evangelical wormhole, I found myself in a new, parallel universe. In church and college parachurch meetings no one explained what we were doing, which left me completely confused. Why does the band stink, and how come people at the concert sing along with the bad band? Why are people raising their hands during the music time— do they have questions, or are we exercising like an aerobics class? Why do they close their eyes when they pray? (Where I grew up, that'd be a good way to get your stuff stolen.) And when I brought a buddy to church and the offering basket came by, he took a few bucks out, not understanding we were supposed to put money *in*.

The insider language believers used made no sense to me. Is "fellowship" some sort of cruise? Why are guys I've never met suddenly calling me "brother" and giving me long hugs in public when no one has died? What in the world is a "quiet time"? Is it like when you get busted as a kid and have to sit in the corner? Who the heck are "Hallelujah" and "Amen," and will somebody find them so everyone will stop yelling for them? I was so confused by the terminology that I walked down to a Christian bookstore in town and asked if there was a book that translated Christianese into English. I bought a compact dictionary of doctrinal words and carried it along with a Bible wherever I went so that if I met Christians, I could understand what they were talking about. I quickly learned that the evangelical Christian world was completely different from the world I knew.

If you've been tucked inside the Christian subculture for a long time, you might not even realize how strange we can look to nonbelievers. And even more, you may have wrongly thought evangelical Christianity was strong and on the rise. And why wouldn't you? Maybe you attend a big evangelical church or participate in one of the many big evangelical Christian conferences held every year. Maybe you enjoy big evangelical Christian concerts and sing the latest prom songs to Jesus led by a clean-shaven guy with frosted hair that perfectly matches the hue of his acoustic guitar. But while evangelicals were busy seeing Christian friends, reading Christian books, surfing Christian websites, listening to Christian music, attending Christian events, and enjoying Christian church, things in our culture were quickly changing in a big way—and they still are. Most Christians are sheltered within their own groups and are too busy arguing with other Christians to notice the sad state of Christianity in a broader sense.

In high school I somehow made the football team as a quarterback. In one of my first games, I dropped back to pass the ball and got hit simultaneously from multiple sides. Assuming I was fine, I went to the bench on the sideline and sat down. A few plays later a coach came and asked me if I was okay. I told him I was fine. Then he informed me

I was sitting on the wrong bench with the wrong team on the wrong sideline. Apparently, I'd gotten my proverbial bell rung and didn't know it. In boxing they call this a standing knockout, where a person is basically unconscious but somehow still standing. Today the church in the West is in a similar daze from several simultaneous hits. We'll explore each of these hits as well as their implications for us and our society. But first, we need to take a look backward.

THE HISTORY OF EVANGELICALISM

The Evangelical Experiment began in the mid-1900s, near the end of modernism and the five-hundred-year reign of Christendom. This development was an effort to create a gospel-centered group of Bible-believing, Jesus-loving, Protestant Christians who professed, practiced, and possessed genuine faith. Evangelicalism came into prominence in the days of Elvis Presley, the bus boycott in Montgomery, the launch of the interstate highway system (which created the suburbs, where large, family-oriented churches have flourished), and the first application to the Food and Drug Administration for something called a birth control pill.[1]

Evangelicalism was perhaps most influenced by the Four Horsemen—Billy Graham the evangelist, John Stott the pastor, J. I. Packer the theologian, and Francis Schaeffer the apologist. Magazines such as *Christianity Today* came into existence, along with numerous Bible colleges, seminaries, publishing houses, record labels, conferences, denominations, and other ministries as part of the Evangelical Experiment. The "Greatest Generation" was behind the Evangelical Experiment. Shaped by the pain and poverty of war, they were, generally speaking, a thrifty, generous, hardworking, long-suffering generation— perhaps the last one of its kind in America.

While not everyone at the time was a born-again Christian, the dominant paradigm in the Western world was strongly influenced by what were called "Judeo-Christian" values. The church was considered a vital part of the social fabric, safeguarding morality that would contribute to a better society.

Then came the critique of postmodernism, which challenged many of the underlying assumptions of modernism, such as the existence of objective truth and morality that applies to all people, times, and places. Within evangelicalism this led to a brief but noisy tribe called the emergent church, which was devoted to critiquing modern evangelism, particularly the megachurch phenomenon. I was at the early stages of this development as a young pastor in the mid-1990s, though I quickly exited this push for "postmodern ministry" because I felt it held a low view of Scripture. It rapidly went apostate, denying the perfection and authority of Scripture, original sin, the death of Jesus for our sins, eternal condemnation in hell, the necessity of Jesus for salvation, and the sinfulness of homosexuality. And, as Judas did, this movement managed to find some rope and a tree.

Following Christendom's funeral, where is our culture today? Outside of evangelicalism, the predominant culture is now pluralism. There is no one dominant cultural ideology or spirituality. It's literally everythingism—what missiological guru Lesslie Newbigin called pluralism.[2] As G. K. Chesterton is quoted as saying, "When a man stops believing in God, he doesn't then believe in nothing, he believes anything."

NEW PAGANISM

In 2009 my church hosted a surreal gathering of personalities for a network television debate on ABC's *Nightline*. I shared the stage with Deepak Chopra, the embodiment of new paganism. During the course of our discussion, Chopra made no attempt to conceal his disdain for the Christian world-view, including traditional notions of right and wrong and truth. He traced the origins of "so-called evil" (his description) back to traditional beliefs. "As soon as you move to the next stage of consciousness," he explained, "there's more turbulence. When there's a phase transition in thinking, then people whose primitive beliefs are threatened, they become even more fearful and therefore destructive."[3]

According to Chopra, the divorce between Christendom and Western civilization is a natural part of the evolutionary process, in which mankind will abandon "primitive" beliefs and achieve a level of higher consciousness.[4] Ironically, the spiritual practices he has helped popularize find their roots in ancient primitive paganism. The Bible explains the origins of pagan beliefs in Romans 1:18-32, culminating in one big idea articulated in verse 25, which speaks of idolaters who "exchanged the truth about God for a lie and worshiped and served the creature rather than the Creator, who is blessed forever!"

This passage draws a line between two competing world-views: the truth, what is often referred to as "two-ism," and the lie, or "one-ism."[5] Two-ism is the biblical doctrine that Creator and creation are separate—like two separate circles—and that creation is subject to the Creator. We were created to worship our Creator by enjoying and stewarding his creation. One-ism removes the line between Creator and creation, as if the two coexist within a single circle. Interestingly, the single circle appears as a sacred motif throughout pagan traditions: Hinduism (the yantra circle), Buddhism and Taoism (the mandala circle of dharma and the yin-yang), Wicca (the sun cross), and Native American spirituality (medicine wheels and dream catchers).

Pagan religions differ greatly in their specific beliefs, but all adhere to the basic principles of one-ism that Paul warns us about in Romans 1. Besides a fresh coat of paint, there's nothing new about new pagan one-ism. But many of its modern manifestations have gained broad acceptance, even within some churches. It's important to understand common varieties of "new" paganism in order to identify attempts—blatant and subtle—to exchange the truth of God for a lie.

Atheistic One-ism

Atheistic one-ism results in the belief that there is nothing and no one beyond physical matter. There is no God who made us or is coming to rescue us; we are here for no reason; we suffer for no purpose; and we will die and simply decompose. "I don't feel depressed about it," said famed self-proclaimed "militant" atheist Richard Dawkins. "Maybe the logic is deeply pessimistic, the universe is bleak, cold and empty. But so what?"[6] This ideology has nearly taken over many college campuses where belief in an intelligent designer of the universe—let alone a personal, biblical Creator God—is akin to academic suicide.

Yet the pull toward atheistic one-ism is different from what many of us would have imagined. *The Atlantic* did a feature story on young atheists based on a national campaign to interview college students who were members of irreligious campus groups—basically the opposite of Campus Crusade for Christ—as they met and proselytized against spiritual belief. The goal was simple: invite young atheists to share their journey of unbelief to see if any themes or trends emerged. And they did.

- The majority of young atheists had attended church and embraced atheism in reaction to Christianity specifically and not another religion.
- The churches they left had weak teaching. The message was more about good works (social justice) than Good News (how Jesus intersects with all of life).
- Their churches did not hit hard issues and gave superficial answers to difficult questions. Former-church-attenders-turned-atheists wanted deep discussions and meaningful teaching about Creation and evolution, sexuality, the reliability of the Bible,

Jesus as the only path to salvation, and so on. But they did not get that in their churches. One student simply said, "I really started to get bored with church."

· They really respected ministers who took the Bible seriously. Related to this, they expect Christians who believe the Bible to try to convert them. They assume Christians who don't evangelize probably don't really believe the Bible. One student said, "I really can't consider a Christian a good, moral person if he isn't trying to convert me."

· Ages fourteen to seventeen were "decisive." The high school period is crucial, as those who chose atheism tended to do so in their teen years.

· The decision to embrace atheism was often quite emotional. One woman reported that she stopped believing in God when her father died. He had been so abusive that the thought of him living forever somewhere tormented her. Another woman said that when God did not answer her prayer to remove her from foster care and return her to her father, she embraced atheism, assuming that God likely did not exist.

· The Internet was an important part of their journey to atheism. YouTube videos and online discussion forums were often mentioned as helping inform their decisions to embrace atheism.[7]

Shallow, entertainment-oriented, self-help, knockoff, consumer Christianity that offers bumper-sticker clichés in response to life's crises fuels the movement to embrace atheistic one-ism. It's weak sauce. Let's say there's a barbecue restaurant known for its super spicy sauce. The restaurant has a loyal fan base and is doing just fine. But the managers somehow get the idea that if they water down the sauce to make it less hot, they can appeal to even more people. Their business will probably die. Why? While some people like spicy sauce and others don't, everybody hates watered-down weak sauce. What is true for barbecue is also true for biblical teaching. Nobody likes weak sauce.

Spiritual One-ism

Spiritual one-ism includes typical New Age, Integrative Spirituality, and Native American spiritual beliefs, along with the broader categories of pantheism and panentheism. Spiritual one-ism sees the universe as a living organism with a spiritual force or world soul present within everything. This life force may manifest as spiritual beings (which Christians recognize as demons) that manipulate the course of world events. Spiritual one-ism practices may include various rites, rituals, incantations, spells, and the use of objects like charms, amulets, crystals, and potions to manipulate spiritual energy and the material world. These spirits can be influenced to serve people by using the ancient magical arts. This view also embraces the idea that humans possess divine power. Oprah Winfrey (who somehow remains popular with some professing Christian women) is one spiritual guru who pushes spiritual one-ism books by authors such as Eckhart Tolle (*The Power of Now* and *A New Earth*), Helen Schucman (*A Course in Miracles*), and Rhonda Byrne (*The Secret*). Consider this: nearly every apologetics book written by an evangelical in recent decades tries to prove that the supernatural world is possible. Today such arguments are not necessary when there is a generation of females who believe themselves to be vampires dating werewolves.

Spiritual one-ism is dangerous because it is naive. It assumes that all spirits are good and does not accept the reality of Satan and demons. In a terrible but insightful example, Katharine Jefferts Schori, the presiding bishop over US Episcopalians, said in a sermon based on Acts 16 that Paul acted in a bigoted and sinful way by casting a demon out of a young woman. In a statement she never apologized for, clarified, or retracted, Schori preached, "Paul is annoyed, perhaps for being put in his place, and he responds by depriving her of her gift of spiritual awareness. Paul can't abide something he won't see as beautiful or holy, so he tries to destroy it." She goes on to explain that God had Paul thrown in prison as punishment for casting the demon out of the young girl. Schori then says, "It makes me wonder what would have happened to that slave girl if Paul had seen the spirit of God in her."[8]

That section of Scripture clearly calls the "beautiful" and "holy" spirit that tormented the young woman a demon. The young woman is simply called "a demon-possessed slave girl" (verse 16, NLT). Her spirituality was "fortune-telling," by which she brought her slave owners "much gain." This poor young woman was both a physical slave of men and a spiritual slave of a demon. Yet the leader of a national denomination cannot see this as a problem because her thinking is so dominated by pagan one-ism that both the Holy Spirit and demons are welcome to indwell people, a spiritual experience we should celebrate in either form. If the word *insane* comes to mind, then congratulations—you are paying attention.

Spiritual one-ism shows up in movies like *Avatar* and *The Lion King*, which make no distinction between creation and Creator. Rather, everything is spiritually connected in the great "circle of life." The teen vampire craze (led by the *Twilight* franchise) is another form of one-ism. These narratives not only blend good and evil and dark and light, but they also introduce pagan concepts to an impressionable audience (ritualistic biting, cutting, eternity without God). Given the strong paranormal element throughout many popular books, movies, and shows, it's no coincidence that witchcraft has gained mainstream acceptance in the form of Wicca. In 2007, for example, the US Department of Veterans Affairs added the Wiccan pentacle to the list of approved religious symbols for veterans' headstones.[9]

Deistic One-ism

Deistic one-ism is essentially functional one-ism without all of the raw emotional and practical conclusions that come with a belief that we're totally alone in the universe.

Sociologist Christian Smith coined the term "moralistic therapeutic deism" to describe the prevailing system of spiritual beliefs that the majority of young people live by, regardless of what religion they profess (including Christianity).[10] The system of beliefs is *moralistic* because the objective is to be a good person, not to approach God as a sinner in need of salvation; it is *therapeutic* because the purpose of life is to achieve happiness through counseling and therapy, not to grow in spiritual maturity through serving Jesus or his church according to Scripture; and it is *deistic* because God exists, but he is not really involved in our lives—we are essentially on our own, with the occasional exceptions of God answering prayers or sending us pithy insights to aid our betterment. This ideology fuels much of the self-help movement with mantras of self-improvement, self-esteem, self-actualization, self-empowerment, and self-love as the answers to life's problems. It is epitomized in television dating shows like *The Bachelor*, with all the contestants' talk of "destiny" and finding your "soul mate" in between hot tub sessions where various women vie for one guy's "love," which is bound to survive about as long as a Popsicle in the sun.

Consequences of Pagan One-ism

Here are some practical implications of one-ism as practiced in its various forms:

- *There is no distinction between God the Creator and creation.* Radical environmentalism is one example of this. It exceeds a healthy desire to steward God's creation and results in worshiping the earth because she is our Mother.

- *There is no distinction between God and humankind.*
  Spirituality does not humbly look outward to
  God for salvation but arrogantly looks inward for
  enlightenment and morality.

- *There is no distinction between good and evil.* All
  we have are perspectives, opinions, and culturally
  embedded subjective values. There's no such thing
  as timeless moral truths that apply to all peoples,
  times, and places. We're left with shifting situational
  ethics, building a moral house on sand.

- *There is no distinction between angels and demons.* All
  spirits and spiritualities are considered good, which
  leaves people vulnerable to demonic influences
  masquerading as angels of light.*

- *There is no distinction between mankind and animals.*
  Radical activists advocate for the rights and rescue
  of animals, often while supporting the murder of
  unborn children, contrary to the Bible's teaching
  that mankind is uniquely made in the image of God
  and that the created order places human life above
  animal life.

- *There is no distinction between men and women.* One-
  ism replaces God-given gender with culturally created

---

* See 2 Corinthians 11:14.

gender: transgenderism, bisexuality, homosexuality, cross-dressing, and the like.

- *There is no distinction between religions.* One-ism usually results in a vague pagan spirituality. As a result, a Christianity that makes distinctions (such as those listed above) is considered a fundamental threat to the entire worldview of one-ism.

Perhaps the most tragic implication of new pagan one-ism is that it results in hopelessness. Functional one-ism may in part explain why the largest category of prescription drugs is antidepressants and why many people self-medicate their pain with drugs, alcohol, sex, gambling, high-risk behavior, and food. Speaking of the ancient implications of one-ism, N. T. Wright explains, "When everything (including yourself) shares in, or lives within, divinity, there's no higher court of appeal when something bad happens. Nobody can come and rescue you. The world and 'the divine' are what they are, and you'd better get used to it. The only final answer (given by many Stoics in the first century, and by increasing numbers in today's Western world) is suicide."[11]

HOMOSEXUALITY

Since the mid-1990s, in every interview I can remember with the local Seattle media, I have been asked about homosexuality. My canned response has always been that all sex outside of heterosexual marriage is sinful, including pornography, fornication, friends with benefits, cohabitation, prostitution, polygamy, bisexuality, homosexuality, and adultery, among other things. I then continue by explaining that I was in sin by sleeping with a girlfriend before I became a Christian and consider others' sin no worse than my own.

It took some years before the national and international media started asking this interview question. But today it is almost a given. And with the cameras rolling, I continue to give the same answer to people like Barbara Walters and Piers Morgan. It's like juggling knives while riding a unicycle on a tightrope over a crocodile pit.

But my traditional answer no longer satisfies these days, as the interviewers continue to press in solely on the issue of homosexuality. They hammer away with the intent of getting any and every evangelical Christian they can to publicly admit they do not support homosexuality or gay marriage. Then that Christian is dismissed as being bigoted, homophobic, discriminatory, hateful, and unloving. These interviewers remind me of the kids in my neighborhood who liked to focus their magnifying glasses to burn ants.

The cultural tide has changed quickly and shows no indication of turning back. Consider this: until 1974 the *Diagnostic and Statistical Manual of Mental Disorders*—published by the American Psychiatric Association, the premier authority for the criteria and classification of mental disorders—listed homosexuality as a mental disorder. Today people commonly see homosexuality as simply an alternative, and equally acceptable, lifestyle. That's a big change in perspective in a short period of time.

According to a 2011 survey by the nonprofit Public Religion Research Institute, 62 percent of adults between eighteen and twenty-nine years old said they supported gay marriage, and 71 percent supported civil unions.[12]

Conversely, every time the Bible speaks of homosexuality it does so negatively.* Jesus says that the only alternative to heterosexual marriage is celibacy.† Jesus lived a celibate life, and in the early years of the church, the celibate lifestyle was common and honored—unlike in our day, in which you would think sex would join air, food, water, and shelter as necessary for basic survival.

Consequences of the Broad Acceptance of Homosexuality

From my vantage point in Seattle, where gay marriage is now legalized, it's clear to see that the rest of the nation and Western world are trending in our direction. And for the sake of clarity, I am speaking about homosexual *activity*, not homosexual *desire*. People have desires to do numerous things that if acted upon would be sinful. But simply being tempted by a desire is not a sin. That said, here are six things I see happening without a serious intervention of God's grace:

- *Gay marriage will be nationally legalized in the United States.* If not at first, it will eventually pass and

---

* See Genesis 19; Leviticus 18:22; 20:13; Romans 1:26-27; 1 Corinthians 6:9-10; 1 Timothy 1:8-10.
† See Matthew 19:10-12.

become national law. The tide is turned. The culture war is lost for the Religious Right on this issue.

- *Younger generations will fully accept homosexuality and gay marriage as an acceptable option.* They have been educated in public schools regarding homosexuality, they have gay friends and family members, their pop culture diet includes plenty of lovable gay characters, they watch a lot of porn that includes no sexual boundaries, and they have themselves experimented sexually. And as a general rule, they don't want anyone making any judgments on sex; they want to do whatever they want to do without being told it is wrong. They don't like sexual inhibitions or prohibitions.

- *We will see polygamy legalized in my lifetime, perhaps even in the next twenty years.* Historically the definition of marriage in Western nations has been one man and one woman. But with that definition obliterated, there is not a replacement but rather a vacuum. Once both heterosexual marriage and gay marriage are legal, there will be no logical reason to prohibit bisexual marriage. The argument will go something like this— if it's legal to be right handed, and legal to be left handed, then it should be legal to be ambidextrous. Sociological experts educated beyond their intelligence will be paraded on news shows, armed with statistics saying that divorce rates would go down and families kept intact if unfaithful partners were allowed to keep both the spouse and the lover, bringing them together as one big nuttier-than-a-Skippy-factory family. The Bible is far more direct on prohibitions against homosexuality than it is on polygamy (though both are sinful), and if professing Christians make the long leap to support gay marriage, it's a much shorter step over the line of biblical faithfulness to arrive at polygamy. Mormon scholars and evangelical leaders with rich Hebrew word studies but poor wisdom will jockey to see who can churn out the first landmark book about how the Old Testament is pro-polygamy.

• *Christians will be hated.* Homosexuality has become a matter of civil rights. The plight of the gay population is now commonly compared with the struggles historically faced by ethnic minorities, women, and other marginalized groups. For Christians, racial issues and sexual issues are very different: the same Bible that says all races descend from one man and one woman and are reconciled together in Christ also says any sex outside of heterosexual marriage— including homosexuality—is wrong. In the same passage, Paul actually says that both slavery and homosexuality are sinful: "We know that the law is good if one uses it properly. We also know that the law is made not for the righteous but for lawbreakers and rebels, the ungodly and sinful, the unholy and irreligious, for those who kill their fathers or mothers, for murderers, for the sexually immoral, for those

practicing *homosexuality*, for *slave traders* and liars
and perjurers—and for whatever else is contrary to
sound doctrine."* The world does not think in such
biblical and theological categories, however, which
means that in the public mind, we Christians might
as well be wearing white cloaks with pointy hoods.

A few years ago I was invited to an event with
Billy and Franklin Graham for ministry leaders.
I sat with a group of Canadian pastors, and over
lunch we started talking about the issue of gay marriage in Canada. It might shock Americans to hear
that our neighbors to the north lack some of the
basic freedoms and protections we still enjoy in
the United States. For example, a colleague of these
pastors had recently been subjected to governmental
investigation after he preached Romans 1. I expect
we will soon face similar challenges here. Already
Christians who work in the wedding industry have
faced accusations and even legal action due to allega-
tions of discrimination and bigotry, simply because
they declined to participate in same-sex ceremonies
that violated their Christian convictions. "Do you
affirm gay marriage?" has quickly transformed from
a question of personal opinion to a mandatory moral
checkpoint that secular culture uses to evaluate the
validity of a person's entire perspective.

* 1 Timothy 1:8-10, NIV, emphasis added.

PORNOGRAPHY

Porn. Its cultural impact has not yet peaked, and we are living amid an enormous social experiment without a clue where it will take us. The *Huffington Post* says, "The Internet is for porn. We all know that," and the statistics could not be more concerning. For example, no less than 30 percent of all data transferred across the Internet is porn, 70 percent of men and 30 percent of women watch porn, the average person visits a porn site twice a week, and porn sites get more visitors each month than Netflix, Amazon, and Twitter combined.[13]

The average age of first Internet porn exposure is eleven,[14] and 90 percent of boys and 60 percent of girls are exposed to pornography before the age of eighteen.[15] Youth with significant exposure to sexuality in the media are considerably more likely to lose their virginity between the ages of fourteen and sixteen,[16] and the mean age of first intercourse in the United States is now 16.4.[17] It is now common for young boys to have nude photos of their girlfriends on their phones to enjoy and show their buddies; about 30 percent of older teenagers engage in "sexting" (sending sexually explicit text messages). Fornication is casually known as "friends with benefits," and watching porn is akin to playing cards—something people do just to pass the time.

Other studies show that human orgasm affects the same parts of the brain that heroin and cocaine do. "Because of this activity, many have referred to being 'addicted' to sex. . . .

Oxytocin and vasopressin are released slowly during sexual activity, and released in much larger quantities in conjunction with an orgasm."[18] As I said in my book *Real Marriage*, I believe that "the natural chemical high, what some call a 'biochemical love potion,' resulting from sex and orgasm was designed by God to bind a husband and wife together. In the best sense of the word, God intends for a devoted married couple to be 'addicted' to each other, bound together in every way."[19] But the norm today is to casually engage in this bonding activity, becoming addicted to the act rather than to a spouse.

Consequences of Pornography

Those are the facts, but as a pastor I also see the faces and hear the stories.

Guys who are so addicted to porn they are unable to meet a woman without seeing her as porn instead of a person. Husbands so addicted to porn and masturbation that they are unable to sexually respond to their wives because they prefer images to intimacy. Women who are so addicted to porn and sex toys that they have no intention of marrying, or wives who are not interested in sex with their husbands because they "take care of" themselves. And, perhaps worst of all, couples who decide that porn should be the center of their marriages, so they watch it together and fantasize about other people like two codependent addicts held together by shared highs.

The implications of widespread porn have only begun to surface. Here's the tip of the iceberg:

- *Pornography promotes sex trafficking and abuse.* Those who are in pornography and prostitution are used and abused, beaten and broken, and often held as modern slaves for the sex industry.
- *Pornography contributes to sexual sin in all forms.* As people crave greater sexual highs through more forbidden and risky behaviors, they engage in all manner of sexual deviance: sinful lust, fornication, bisexuality, homosexuality, bestiality, pedophilia, adultery, and sexual assault, to name a few.
- *Pornography downplays the severity of sexual sin.* With so many people becoming ensnared by sexual sin, especially Christians from younger generations, we are increasingly less likely to see this behavior as sinful and more likely to see it as normal. This helps to explain why the younger a person is, the less likely he or she is to see sexual sin as a problem, let alone sinful. Engaging in sexual sin is simply an acceptable lifestyle and recreational activity.
- *Pornography deteriorates one's ability to be faithfully content in marriage, which leads to painful marriages and broken homes.* God did not give our first parents a standard of beauty but rather a spouse. This is because our spouses are to be our standard of beauty. When this is not the case, we are guilty of coveting and what

Jesus referred to as adultery of the heart.* This explains the uptick in adultery and the trend of older men divorcing their wives to pursue younger women and live out their porn fantasies.[20]

- *Pornography corrupts relationships between parents and children.* The "cougar" phenomenon celebrates older women who are sexually involved with guys the same age as their own sons. Fathers into "barely legal" porn, or porn stars dressed up like young girls in school uniforms with their hair in pigtails while sucking on lollipops, are prone to lust after their daughters' friends or even their own daughters as they enter the teen years.

Regarding this last point, this trend leads to a devastating cycle of abuse. One father explained to me that as his daughter matured physically, she started to look like the porn stars he enjoyed, which made him feel uncomfortable around her. He stopped hugging her, kissing her on the forehead, sitting next to her on the couch, and showing other appropriate forms of affection that he had shared with her since she was young. Not knowing her father's sin problem, the daughter began to think there was something wrong with her and started craving male attention. She found a boyfriend—who, interestingly enough, was into porn—and she began watching it with him at his request. He pressured her to do some things from the movies, which made her uncomfortable.

* See Matthew 5:27-28.

When she declined, he sexually assaulted her. This made her feel dirty and worthless, which led to a series of bad dating relationships and more sexual assaults.

As a father of two girls and a pastor to thousands of women, I wish I could say this kind of story was rare. It's not. Sexual assault happens to one in four women and one in six men at some point in their lifetimes.[21] If everyone left my church but those who have been sexually assaulted, I would still have a megachurch. Because it is one of the most underreported crimes, those numbers are likely very low—probably only 5 to 40 percent of the actual total.[22] Sexual assault is often the initial tragedy that leads to prolonged pain and grief in other forms. At Mars Hill Church, we've found that people who struggle with self-mutilation, depression, suicidal thoughts, self-medication (food, drugs, alcohol, sex, gambling, shopping), remaining in abusive relationships, anger, bitterness, the idolatry of dependence ("I must always be in a dating relationship"), and the idolatry of independence ("I won't allow anyone close enough to hurt me") are often trying to cope with the effects of sexual assault they endured at some point in life.[23] Unfortunately, as the collateral damage of pornography and sexual deviance proliferate, sexual assault and all of its subsequent symptoms will undoubtedly increase as well.

This is doubly true on college campuses that foster a rape culture. Young women away from parental support are prone to eating disorders, out-of-control drinking, and pressure to perform sexually in order to attract the interest of popular males. Underage men without adult supervision or godly male role models drink a lot, watch a lot of porn, and compete with one another sexually, treating young women as, as one frat guy told me, "toilets for fluids." Having worked with college students for more than twenty years and now as a dad of an adored daughter just a few years from college age, I find this horrifying, devastating, infuriating, and terrifying.

My wife was sexually assaulted before we met. I grew up by the airport down the street from strip clubs, cheap massage parlors, and hourly rate motels. The Green River Killer and Ted Bundy—both serial killers obsessed with pornography—picked up many of their victims down the street from my house. These issues are deeply personal to me and close to the heart of Father God. We have an entire generation of young Christian leaders sitting on the sidelines feeling discouraged and disqualified because they were defeated by lust. Jesus died for our sin and cleanses us from our unrighteousness. Without the gospel, we are dirty, defiled, damaged, discouraged, distracted, and defeated. Sexual addiction and sexual assault fueled by porn is the cultural issue for this generation. It's a digital plague that has become an epidemic.

INTOLERANT TOLERANCE

After the release of our book *Real Marriage*, Grace and I had media interviews set up with a number of folks in the mainstream press, but the interview I was most concerned about was with CNN's Piers Morgan, who seems to enjoy kicking evangelicals as much as David Beckham likes kicking soccer balls.

A few days prior to my interview, Kirk Cameron had been a guest on the show, and Piers took him to the proverbial woodshed for his biblical views on homosexuality and gay marriage. I decided to handle the show alone, rather than subject my lovely wife to what I was sure would amount to juggling live grenades in front of an international audience. To be honest, I feared that if Piers Morgan was unkind to my wife, I would lose my cool and our interview would result in a legendary YouTube clip featuring me vaulting over the desk while yelling my dad's old construction-worker words to extend what the apostle Paul calls "the right hand of fellowship."

By God's grace, however, things went well with Piers. He was an enjoyable guy for the most part. We are both Irish, formerly Catholic, and stubborn, so it felt familiar. I brought him a nice study Bible, and he thanked me, saying I was the first person to ever give him such a gift. The show was edited fairly, though I was bummed they took out the segment where I told him that one day he would be sitting across the desk from Jesus Christ to answer God's questions and that he was not ready for that day.

At one point, our discussion turned to the subject of tolerance. Piers gave a lot of weight to the issue, as do many in our culture today:

MORGAN: Do you think you're a tolerant kind of guy?

DRISCOLL: I love people very much and—

MORGAN: That's not the same thing.

DRISCOLL: Well, how do you disagree with people that you love? That's a very difficult issue for everybody, but for a pastor in particular, because—

MORGAN: But do you preach tolerance?

DRISCOLL: I've preached that we should love our neighbor, that we should accept—

MORGAN: But tolerance. Tolerance in particular.

DRISCOLL: You keep hammering it. What do you mean by tolerance?

MORGAN: Tolerating people who may have a lifestyle or a belief that you don't agree with.

DRISCOLL: Yes, we have to. When Jesus says "Love your neighbor," he knows you're not going to agree with all your neighbors, but he wants you to love them, to seek good for them, to care for them.[24]

Our conflict was around the old definition of tolerance (which I hold) and the new definition of tolerance (which he holds). Theologian D. A. Carson explains how the definition of tolerance has changed from accepting that lots of people have different views, some of which are wrong, to agreeing that all views are equally true.[25]

The old view of tolerance assumed that (1) there is objective truth that can be known; (2) various people, groups, and perspectives each think they know what that objective truth is; and (3) as people/groups disagree, dialogue, and debate their conflicting views of the truth, everyone involved will have an opportunity to learn, grow, change, and possibly arrive together at the truth.

The new tolerance is different from the old tolerance. The new view of tolerance assumes that (1) there is no objective truth that can be known; (2) various people, groups, and perspectives do not have the truth but only what they believe to be the truth; and (3) various people, groups, and perspectives should not argue and debate their disagreements because there is no truth to be discovered and to assume otherwise only leads to needless conflicts and prejudices.

A few things are perhaps most curious about the new tolerance. One, it denies moral absolutes while holding to the moral absolute that there is no moral absolute. I know that's confusing. It's like saying, "There is no such thing as absolute truth"—to which the question should be asked, "So does that mean you're lying when you want us to believe your absolute statement that truth does not exist?" You cannot say absolutely that there are no absolutes. I hope you see that the statement itself saws off the very limb it's sitting on. Two, the new tolerance is dreadfully intolerant. Ask average people arguing that every moral view is equally valid and respectable whether they think it's right for big corporations to destroy the planet, that women at one time could not vote, or that people once smoked on airplanes, and see if they are willing to truly welcome, embrace, celebrate, and tolerate everyone and everything. I'm pretty sure if an old guy smoking a cigarette while buying stocks in oil companies and gun makers and bemoaning that it was a big mistake to let women learn to read was sitting on a plane next to a feminist on staff with Greenpeace, she would not defend his equally wise and welcomed alternative lifestyle to the flight attendant who was being intolerant for asking him to put out his cigarette.

Today morality is more like wine tasting than banking. In banking, there is a right and wrong answer. If you deposit a thousand dollars in a new bank account and a week later try to withdraw eighty dollars, you would not be willing to agree to disagree when the teller says your account is empty. But we don't see morality like banking anymore. Instead, we see it more like wine tasting. In wine tasting, everyone has their favorite blends and no one is necessarily right or wrong—it all depends on individual palates. No one has the right to declare as an absolute truth that simply because they prefer a specific grape or vintage, it is superior to all other wines. The problem is, the God of the Bible sees morality like banking, not wine tasting. This is why Jesus referred to sins as "debts" in the world's most famous prayer.[*]

---

[*] Matthew 6:12.

Consequences of the New Tolerance

Today there are not sins. There is only one sin, and that is calling anything a sin.

When I was a kid, it was common when we disagreed with other kids to simply tell them to shut up. Today those kids have grown up, gone to college, and learned that saying, "You are being intolerant" is a more shaming and winning way of saying, "Shut up."

In response to accusations of intolerance (or bigotry or fundamentalism or hatred or any other criticism, for that matter), some will want to give Jesus an extreme makeover that glosses over the very statements that got him killed, such as, "Repent," "I tell you the truth," and "I am the truth." Evangellyfish with no backbones will propagate the myth that God and Jesus are infinitely tolerant. This process is well under way.

A Christian may mean well in responding to criticism, but without certain doctrinal guardrails, attempts to pacify critics and enemies almost inevitably end in capitulation, compromise, or apostasy. "Christian heresies vary wildly in their theological substance, but almost all have in common a desire to resolve Christianity's contradictions, untie its knotty paradoxes, and produce a cleaner and more coherent faith," says Ross Douthat. He explains that would-be heretics "tend to see themselves, not irrationally, as rescuers rather than enemies of Christianity—saving the faith from self-contradiction and cultural irrelevance."[26]

In the trailer for his book *What We Talk about When We Talk about God*, Rob Bell illustrates Douthat's painful point perfectly:

> Things have changed. We have more information and technology than ever. We're interacting with a broader, more diverse range of people than ever, and the tribal God, the only one many people have ever heard of, appears more and more small, and narrow, and irrelevant, and in some cases just plain mean, and other times not that intelligent. . . . Is God going to be left behind like Oldsmobiles? I don't think so, because I believe there are other ways, better ways of talking about God, and understanding God.[27]

Apostates with good intentions have plenty of company throughout history. They try to make Christian faith timely but forget that, since it is timeless, it is already and always timely and never needs to be made trendy. This is an old pile, and once you step in it, it's very tough to get it off your shoe. In the earliest days of the Christian church, it was the Gnostics who sought to upgrade biblical truth with cultural trends by making it more supernatural and less natural, more heavenly and less earthly, more spiritual and less physical. Many years later, during the age of reason, it was the deists and Unitarians—like Thomas Jefferson, who literally cut out portions of his Bible—who sought to liberate the Bible from old myths like miracles and the supernatural realm. The goal to make Christianity more appealing to naturalists was led by David Hume, who denied that God, if he exists, involves himself in our world but rather functions more like an absentee landlord who left natural laws in place as his property manager. All attempts to rescue Christianity from "primitive" parts of the Bible are efforts by people to save God. But the entire story of the Bible is that we need God to save us and he needs no one to save him. These sorts of rescue attempts may be appealing to the world, but they are appalling to the Lord.

The intolerance of tolerance is nothing new. As G. K. Chesterton quipped, "Tolerance is the virtue of the man without convictions." For thousands of years, Christians who crave the acceptance of the world have abandoned their belief in the true God of the Bible. The present day is really no different; we just get to watch it unfold on YouTube.

BAD DADS

Good dads are an endangered species. Bad dads are an epidemic.

Tonight roughly 40 percent of kids will go to bed without a father.[28] For the first time in America's history, the majority of children born to women under thirty are born out of wedlock.[29] As a dad to three boys and two girls I love with all my heart, I find it devastating to think that the normal childhood for children going forward will be to have no father. Making matters worse, some who *do* have a father have a bad dad.

There are various kinds of bad dads. Some dads abuse their authority by being harsh and even violent with their children. Some dads avoid their responsibilities by not providing for the physical, emotional, mental, and spiritual well-being of their children. Some dads abdicate their responsibilities and are just bums you can't depend on for much of anything. And some dads abandon their responsibilities by walking out on Mom, expecting her, the grandparents, the school, the foster care system, the church, the treatment center, or the legal system to correct and raise their children.

The Bible often refers to the husband and father as the "head" of the family.* This does not mean he is better, superior, or the king. Rather, it means that God holds him accountable for the well-being of his family. This does not imply that his wife and kids bear no responsibility for their sins and failures. Rather, it means that, to some degree, the father is responsible for his own sins and failures as well as the sins and failures of his family. This explains why, though Eve sinned first, God sought out the man, asking, "Where are you?"† And God has that same question for the bad dads today: Where are you when your children are being harmed, neglected, and not fathered?

The husband and father is the most dominant person in the family. Even if he is absent, his absence dominates the family system.

This is covenantal thinking. In covenantal thinking, the

---

* See Genesis 2:18; 5:2; 1 Corinthians 11:2-16; 14:33-34; Ephesians 5:21-33; Colossians 3:18; 1 Timothy 2:11-15; Titus 2:3-5; 1 Peter 3:1.
† Genesis 3:9.

head of the covenant is responsible for everyone in the covenant. For a covenant family, this means that the mother and father are both responsible for the well-being of the children but that the father bears the greatest responsibility of all and will give an account to the God who reveals himself as Father and Father to the fatherless. Thinking covenantally means a man is not thinking about a good time as much as a good legacy and does not see children as a burden but rather a blessing. By God's grace, covenantal thinking compels a man to be the kind of man his sons should become and his daughters should marry, as that's likely exactly what will happen.

Christian dads who think covenantally and accept their responsibilities actually make the best fathers.[30] To be a good dad means a man has to be tough and tender. He has to be tough enough to go to work, fight to provide for his family, protect them from harm, and contend against all the worldly influences seeking to undermine God's plan for his children, such as sexual assault, drugs, alcohol, pornography, lethargy, and plain old folly. And he has to be tender enough that his daughters are deeply cherished without any fear of him and his sons are lovingly encouraged to become men. In short, he should be tough *for* his family and tender *with* his family.

Consequences of Bad Dads

The bad dad epidemic is having a profound impact on how newer Christians and younger people are seeing God and church. In a day when families are broken and people are constantly moving, nowhere feels like home and no one feels like family. I believe there is a correlation between the rising tide of bad dads and the rise in moralistic therapeutic deism among younger generations. This view of God is much like their experience of their earthly fathers—distant, uninvolved, and essentially having abandoned them to figure out life on their own. Bad dads and broken families mean that a lot of people have never had a family and had to in essence raise themselves, which results in immaturity, pain, and loneliness.

Today a single woman is more likely than her male counterpart to go to college, have a job, attend church, and have a driver's license. Apparently guys are increasingly more likely to ride than drive so they can play video games and download pornography, as their phones are now more important than their futures.

The *New York Times* magazine ran a story called "What Is It about 20-Somethings?" which looked at the new life stage of emerging adulthood.[31] The article echoed what other recent studies are showing and something I've been saying since we launched our church in 1996: the world today is filled with boys who can shave.

Between boy and man is a new, indefinite life stage called adolescence. Too old to be boys and too irresponsible to be men, those in this stage are just called "guys." During this time, which can last from years to decades, a guy has all the benefits of being a man and none of the responsibilities as he avoids work, marriage, and children like they are diseases.

These guys tend to laugh a lot, not knowing that their lives are the joke, and it ain't funny.

The marketing sweet spot for many companies is young men ages eighteen to thirty-four. These guys don't know what it means to be men, so marketers fill the void with products that help them to define manhood by what they consume rather than what they produce. But men are supposed to be producers, not just consumers. We're defined by the legacy, the life, and the fruit that come out of us, not by what we take in.

What happens if you walk into a church and try to find out what a man looks like? First of all, you're not going to find a lot of competent, responsible, single, godly men ready for marriage and family in most evangelical churches. The least likely person you'll see in church is a single twenty-something male. He is as rare at church as a vegan at a steak house.

In the world, boys who can shave are children who are consumers. In the church, boys who can shave are cowards who are complainers. The church has to pick up this slack. Where else can a young man go to figure out what to do with the rest of his life? There is no National Organization for Men to join or Men's Studies minor in college.

I have no hope in guys. But I still have hope *for* the guys because they are "the image and glory of God."* God wants his glory to shine through men. God wants his Kingdom to be made visible through them. God wants them to be his

* 1 Corinthians 11:7.

sons. God wants them to follow, by the power of the Holy Spirit, in the example of Jesus.

I don't care if you buy a truck or play some video games or rock out on your guitar. But the problem is when those are prevalent, predominant, and preeminent in your life. Some of you would argue and say, "It's not a sin." No, but sometimes it's just dumb. You got fired because you fell asleep at work after staying up too late to get to the next level of some online game and become a guild leader. That's dumb. You work one part-time job so you can play more guitar or Frisbee golf. That's dumb. You spend all your money on a new car or truck or toys or gear or clothes or gambling or fantasy football. Dumb. Some of you say, "Well, it's not a sin." Neither is eating your cereal box instead of the cereal. It's just dumb. There are a lot of things that Christian guys do that aren't evil; they're just dumb and childish. There's nothing wrong with being a boy—if you are a boy. There is a big problem if you are a boy with a beard and a condo.

In light of the increase of boys who can shave, it is not surprising that for the first time in American history, single adults outnumber married adults.[32] That is part of a global trend across many Western first-world nations. And the results are numerous.

First, people are waiting longer to marry. For men, the median age of first marriage for those who do marry is around thirty. For women, the median age of first marriage is the late twenties. This is considerably higher than at any point in American history.[33]

Second, people are sexually active during their single years, using birth control and abortion to ensure they do not have children. Simply put, the issues of marriage, sex, and children are no longer related in our culture for most singles who spend their time dating, relating, and fornicating.

Third, people are cohabiting during their single years. It is estimated that about a quarter of unmarried women between the ages of twenty-five and thirty-nine are currently living with a partner and about half have lived at some time with an unmarried partner (the data are typically reported for women but not for men).[34] Over half of all first marriages are now preceded by cohabitation, compared to virtually none earlier in the century. The most likely to cohabit are people aged twenty to twenty-four.[35]

David Popenoe and Barbara Dafoe Whitehead, marriage experts with the National Marriage Project, say, "What makes cohabitation so significant is not only its prevalence but also its widespread popular acceptance."[36] In studies, nearly 66 percent of high school senior boys and 61 percent of the girls indicated that they "agreed" or "mostly agreed" with the statement "It is usually a good idea for a couple to live together before getting married in order to find out whether they really get along." And three-quarters of the students stated that "a man and a woman who live together without being married" are either "experimenting with a worthwhile alternative lifestyle" or "doing their own thing and not affecting anyone else."[37]

Fourth, churches that advertise themselves as being a

great place for the entire family, with service times on Sunday morning that work for young families, a great kids' program, rocking student ministry, family camps, and daytime Bible studies for stay-at-home moms, are inadvertently telling the majority of Americans—singles—they are not welcome and to stay away. And singles do, especially single men in their twenties, the least likely demographic to attend church. The unintended message to singles is, "Go ahead and do what you want, and if you ever get married and have kids, then visit our church, because we are basically a social club for families."

Studies from Josh McDowell, LifeWay Research, Barna Group, and secular researchers report that somewhere between 69 and 80 percent of evangelicals in their twenties leave the church.[38] Some people suggest that even if young people leave the church, they still maintain an internal faith. However, sociologists Christian Smith and Patricia Snell believe the evidence suggests that "when young people leave on the outside, they've left on the inside, too."[39] Young evangelicals are likely to leave their faith because they are not able to articulate their own faith, and many lack a biblical worldview.

Another argument is that many evangelicals who leave in their twenties will come back. However, using estimated numbers of evangelicals' true size, of the 3.7 million evangelicals in the United States who are between eighteen and twenty-nine years old, 2.6 million will leave the faith at some point by their twenty-ninth birthday. Moreover, 1.7 million of the 2.6 million will not return to an evangelical church, based on the evidence at hand. While young people are leaving the evangelical church at the highest rate, singles over thirty-five years old and single moms are also leaving the church. These specific groups are leaving because "'they are fed up with their needs never being addressed.' . . . We are failing to disciple our people into transformed thinking or living."[40]

Jesus was single, and we cannot afford to present faithful followership of him as something only for the now-minority group of married couples with children.

In addition to fewer marriages, people are also having fewer children.[41] In recent years, the birthrate in the United States has dropped lower than at any other time in the nation's history.[42] Where I live, there are cats, dogs, and children in that order, numerically speaking.[43] In fact, there are 50 percent more cats than children. We, along with San Francisco and Washington, DC, are the only American cities where fewer than 20 percent of all households have a child.[44] Children make up only 15.3 percent of Seattle's population, and that number drops to 13.4 percent in San Francisco.[45] That trend will increase across major cities and Western nations.

It is not uncommon these days for people to refer to their pets as their "babies." In Seattle, Green Lake is a popular urban spot for people to walk, jog, skate, and ride bikes. Curiously, I have seen people pushing their pets (usually a cat or dog) in baby strollers around the lake. I have seen other people carrying their pets in front packs made for babies.

These same types of people are also pressing to have their pets allowed into restaurants, added to their wills, and given greater legal rights. What is getting lost is a biblical worldview, which teaches that our place as God's human image bearers is below God and above animals. We are not equal to God but rather created by God and under his rule. And animals are not equal to us but rather created by God and under our rule.

There is a growing vocal contempt of motherhood in cities that has not hit the kid-friendly suburbs where most Christians live. Mothers in the cities are referred to as "breeders," a pejorative term. In fact, in the week I am writing this chapter, in God's providence our church is being picketed . . . again—this time by a women's rights group. They will meet in a park to hear some lectures from people who somehow forgot that they entered this world through a mom, then march to our downtown church to protest what they call "breeders" before proceeding to their final stop—an enormous strip club—to protest the objectification of women. That we and the strip club ended up on the same team just goes to show that common sense is anything but common.

One article titled "Why I Am Not Having Kids," written by a married woman in Seattle who decided she would never have children, caused quite a stir as she pondered, "To breed or not to breed, this was the question." One of her primary answers for not having kids was "Not having a child is the most important thing I could do to reduce my carbon footprint."[46] I might add, another way is to stop writing for newspapers printed on murdered trees.

This is a trend we've seen in our church as well. As young, urban, educated married couples meet Jesus, they like to say things like "We don't feel called to have children," as if motherhood were a special calling from Jesus reserved solely for "breeders." I always thought we called them by the more affectionate title "moms," but I guess the world has really changed, and it's time to start buying my mom a "Happy Breeder's Day" card. Thankfully, we know the Person who created the world, and he said to fill it up with people.*

CHEAP CHRISTIANS

Like many people, you have probably lost money in recent years. If you own a home, the value is down. If you have investments, the value is down. If you have retirement savings, the value is down. Just thinking about it probably has *you* down.

You are not alone. Lehman Brothers went out of business due to bankruptcy, General Motors and Chrysler went bankrupt and only stayed afloat by the Treasury Department, Washington Mutual no longer exists after the largest bank failure in US history, and the list goes on and on. We've even got a name for this phenomenon—the Great Recession.

In hindsight, there were signs indicating trouble was on the horizon. However, we didn't heed those warnings. Some

* See Genesis 1:26-28.

of us likely ignored the warnings, others waited too long to make changes, and still others just hoped things would get better somehow.

They did not. Things got worse. Much worse.

Today the church of Jesus Christ finds itself in a similar place.

Tom Brokaw referred to the generation that emerged from the Great Depression, put down Adolf Hitler, and created modern America as the "Greatest Generation." Those of the Greatest Generation were marked by hard work, sacrifice, frugality, and generosity. They built our nation. And they built the churches, denominations, parachurch ministries, mission organizations, Bible colleges, and seminaries that constitute American evangelicalism today and which in some regard funded and fueled the spread of Christianity around the globe.

That generation—my grandparents' generation—is finishing its race, and my generation and my children's generation are dropping the baton. Today we demand rights and avoid responsibilities, we take instead of give, and we expect entitlements without obligations. Generosity is considered a function of the government, which collects money from rich people in order to provide goods and services for the "99 percent." We've replaced capitalism with cannibalism. Hipsters may have kept their grandparents' clothing, but they have lost their grandparents' frugality and generosity.

Churches and ministries feasting on the final generosities of the Greatest Generation are in for a rude shock. And new churches and new ministries hoping to one day see the kind of donations that marked the Greatest Generation will be greatly disappointed. Many churches and ministries have seen donations decrease by 20 to 30 percent each year since the Great Recession began around 2007. Economic difficulties can be used to explain a decrease in donations to an extent, but John Dickerson notes that during this same time period, "the generation that gives almost half of total donations began passing away." He predicts that "over the next twelve years, this faithful and reliable generation will pass away. As they do, total giving will decrease by as much as half for typical evangelical ministries—nationally, regionally, and locally."[47]

Simply put, younger people give less money than older people do. According to data published in 2008 by the Pew Research Center, even though the older generation accounts for only 19 percent of the national church, they give 46 percent of the donations. Young evangelicals will likely "become more generous as they age [but] that does not mean they will become *as generous* or consistent as the present-day older generations."[48] For one thing, younger generations tend to have greater consumer debt, negative equity, and overall less trust in institutions, which translates into less giving.

We've got a serious generational slide. Baby Boomers were rebellious and did not want to be tied to an establishment but did enjoy some financial earnings in their power years. Generation X (I still hate that term) tends to be a greedy and selfish bunch, wanting to make money and live lavishly if possible. Millennials have a completely different mind-set, as they do not have a strong work ethic but rather a strong play ethic. They are less concerned with working hours and making dollars than having fun, building relationships, and enjoying entertainment. Among these groups, some have a lot of money and some have little money, but no group is proving generous to the church or the cause of the gospel.

The future is bleak. Of course there will be exceptions, and change can happen. But if my experience and the experiences of the hundreds and hundreds of church planters I work with are any indication, things will not get better overall. We have to learn to do more ministry with less money.

Consequences of Lower Charitable Giving

The impact of this particular trend is fairly obvious (less money), but there are some additional, subtler ways that it is already compromising the church's mission:

- *Consumer Christians are consuming programs rather than committing to a church.* The prevailing sense of entitlement in our culture today leads to people who show up in church expecting to give nothing but receive everything. Coupled with a consumer mentality, this means that if one church presses for giving or is unable to provide the desired religious goods and services, another church nearby can potentially attract "customers" by talking less about

money and providing better goods and services.
Many modern Christians will take the best programs
from every church while committing to no church.
They even have a name for it: "church shopping."

- *The church promotes causes instead of Christ.* Young
  people tend to get excited about causes more than
  they do churches. In the age of social media, it is
  easy to identify with a cause and enjoy the public
  perception of goodness through commitment to a
  cause. This commitment, however, is often as shallow
  as it is public. Personal investment is neither long
  term nor generous. People are prone to not give to
  any church or ministry consistently, and when guilt
  sets in, they'll jump on the latest cause bandwagon
  for some public recognition, donate a few bucks,
  and assuage their consciences for a while.

- *Parachurch ministries siphon resources and undermine
  the health of the church.* Parachurch ministries include
  Bible study ministries, mom groups, student groups,
  singles groups, and other similar organizations.
  Not all parachurch ministries are bad; in fact, the
  best ones foster collaboration across churches for
  important ministry and unity. But many operate
  without any standard for membership or biblically
  qualified spiritual authority. Parachurch ministries
  borrow church facilities and could potentially
  steer donors away from churches, with the end
  result being people who are no longer actively and

sacrificially participating in a local church. Cheap Christianity promotes the idea that we can pick and choose from a variety of local ministries and churches, much like a salad bar where we can snack on whatever suits our own personal convenience and preference— and then skip the cash register at the end.

- *The supply line for global missions and ministry is drying up.* A cash-strapped church in America will affect more than our own country. This is an international issue. For years, American Christians have been the supply line that funds the front line of global missions and ministry. From supporting theological education around the world and funding missionaries, to participating in mercy and justice projects and translating the Bible into various languages, American Christians (led by the Greatest Generation) have provided a huge financial base. Unless something changes, however, there will soon be fewer Christians, giving less generously, while the global population and need rise.

A CALL TO RESURGENCE

Apart from the Holy Spirit dropping a grace bomb with a mushroom cloud of revival, the good days are behind us and hard days are ahead. Fewer Christians and more quitters. Fewer givers and more takers. Less cultural acceptance and more cultural resistance.

And it's awesome! Praise God. We need something big enough to live for. We need a mountain to climb. We don't need more bored church people falling asleep, filling the blanks in some outdated discipleship manual in a musty church basement while humanity outside is getting stacked up like kindling for an eternal fire.

The church is facing a great opportunity—or harvest, to use the biblical term—to be part of a far-reaching and sub-stantial movement of the Holy Spirit to see many come to Jesus. You're invited to be a part of this resurgence of timeless truth for troubled times. In fact, you're *key* to it. The world is changed by influential ideas embodied in families, institu-tions, and networks—all of which are made up of ordinary people ready to be part of something extraordinary.

At the end of the day, we don't need more celebrities and more debate. We need more Spirit-empowered Christians who take seriously their call to witness to God's work in this world, and to do so in unity with other Christians, even if they don't agree on some secondary matters. This means modeling the implications of the gospel in our relationships, in our families, in our interactions with one another, and in the way we engage the world with the message of hope found in the good news of Jesus Christ.

How about you? How's it going? Do you love Jesus? Are you living a generous life by the Spirit's power on God's mis-sion? Or are you simply a cultural Christian or yet another consumer taking goods and services from churches and min-istries but giving little to nothing of your wealth and works?

How is your family? How is your church?

Are you spending more time making plans or making excuses?

Are you spending more time critiquing what others are doing than doing what you are supposed to be doing?

Whatever you do next, don't call for yet another theologically flawed prayer meeting. You know the kind. Christians get together to beg the Holy Spirit to show up and empower them for ministry. The entire assumption is flawed. In the opening chapters of Acts, the early church prayed, and then the Holy Spirit showed up and has not left God's people since. We are never out ahead of the Holy Spirit. He is never the one unwilling to advance the gospel. We do not need to pray loudly to wake him up from his nap, or pull him down from heaven by our fervent prayer. *Pray*, but not that way. The main point of a prayer meeting is not to move God but to allow God to move us. The Bible says we Christians grieve, quench, and resist the Holy Spirit.* So, we pray to repent of our sin against him and align our will with his. The Spirit is always available to us, and in prayer we make ourselves available to him.

Chapters two and three of Revelation record Jesus speaking from heaven to churches on earth, saying no fewer than six times, "Hear what the Spirit says to the churches."

Are you listening?

What is he saying?

---

* See Acts 7:51; Ephesians 4:30; 1 Thessalonians 5:19.

Chapter 3

A NEW REALITY
FROM MODERNISM TO EVERYTHINGISM TO TRIBALISM

OVER THE YEARS, I have endured and enjoyed a lot of controversy over things I've said. But one event I participated in brought more tension, conflict, and controversy than anything else I'd ever been involved in. People absolutely freaked out, as if I'd tasered their mom just to see what would happen.

That event was Elephant Room 2012.

It was organized by Pastor James MacDonald of Harvest Bible Chapel in Chicago. He'd hosted the event for a few years, and I had always enjoyed being part of it.

The big idea was pretty simple: get Christian leaders to sit down and talk to one another in an informal and respectful way. The hope was to model civility among Christian leaders and the importance of talking with people instead of just about them in an effort to build mutual understanding, if not affection, among leaders for the good of the church. An invitation to speak at the Elephant Room was not an endorsement of anyone, handing the pulpit to anyone, or just listening to anyone. This was a moderated forum for respectful but pointed discussion over matters of disagreement among various leaders.

In past events, we had enjoyed frank and fun conversations with numerous guests, including Greg Laurie, one of the leading pastor-evangelists in the United States; Jack Graham, the former two-term president of the Southern Baptist Convention; Perry Noble, the founding pastor of NewSpring Church; Steven Furtick, leader of Elevation Church and Code Orange; David Platt, pastor and bestselling author; Matt Chandler, leader of The Village Church and Acts 29; Wayne Cordeiro of the New Hope churches; and Crawford Loritts, pastor and former staff member of Campus Crusade for Christ.

Then Bishop T. D. Jakes was invited to attend. And he accepted.

The pin was pulled from the grenade.

Reformed complementarian leader Mark Dever quickly opted out of the event, likely sensing impending radioactive fallout. Soon members of various groups grabbed dead cats and started flinging them from every direction, criticizing everyone and everything over something that had not yet happened. Just the fact that differing Christian leaders would sit in the same room without an octagon and a bloody battle to the death was considered a Judas move.

Opting not to wear an athletic cup or helmet—although I strongly considered it—I boarded a plane for Chicago. The Christian leaders spent the first night together over an informal dinner, just getting to know one another. I found it to be a great time and very insightful. Each man at the table demonstrated genuine humility and was really open and enjoyable. I was seated near Bishop Jakes and found him to have a great sense of humor and some unique insights.

Partway through dinner, Bishop Jakes leaned over and kindly asked me about myself. He clearly had no clue who I was, and when I told him I was part of the Reformed tribe, he looked at me like a beagle who heard a whistle. I tried to explain that guys like John Piper and Wayne Grudem were influential to me and that I spent time with groups like Resurgence, Acts 29, and the Gospel Coalition.

He still had no idea who or what I was talking about. He had never heard of any of these ministries or leaders. I then said something I won't repeat and probably should not have said (but it was funny), and he said, "Oooooh . . . yeah, I *have* heard of you." I guess if you don't make famous, there's always infamous.

The point of this story is not my reputation for sticking my foot in my mouth. The point is that Christianity has become so splintered and separated that even Christian leaders don't know one another. I likely had as little knowledge of

T. D. Jakes's ministry as he did of mine. If he started dropping names of well-known leaders in his circle, books they'd written, churches they pastored, and conferences they held, I, too, would have been oblivious.

In this culture of everythingism, the Internet has allowed people to self-organize around religions big and small, revive ancient pagan practices, create their own spiritualities, and combine aspects of various belief systems. You could perhaps not think of any kind of spirituality without being able to find some group devoted to it online. Each is what Seth Godin would describe as a tribe:

> A tribe is a group of people connected to one another, connected to a leader, and connected to an idea. For millions of years, human beings have been part of one tribe or another. A group needs only two things to be a tribe: a shared interest and a way to communicate.[1]

Tribes come in all sizes, from a handful of people to millions. Inside of evangelicalism, the predominant culture is now tribalism. We aren't one big group anymore with one key leader. We live and worship in tribes, which is not necessarily a bad thing. But because tribes have a tendency to circle the wagons and fight against one another rather than mobilize together for growth, we've unknowingly contributed to the rapid demise of Christendom in America—in spite of ourselves. We've lost sight of what's really important, and the priority of the gospel has gotten lost in the shuffle as each tribe tries to shout the loudest to make its own particular point about something else.

One of the most isolated literal tribes on the earth today is the Sentinelese islanders. They live on a small island in the Indian Ocean. They have no contact with the world beyond their tribe. In 2004 a tsunami washed over their island. A rescue helicopter seeking to discover if they had all perished soon realized the tribe had lived through it, as the men aimed arrows with poison darts to discourage the rescuers from landing. The tribe has survived with their way of life for generations. But they have no idea what is going on around the world and no impact on it. Some Christian groups are much like this—isolated and shooting at even friendly visitors while making little or no impact on the world, which is not what Jesus had in mind when he told us to bring the gospel to the ends of the earth. Nevertheless, Christian tribes do exist and are held together by a tribal way of life, which we will now explore.

TRIBAL COMMUNICATIONS

Tribal beliefs are determined, clarified, and multiplied in the tribe through tribal communication. This communication can be tribal chief to tribal chief, tribe to tribal chief, tribe member to tribe member, or tribe member to outsider from another tribe.[2]

As a result of technology, new tribes are forming all the

time. But before you blame our current state of affairs on advancing technology, you need to know that throughout history God's people have consistently adapted new technology as a means of tribal communication.

The invention of the printing press in the fifteenth century was in large part responsible for the Protestant Reformation. Before then, although the ideas raised by the Reformation did exist, they lacked the means to be widely communicated. The printing press changed everything, as information (e.g., books, pamphlets, magazines, Bibles) for the first time could be widely and less expensively distributed, thereby allowing an enormous tribe called Protestantism to come into existence in a more formal and organized way.

With the twentieth century, electricity, loudspeakers, and microphones forever changed church services, conferences, and concerts. Billy Graham's emergence as a high-profile evangelical tribal chief would simply not have happened without the innovations that allowed him to preach to stadiums of people.

By the early twentieth century, the human voice was sent over radio. This allowed preachers to reach a tribe of people without physically gathering them in one room to hear a sermon. Before long, people scattered around the world could listen in their homes and cars to their tribal chiefs preach sermons, teach classes, and host call-in radio programs.

Around that same time, the first public movie theater opened, and Christians were among the first to utilize the new technology. Many of the first films ever made focused on the story of Jesus, as various Christian tribes sought to tell about the life, death, and resurrection of Jesus Christ.

Television created a ready-made tribe, as Christian leaders again took advantage of the technology to create their own television programs and channels. Not long after the Internet went public in the early nineties, my wife, Grace, and I planted our church near the Microsoft headquarters. We wanted to reach out primarily to young college-educated singles working in the tech industry. We did not at that time see the providence of God, as the Internet has forever redefined how people access information and one another.

Now, with the advent of the Internet, we have an unprecedented opportunity for forming and growing various tribes. Geography is no longer a limiting or defining factor for tribal involvement. In the past, evangelical tribes were better able to control communication to and from their tribes, since such communication had to be delivered through Bible colleges, seminaries, magazines, conferences, publishers, and radio and television programs. Today, however, social media, e-mail, blogs, podcasts, e-books, YouTube, and other various websites have significantly reduced the influence of such gatekeepers. Today, anyone, anywhere, at any time can say anything to conceivably any-one via the Internet for free. Add to that the immediate and constant access we have through smartphones, and it's easy to see how now, more than ever, tribes are forming and mobilizing so quickly.

Communication today is instant, constant, global, and permanent. This means that content—both good and bad—can be delivered immediately. And that content is flowing every minute of every day, all around the world. Once something is posted online, it lives forever—even if it is untrue or later repented of.

This means that every tribal leader and all tribal communication is now under constant scrutiny and open to interpretation. Our tribes often find themselves caught up in controversies as crowds gather to watch the conflict and online flame throwing. Simply stated, everyone loves a good old-fashioned fight; we've just moved the fight from the playground to the web.

One result of this online warring is the development of tribes that are almost entirely negative. They define themselves more by who or what they are against than by who or what they are for. The feminists have a short list of men to follow and harass, the Calvinists have a short list of Arminians to follow and harass, the cessationists have a short list of charismatics to follow and harass—and the list goes on and on. Such people know that individually they are like bees—annoying and pesky, but not deadly. Hence they tend to create swarms for greater effect. This is what Charles Haddon Spurgeon meant when he referred to his critics' tactics as "death by a thousand bee stings." The target of such stings is almost always the tribal chief. The one who calls the shots is also the one who takes the shots.

TRIBAL COMMITMENTS

Tribal commitments are the beliefs that define and establish tribal boundaries. Within various evangelical tribes, these include theological beliefs on both primary and secondary issues, as well as philosophies of ministry and political affiliations. The tribal chief defines and defends these tribal commitments through tribal communications. Let's look briefly at some examples.

- *Bible translations.* Sometimes a tribe can be defined by which Bible translation it prefers. Such preferences are usually the result of the tribe's feelings regarding translation principles. While there are exceptions, the following are generalized examples. Tribes that lean more toward fundamentalism often stick to the New American Standard Bible. Mainline and egalitarian tribes tend to use the New Revised Standard Version. Within the Southern Baptist Convention, the Holman Christian Standard Bible is most popular. More traditional and fundamental tribes still use the King James Version. Within mainstream evangelical, Pentecostal, and charismatic tribes, the New King James Version, New International Version, and New Living Translation are popular. My preference is the English Standard Version, which is often used in Reformed tribes, who jokingly refer to it as the Elect Standard Version.

- *Creeds, confessions of faith, and doctrinal statements.*
  Such statements formalize tribal commitments and
  help to clarify who is in and who is out of the tribe.
  In the early days of the Gospel Coalition, tribal
  leaders spent a number of years working on a joint
  confession of faith under the leadership of Tim Keller
  and Don Carson. Joining them were roughly forty
  pastors who met in Chicago multiple times and
  carefully worked through the founding documents
  for doctrine and mission. It was an honor to sit at
  the table to witness firsthand the careful work that
  was done in the early formation of that tribe. Most
  Christian tribes have similar documents.

- *Books.* Landmark books are vital to the creation and
  preservation of a tribe's commitments. Some books
  are so important that the tribe considers them to be
  the defining work on an issue. Because publishing
  is an important component of disseminating and
  defending a tribe's core beliefs, some tribes go so
  far as to start their own publishing houses.

- *Christian education.* Within each tribe, Christian
  colleges, Bible colleges, seminaries, and other
  schools serve as the gatekeepers for determining
  what future leaders will believe and ultimately
  teach. Like publishing, tribal education is seen as
  a key component for protecting and promoting
  each tribe's core commitments—so much so that

it is not uncommon for larger tribes to found and
support their own schools.

- *Conferences.* One of the most visible and effective
means of sharing and spreading tribal commitments
is through conferences. The tribal leader often
serves as the host of the event, inviting the speakers
who will best empower fellow tribal leaders. Tribal
commitments are spoken from the stage and sold
from the bookstore. When a tribal leader quotes
someone positively from the stage (usually an author
or a fellow leader), this endorsement holds great
weight within the community.

The communications we pay attention to and commitments
we hold help reveal what tribe we are in. It's important to understand which tribe we belong to because only when we acknowledge where we are can we determine where to go from here.

So which tribe are you in? (For those of you who hate being
labeled, just so you know, that is now a tribe as well, so enjoy
the stereotyping and make friends with the other people painted
into your box.) Everyone is in a tribe, and the sooner we realize
we are not each unique, like a snowflake—a special, one-of-a-
kind person, just like Mama said—the sooner we will make
sense of ourselves and the spiritual cul-de-sac we call home.
You are likely not unique, particularly special, or a maverick
innovator. One of the most truthful, helpful, and controversial
commencement speeches of all time says it this way:

You are not special. You are not exceptional.

Contrary to what your soccer trophy suggests, your glowing seventh grade report card, despite every assurance of a certain corpulent purple dinosaur, that nice Mister Rogers and your batty Aunt Sylvia, no matter how often your maternal caped crusader has swooped in to save you . . . you're nothing special.

Yes, you've been pampered, cosseted, doted upon, helmeted, bubble-wrapped. Yes, capable adults with other things to do have held you, kissed you, fed you, wiped your mouth, wiped your bottom, trained you, taught you, tutored you, coached you, listened to you, counseled you, encouraged you, consoled you and encouraged you again. You've been nudged, cajoled, wheedled and implored. You've been feted and fawned over and called sweetie pie. Yes, you have. And, certainly, we've been to your games, your plays, your recitals, your science fairs. Absolutely, smiles ignite when you walk into a room, and hundreds gasp with delight at your every tweet. . . .

But do not get the idea you're anything special. Because you're not.[3]

As that great prophet Pink Floyd once declared, "All in all you're just another brick in the wall."[4] But do not dismay. This realization is liberating and not discouraging. The pressure is off to be Jesus 2.0, one of a kind and without peer.

You can be yourself, enjoy the tribe you are in, and get to know some brothers and sisters in Christ from other tribes.

WHICH TRIBE ARE YOU IN?

I still remember the wonder of learning how to mix colors with paints when I was young. It was fascinating to see what happened when two colors came together as one. Blue and yellow make green. Red and yellow make orange. Blue and red make purple. You know how this works. Furthermore, as you also know, there are hues within the colors. Darker and lighter shades occur when each color is mixed in differing proportions to the other colors.

Evangelical tribes are kind of like that. Various doctrines are like colors, and when you mix them together, it colors your theological commitment. Depending on what is heavily stressed in the mix, some things become stronger and others weaker in their coloring.

I admit that my analogy breaks down in many ways, not the least of which is the fact that God's black-and-white truth cannot be manipulated or changed. But for the sake of this chapter (and my analogy), I will be talking about various evangelical tribes that all agree on these black-and-white issues:

- the Bible as God's perfect and authoritative Word
- one God in three persons (Trinity)
- human sinfulness by nature and by choice

- Jesus as fully God and fully man who lived without sin, died in our place for our sins, and rose from the dead
- salvation bestowed by the grace of God when a sinner turns from sin and trusts in Jesus alone through faith
- new birth through the Holy Spirit
- eternal heaven for believers and eternal hell for unbelievers

Agreeing that these points are black and white and non-negotiable, we'll look at the other preferences, beliefs, and commitments that shade the various tribes within evangelicalism. While these questions do not get into all areas of theology, they do address the areas that most commonly color tribal affinity.

Although these four questions aren't going to make or break anyone's salvation (there is room for disagreement among the tribes), they are difficult, hotly debated, and therefore have the potential to be hugely divisive.

To keep this book at a readable length, I have chosen not to delve into all of the nuanced tribal positions. Rather than treat big issues in a little way, I've provided a very lengthy and detailed recommended reading list in appendix B to help you study these four questions from a wide variety of perspectives.

Admittedly, I do not write from a position of neutrality, as could no one else. I am gladly Reformed, complementarian, continuationist, and missional. These convictions are drums I have beat since the mid-1990s.

How about you? Which tribe are you in? Let's find out.

1. ARE YOU REFORMED OR ARMINIAN?

The basic difference between Reformed and Arminian Christians is their belief about salvation. This big issue of how someone enters into relationship with God is connected to numerous related issues, such as whether a Christian can lose his or her relationship with God and how a Christian grows in relationship with God. Simply put, this is no small matter, theologically or practically.

Synergism is the belief that, in varying degrees (depending on who is advocating this position), God and man work together in the process of saving a sinner (justification). Conversely, *monergism* is the belief that God alone works for our justification and we play no part whatsoever in our salvation. Think of it this way: Does God reach down to grab sinners and save them solely by the work of his hand (monergism), or do sinners also reach up and grab God's hand if they are to be rescued (synergism)? Is salvation one-handed (God alone) or two-handed (God and us)?

There are now, broadly speaking, two general Christian schools of thought regarding salvation in general and predestination in particular. These schools follow the teachings of either John Calvin or Jacob Arminius. They are called Reformed (Calvinists) or Arminians, respectively. It is important to note that both tribes, generally speaking, believe that God is the one who initiates salvation with sinners. In fact, this is the biblical pattern from the Garden of Eden forward, when our first parents hid from God after their first sin, and God took the initiative to pursue them. Principally, this is what 1 John 4:19 means: "We love because he first loved us."

Arminians can trace their modern history to a theological council that met in 1610, known as the Remonstrance. The term refers to the fact that they were protesting the Reformed view of how God saves sinners. The council promoted the Five Points of Arminianism, which stress the freedom of the human will in salvation:

1. Free Will
2. Conditional Election
3. Universal Atonement
4. Resistible Grace
5. Perseverance of Some Saints

In response, the Calvinist theologians met some 154 times at the Synod of Dort (1618–1619) and responded with the Five Points of Calvinism, which stress the sovereign choice of God in human salvation:

1. Total Depravity
2. Unconditional Election
3. Limited Atonement

4. Irresistible Grace
5. Perseverance of All Saints

Admittedly, both the Arminian and the Calvinistic camps are broad and include many hues of color that create various nuanced positions. For example, many Arminians would disagree with the fifth point of Arminianism, not believing that Christians can lose their salvation, and many Reformed people (including me) struggle with the third point of Calvinism, that Christ died only for the elect, depending on how the issue is articulated (I prefer unlimited/limited atonement) and would prefer single predestination over double predestination (God predestines people for heaven but not hell).

Modern-day Reformed tribes include Acts 29, Together for the Gospel, the Gospel Coalition, Reformed Baptists, Presbyterian Church USA, Missouri Synod Lutherans, and New Frontiers. Reformed tribal leaders include past preachers such as Martin Luther, Jonathan Edwards, and Charles Spurgeon, along with the Puritans. Popular modern-day Calvinistic preachers include John Piper, John MacArthur, R. C. Sproul, Terry Virgo, C. J. Mahaney, and Tim Keller. Popular modern-day Reformed theologians include Wayne Grudem, Al Mohler, Michael Horton, and Don Carson. Well-known younger tribal chiefs who lean more toward the Reformed view include Lecrae, Matt Chandler, Francis Chan, and David Platt.

Those in the Arminian tribe include John Wesley (the

founder of Methodism), Free Will Baptists, Nazarenes, and many Charismatic and Pentecostal Christian networks and denominations such as the Assemblies of God and Foursquare. Popular modern-day Arminian theologians include Stanley Hauerwas, Will Willimon, and Thomas Oden. Popular modern-day Arminian preachers include Bill Hybels; Billy Graham; Calvary Chapel tribal leader Chuck Smith; the Surratt brothers (tribal leaders in the Association of Related Churches); Brian Houston, the tribal leader for Hillsong; Foursquare tribal leaders Jack Hayford and Wayne Cordeiro; and Joel Osteen, Joyce Meyer, and T. D. Jakes (who all have leadership influence across multiple charismatic and Pentecostal tribes). Well-known younger tribal chiefs who lean toward the Arminian view include Joseph Prince, Perry Noble, and Steven Furtick.

So, are you Reformed or Arminian?

2. ARE YOU COMPLEMENTARIAN OR EGALITARIAN?

Ever since sin entered the world, women have suffered much cruelty and abuse. Likewise, children have been abandoned, left to die, and treated like commodities. Though men have suffered, too, they've also been the cause of much of the suffering that women and children endure.

Because the world can be a tragic place for women and children, a biblical understanding of how men should relate to them is very important. In our age of great gender confusion—from belittling, misogynistic chauvinism to man-hating feminism—the issue of God-designed gender roles is incredibly timely and vital for the well-being of God's people.

Masculinity and femininity are important issues, and it's crucial that we derive our understanding of them from the Bible rather than from our cultural identity and assumptions. Faith doesn't exist in a vacuum, and there is no cultureless expression of Christianity. What this means is that many people—knowingly and unknowingly—allow what they've been taught, experienced, or supposedly known for their whole lives to effectively trump the Bible's authority. We live in a culture that is a product of the implications—both positive and negative—of the feminist movement. But as Christians, we are to have our thoughts and actions shaped by the Bible.

Because this can be a very emotionally charged topic with practical implications for people's lives, both sides will be well served to be gracious in their disagreement—something I'm sad to report I've not always been. For starters, there are different hues in both tribes. For example, some people are egalitarian in respect to general male-female relations but still think certain offices in the church are limited to men (or women) only. On the other hand, one could think that all of the church offices are open to both men and women while at the same time being committed to relational complementarianism in the home. This needs to be said because while biblical faithfulness to the roles of men and women is extremely important, people can hold differing views on the relationship of men and women in the church, home, and society while still being committed Christians. Though a significant issue, this is not a salvation issue. Here it's important to briefly outline a sketch of the common positions taken concerning male-female relations.

Chauvinism and Hard Feminism

Sadly, some critics of complementarianism confuse it with chauvinism. Chauvinism wrongly sees men as created above women and superior to them. This kind of thinking does not accept that women are equal and equally bear God's image. Chauvinism denigrates, disrespects, and dominates women. In chauvinism, essentially every man is considered above every woman, and women should not aspire to leadership over any men. The Christian form of this false teaching wrongly extends the Bible's commands for wives to respect their husbands to women in general respecting men in general. This is foolish and endangers women. As a complementarian father of two daughters, I could not fathom telling my daughters to submit and defer to men in general.

Hard feminism, particularly in secular forms, holds the same basic beliefs as chauvinism but flips the roles. In varying degrees, hard feminism says that men are now the lesser gender, as men have been responsible for most of history's evils (war, sexual assault, murder, and so forth) and women have become more advanced and civilized. This is supported by the fact that women are more likely to attend college and live responsible lives than men, who are taking longer than ever to grow up into responsible adults—if they ever do. The case is then made that since men have proved themselves unable to evolve, women should rule over them.

Both views idolize one gender and demonize the other. Both are wrong. And the Scriptures are clear that men and women carry equal value by virtue of the fact that all men and women were made in the image of God.* For the purposes of this book, we'll dismiss chauvinism and hard feminism as alternatives for God's people, which leaves us with egalitarianism and complementarianism to consider.

Egalitarianism

The common position held by many Christian tribes today is often referred to as *egalitarianism*. Those who hold this position say there is no God-ordained structure of how men and women ought to function in the church, society, and the home.

The egalitarian position teaches that because men and women were created as equals and because differences like race and gender have been eliminated through Christ, there is no need for a specific structure regarding how the sexes relate to one another and the church. Practically speaking, this means that either a man or a woman can be a pastor in the church and that either the husband or the wife can be the family leader.

Egalitarian tribes include denominations such as Methodists, Nazarenes, Quakers, Seventh-Day Adventists,

* See Genesis 1:26-28.

Assemblies of God, Foursquare, Hillsong, the Association of Related Churches (ARC), most charismatic and Pentecostal groups, and pretty much any tribe that includes women pastors. Egalitarian tribal chiefs include Linda Belleville, Gilbert Bilezikian, Gordon Fee, Scot McKnight, Bill Hybels, Ben Witherington III, N. T. Wright, Joyce Meyer, Brian Houston, T. D. Jakes, Joel Osteen, Paula White, and Christine Caine.

Complementarianism

Complementarianism teaches that men and women are equal and work together in every area of life. However, in the government of the home, husbands are to lovingly, humbly, and sacrificially lead their families as Christlike heads and wives are to submit to their husbands as patterned after Jesus' relationship with the church.

According to complementarians, there is no difference between the government of the home and the church. So in the government of the church, only men are called to lovingly, humbly, and sacrificially serve as pastors.

To be clear, the Bible speaks to the role of men and women only in the context of the home and the church. Practically, this means that women do not submit to men in general, but wives do submit to their husbands. Women are free to pursue positions of leadership in the church such as being deacons, and they are free to lead over men in other arenas outside of the church such as in government and business.

Complementarian tribes include Southern Baptists,

Calvary Chapels, fundamentalist groups, the Gospel Coalition, Together for the Gospel, conservative Reformed denominations (for example, the Orthodox Presbyterian Church and Presbyterian Church in America), Missouri Synod Lutheran, New Frontiers, Roman Catholics, and Acts 29. Complementarian tribal chiefs include Wayne Grudem, John Piper, R. C. Sproul, Al Mohler, Mark Dever, John MacArthur, Tim Keller, Don Carson, Elisabeth Elliot, Bruce Ware, Ligon Duncan, and James MacDonald.

So, are you complementarian or egalitarian?

3. ARE YOU CONTINUATIONIST OR CESSATIONIST?

Spiritual gifts are talents or abilities, whether supernatural or natural, that are used for the building of the church of Christ.* They are sometimes divided into the categories of sign gifts and service gifts, or the categories of sign gifts, service gifts, and speaking gifts. The New Testament includes four separate lists of gifts, though these lists are almost certainly representative rather than comprehensive, since they differ from one another. Within the church, there are two categories of belief with regard to whether all of the spiritual gifts continue to function in the church today.

Cessationism

Cessationists believe that the sign gifts of the Spirit (for example, miracles, healings, speaking in tongues, private

---

* See Romans 12:6-8; 1 Corinthians 12:8-10, 28-30; Ephesians 4:11.

extrabiblical revelation, casting out demons) have ceased. According to cessationism, these sign gifts served a unique role in the first century as a confirmation both of apostolic authority and of the apostolic message prior to the close of the canon of Scripture. Since the Bible is complete, we no longer need sign gifts in order to know what the message of God is. We can simply read the Bible, which has God's completed message. It is important to note that cessationists do not believe that all spiritual gifts have ceased, as some people have charged. Cessationism deals only with the sign gifts.

A subsection of cessationism includes those who are "open but cautious." This is a growing group of people who believe that sign gifts and the miraculous are possible but highly unlikely today. Consequently, when the presence of such a gift is claimed, it is to be treated with some skepticism. Cessationists typically believe that the sign gifts no longer function as they did during the New Testament era but that God can, as he desires, theoretically perform similar miracles. They are theoretical continuationists but practical cessationists. Commonly, leaders in this tribe are prone to give credit to the gospel rather than to the Holy Spirit.

Cessationist tribes include most fundamental groups, Conservative Baptists, the more conservative wings of the Reformed tribe (such as the Orthodox Presbyterian Church), and those holding to older forms of dispensational theology. Cessationist tribal chiefs include John MacArthur, Richard Gaffin, and Daniel B. Wallace.

Continuationism

Continuationists believe that the sign gifts of the Spirit continue. The Spirit still works through gifts such as prophecy, knowledge, tongues, and healings in various ways. Sometimes continuationism is also referred to as being charismatic.

Continuationists teach about and practice the supernatural gifts in a wide variety of ways. Conservative continuationists prefer order in their gathered church services and place Scripture and godly church leaders in the position to discern what is from the Holy Spirit and what is not. Those who are less conservative are much more open when it comes to claims of prophecies, promises, and healings.

Some conservative tribes broadly label continuationists as charismatics and dismiss them all as dangerous to the church. This notion is simply incorrect. Continuationism, as with any of these tribal traits, has several strands with different hues. To avoid confusion, I prefer to use the term *Spirit-empowered* to refer to conservative continuationists. Jesus was Spirit-filled, Spirit-led, and Spirit-empowered and said he would send the Spirit to us with power to live a life patterned after his, by his power, for his glory. This keeps Jesus at the center of our lives and doctrine without grieving, quenching, or resisting the Spirit.

Conservative continuationist tribal leaders include Chuck Smith, Jack Hayford, Wayne Cordeiro, Steven Furtick, Brian Houston, Wayne Grudem, Greg Laurie, John Piper, C. J. Mahaney, and Terry Virgo. Conservative continuationist tribes include Calvary Chapel, Acts 29, Assemblies of God, Foursquare, and most Bible-based charismatic and Pentecostal groups.

So, are you a cessationist or a continuationist?

4. ARE YOU MISSIONAL OR FUNDAMENTAL?

The primary difference between missional and fundamental churches is their understanding of a faithful Christian relationship with mainstream or "secular" culture. Missional believers emphasize the need for Christians to adopt the posture of missionaries in the culture in which they live—by appropriating, insofar as Scripture allows, the customs, dress, language, and other cultural elements. Fundamentalist believers emphasize the worldliness of the surrounding culture and generally avoid participating in it for fear of compromise. (This is one reason why home-schooling is often associated with fundamentalism, though obviously this educational option appeals to many different families for many valid reasons.) Fundamentalists argue for a cultural retreat, where mainstream movies, music, fashion, language, and other aspects of culture are to be rejected for the purpose of holiness. Some fundamentalists will jettison this label, and as one who believes in the fundamentals of the faith, I would say that fundamentalism focuses primarily on training up believers and is weak on reaching unbelievers.

When trying to evangelize, fundamentalists are more

prone to use methods such as tract bombing and aggressive street witnessing, which are devoid of relationship and which unbelievers experience as the spiritual equivalent of a flasher in a trench coat. One of the most vocal issues for fundamentalists is a very literal six-day Creation and a young earth, and for some, a commitment to a literal thousand-year premillennialism, often with dispensational commitments to other eschatology issues such as the Rapture. Some have explained fundamentalism as "militant evangelicalism" because it holds to mostly common evangelical beliefs but does so with a more battle-ready attitude, seemingly looking to fight with other tribes they see as being guilty of theological compromise on primary or secondary issues (a distinction some fundamentalists hardly recognize as they will war over alcohol, worship styles, age of the earth, and speaking in tongues just as fervently as they'll defend the Trinity and the Resurrection).

Both missional and fundamental churches do missions—sending people and money from their tribe to reach other people groups around the earth. The difference is how they behave in their home culture. A fundamental church sees itself primarily as a *sending* tribe. They send people and money across the world for missions but do not live as missionaries across their city. They may evangelize lost people where they live by witnessing, street evangelism, handing out tracts, or holding evangelistic meetings, but they are not intentionally aware of or deeply involved in the local culture and its customs.

Conversely, a missional church sees itself as both a *sent* and a *sending* tribe. People in this tribe see themselves as having been sent across the street and as sending money and people across the globe. Missional churches emphasize contextualization in the culture, rather than retreating from it, so as to transform it by the power of the gospel. Consequently, missional churches generally have more converts than fundamental churches. Most evangelical churches are good at one or the other—sending *or* being sent—with most churches leaning more toward sending.

Missional tribal leaders with influence across multiple tribes include Andy Stanley, Ed Stetzer, Tim Keller, Greg Laurie, Rick Warren, and Craig Groeschel. Missional tribes include Catalyst, Acts 29, Passion, Resurgence, Purpose Driven Network, and numerous church-planting tribes.

Fundamental tribal leaders include John MacArthur, Ray Comfort, Voddie Baucham, and Ken Ham. Fundamental tribes include many Southern Baptist churches, numerous smaller fundamentalist networks, and Together for the Gospel.

IDENTIFY YOUR TRIBE

To help you navigate the complicated world of evangelical tribalism, I've devised a handy reference chart (see pages 112–113). Admittedly, this chart is exceedingly imprecise. It is filled with generalizations and stereotypes, all designed to help you discover what tribe you are in while giving fits to nerds who like their charts as tight as the top button on their well-starched shirts.

Solely by God's grace, I've had the great honor of meeting other tribal chiefs from around the world. I have been criticized by some tribes and chiefs, and I have done my share of criticizing. Over and over people have asked me why certain people and groups hug and why others punch. After having this conversation maybe hundreds of times, I realized that *this* really is a key issue for Christians today. And this is not a new problem. Unholy jealousy, unhelpful rivalries, and ungodly acrimony are the worldly ditch into which all who resist the Spirit fall. Addressing this very issue, Paul said to the immature church in Corinth who wrongly thought they were spiritually mature,

> I, brothers, could not address you as spiritual people, but as people of the flesh, as infants in Christ. I fed you with milk, not solid food, for you were not ready for it. And even now you are not yet ready, for you are still of the flesh. For while there is jealousy and strife among you, are you not of the flesh and behaving only in a human way? For when one says, "I follow Paul," and another, "I follow Apollos," are you not being merely human?
>
> What then is Apollos? What is Paul? Servants through whom you believed, as the Lord assigned to each.[*]

The names have changed, but the problem remains.

---

[*] 1 Corinthians 3:1-5.

	REFORMED	ARMINIAN	COMPLEMENTARIAN	EGALITARIAN	CONTINUATIONIST	CESSATIONIST	MISSIONAL	FUNDAMENTALIST	
Charismatic Pentecostal		x		x	x				
Reformed	x		x			x		x	
Reformed charismatic	x		x		x			x	
Reformed egalitarian	x			x	x				
Reformed missional	x		x			x	x		
Arminian missional		x	x		x		x		
Arminian egalitarian missional		x		x	x		x		
Fundamental Baptist		x	x			x		x	
New Reformed	x		x		x		x		

DESCRIPTION

You probably like Joel Osteen, T. D. Jakes, *Charisma* magazine, raising your hands in worship, Joyce Meyer, and phrases like "next level," "breakthrough," and "sow a seed."

You probably like Together for the Gospel, the Gospel Coalition, Nine Marks, R. C. Sproul, reading books by dead guys, expository preachers who wear suits and have bad bands at their services, and wish this book had more footnotes and fewer jokes.

You probably like New Frontiers, Wayne Grudem, John Piper, and reading dead guys like Jonathan Edwards while listening to modern praise music and anything from Reach Records.

You probably like reading Gordon Fee and feel very lonely as your tribe could have its international conference in a phone booth.

You probably like Tim Keller, planting churches, footnotes, and NPR and don't talk about the Holy Spirit nearly as much as the gospel.

You probably like Calvary Chapel, Andy Stanley, Craig Groeschel, Rick Warren (even though he's actually more Reformed than Arminian), and driving to Catalyst conferences while listening to music from Passion conferences and wearing a T-shirt raising awareness about some poverty-related issue.

You probably like Hillsong, New Hope, Perry Noble, Steven Furtick, well-played music, smiling, and seeing people get saved and prefer short books with lots of illustrations over long books with lots of Greek words.

You probably like discernment websites run from caves deep in the woods; the words *illuminati, Armageddon, last days,* and *one-world order*; not having any fun; trying to connect current events to the book of Daniel; and sketching out an end times chart on an ammo box while your wife churns butter and your kids save up enough money to run away from home.

You probably have an occasional bad attitude, tattoo, impressive theological library and liquor cabinet, *ESV Study Bible*, entire collection of the latest indie rock, and flannel shirts and boots for no reason as you do zero logging.

That word *servant* is an interesting one. It often refers to the person who brings food to your table and sets it before you. Paul's point is that if Jesus is the Chef cooking up the banquet of truth for us to enjoy, isn't it silly for tables at the same party to fight and throw their food at one another over which table has the best waiter?

It is simply unreasonable for us to expect that all Christians in any tribe will act maturely. As one commentator said of this section of Scripture, "The church is a school for sinners, not a museum for saints."[5] But in love for the immature (who are often the last to see their immaturity) and for unity across tribes, tribal leaders must model civility with other godly tribal leaders and rebuke their own tribes as Paul, the founder of the church at Corinth, was doing publicly to his own converts. In this instance, the ongoing skirmishes were between immature members of various tribes, not between tribal leaders such as Paul, Apollos, or Peter. This is why Paul could go on to say, "So let no one boast in men. For all things are yours, whether Paul or Apollos or Cephas [Peter] or the world or life or death or the present or the future—all are yours, and you are Christ's, and Christ is God's."* Bible commentator Leon Morris rightly says,

> [Paul] reasons, "Why do you limit yourselves by claiming that you belong to a particular teacher? Do you not realize that all teachers, indeed all things that are, belong to you in Christ?" So far from enriching

---

* 1 Corinthians 3:21-23.

themselves by staking their claim to exclusive rights in one teacher, the Corinthians were impoverishing themselves. They were cutting themselves off from greater treasures that were really theirs.[6]

It's important to ask yourself this one final question: Is your tribe a prison or a home? If your tribe is a prison, you rarely get out to meet Christians from other tribes, read anything from anyone not in your tribe, listen to any outside preachers, or sing any songs not created or endorsed by your tribe. If your tribe is a prison, you may not know that your nation is becoming increasingly anti-Christian, because you have been busy working within your tribe and battling against other tribes. If your tribe is a home, you are free to enjoy friendships with Christians from other tribes, read books and sing songs from believers outside your tribe, and pay attention to what is going on in the world.

I'm not talking about tolerating false-teaching wolves who, in the name of false unity, love the sheep in order to feast on them. The same Paul who admonishes unity through maturity is also responsible for some of the most vehemently debated teaching in the Bible (about women in ministry, tongues, predestination, homosexuality, and wives submitting to their husbands, to name just a few). He also models using God-given leadership authority to sternly rebuke false teaching, as he does in Galatians (where he says false teachers might as well emasculate themselves), and elsewhere he even names heretical tribal leaders Hymenaeus and Alexander.

Paul was willing to fight some tribal leaders, but not many tribal leaders. Paul was willing to fight over some issues, but not many issues. Similarly, we need to stop following Corinthian carnality and learn to choose our battles wisely.

Clearly, we are all in one tribe or another, with some of us straddling a line or two between tribes. How confusing all this must be to the outside world. No wonder they think we're strange! If they eavesdrop on our debates, they will hear fighting over secondary things and not a focus on the gospel that can save them. It's easy to get wrapped up in the politics, drama, and discussions of your own particular tribe, inter-acting only with your own tribe as your tribe goes to war with some other tribe. Meanwhile, as the world becomes more anti-Christian, the church is filled with more carnal Christians. Making matters worse, today the Corinthians have Internet connections, which ensures that the clowns never lack a carnival.

How we get out of this mess without falling into the well-worn ditches of theological hard conservatism (which fights for too much) and theological hard liberalism (which fights for too little) will be the subject of the next chapter. Similarly, we have to be known for who and what we are *for* more than who or what we are *against*. If we fail, Christianity will have a funeral rather than a future.

Chapter 4

HOME SWEET HOME
UNDERSTANDING OUR BORDERS

Where do you live?

It seems like an easy question to answer. But the farther you travel from home, the more different your answer to the question will be.

For example, when I'm traveling internationally, people often ask where I'm from, and I say, "The United States."

When I'm traveling in the States and am asked that question, I never say, "I'm from the United States," for the obvious reason that if I have no foreign accent and am in the country, people assume that's home for me. So instead I say, "Washington," or even "Seattle."

When I'm home in Seattle and someone asks where I'm

from, I answer with my neighborhood. And if I'm in our neighborhood and someone asks where I live, the answer is something like "We're up the street three blocks and then to the left."

Where do you live?

It's actually a complicated question. When I was in Turkey and was asked, "Where do you live?" I never answered, "Two doors down from the Johnsons, who have the big tree." And when I'm walking the dog and a neighbor asks me, I never answer, "In the United States."

We define where we live in relation to how close the people we're talking to live to us. The closer they live to us, the more detailed and specific we can be regarding where we live, because they're familiar with our world.

Spiritually speaking, where do you live?

Your local church or ministry is like your home.

The churches or ministries you partner with are like your neighborhood, with some neighbors you know fairly well.

The denomination, network, or other affiliations you align with are like the city where you live.

The tribe you identify most closely with is like the state where you reside.

The tribes most like yours are like the regions of a nation. For example, I live in the Northwest, which is a group of states that have much in common, such as geography and climate. You'll find similar commonalities in the Southeast, Northeast, Midwest, and other regions of the United States. To some degree, you can think of the various kinds of Baptists,

Reformed tribes, Charismatic and Pentecostal tribes, styles of churches (e.g., seeker or liturgical), and so on as regions with a lot in common.

And Bible-believing, Jesus-loving, sin-repenting, Kingdom-serving Christianity is like the nation in which you are a citizen.

The spiritual question of where you live is as complicated as its physical counterpart.

Physically speaking, the borders between neighborhoods, cities, and even states are barely noticeable. For those outside the United States, I apologize for the illustration from a solely American context; you'll need to rework my analogy for your culture. But you are probably used to us Americans being like this anyway, as eating French fries and Belgian waffles is as close as many of us get to a global understanding. Nonetheless, anyone who has driven in the United States knows that you can pass between neighborhoods, cities, and even states without being aware of the transition. At most there is a simple sign on the side of the road, and if you miss it, you're oblivious to the fact that where you are has even changed.

But it's very obvious when you pass from one nation into another. Those borders are fixed, obvious, and patrolled. Passing from one nation to another can be difficult, as both sides often have good reasons for living separately and controlling how much one side affects the other.

This brings us to two important questions:

One, where do you live, spiritually speaking? Or to say it another way, what is your tribe? How do you define yourself?

Who is closest to you, and who lives far away? Odds are the farther a tribe lives from you, the less you know about it, and the more you are suspicious regarding it.

Two, what borders do you and your tribe tend to fight over, discuss, teach on, publish about, and push against? What topics and other tribal leaders are dominating the conversations in your tribe? Is your energy spent on issues about the boundaries of your home, neighborhood, city, state, region, or nation? How much time and energy is wasted in warring that could be better invested in witnessing?

In some tribes all borders are treated as national borders, with wars fought over anything and everything, even if the issue is seemingly insignificant. In other tribes all borders are treated as neighborhood borders—little or nothing is fought for or over.

Each border is important, but they are not all equally important. For example, Mars Hill Church is my home. Like-minded churches are our neighborhood. Our commitment to being Reformed, complementarian, continuationist, and missional constitutes our four state borders. Because of our commitment to evangelism and church planting, we work with other evangelical churches who love Jesus, believe the Bible, and are led by Bible preaching. These are our regional connections. And the nation we are part of is Protestant Christianity as defined by the doctrines of the Bible and articulated in the major church creeds. This nation includes the Arminian, egalitarian, cessationist, and fundamental tribes with whom we lovingly disagree but work with for the sake of evangelism.

Now more than ever God's people must be committed to being gospel centered. Jesus can no longer be out there somewhere on the horizon as we look to culture, religion, politics, spirituality, or morality for our true north. To be gospel centered means to acknowledge that Jesus alone sits above all, rules over all, sees all, judges all, and is alone the object of our affection and the center of our devotion.

As secular culture becomes less and less warm toward Christian faith, it becomes more and more important for every tribe to be clear about national border issues for three reasons: One, we want Christians to know where the line is. There is a line between Christianity and apostasy, heresy, cult, or different religion. One example of a line is the doctrine of the Trinity, as this alone is the Christian concept of God; without it a person no longer has a Christian view of God. Two, we want new Christians to mature in their understanding of the faith. We cannot assume anything anymore. The growing rates of biblical illiteracy and theological ignorance mean that if we are going to err on the side of either too much or too little practical, biblical teaching, we should err on the side of too much. Every generation needs to be theologically trained, or, as the old Christians used to say, "catechized." Three, we want non-Christians to understand the essentials of our faith so that whether they receive or reject Jesus, they at least do so from an informed perspective. The remainder of this chapter is dedicated to these ends.

Every generation has its tribes that, sadly, become apostate or even cults. They do so by denying a border issue. Today is no different. Tomorrow will be no different. In response, there are always tribes that become fearful and wonder if they are the only ones who have not bowed their knees to Baal.

My aim in this chapter is not complicated. I want to carve out the national boundary issues of Christianity and distinguish them from the regional, state, city, neighborhood, and home boundaries. To keep things simple, I will refer to the national borders as the primary issues and all other borders as the secondary issues. My hope is to clarify a reasonable basis for the kind of unity that Jesus prayed for in John 17—the unity that occurs when tribes gather around the truth.

What follows are thirteen theses that constitute the border issues for biblically faithful and culturally missional Christianity. I know thirteen seems like a lot, but it's somewhere between the typical preacher's three-point sermon and Martin Luther's Ninety-Five Theses. Some of these issues define and defend Christian faith, while others evangelize and extend Christian faith. Admittedly, the rest of this chapter will get a bit theological and technical. But we're talking about very important issues—the kinds of things people have fought over and died for. Those with nerd tendencies (like me) will be excited about this. Those without nerd tendencies will be tempted to skip to the next chapter right about now. But please hang in there. Ask yourself, *Is there anything I would add to or delete from this list?*

The format of the rest of this chapter is simple—I define a primary border doctrine and then explain the secondary border issues related to that doctrine. I cover the same doctrinal ground in much greater detail in my book *Doctrine*.[1] (I've also included the biblical basis for each doctrine in the footnotes.) Primary border issues are points of division between Christians and non-Christians. Secondary border issues are points of distinction among Christians. These issues merit discussion, debate, and distinction among tribes, but they should not be a point of division if we are to see a resurgence of real Christianity. Lastly, what I am trying to do is force a bit of deep thinking. In our age of spiritual entertainment, self-help sermons, and [insert your number here] steps to improve [insert your felt need here], let's just admit that most people stink theologically and are about as ready to articulate basic Christian belief as a basset hound is ready to fly a helicopter.

TRINITY: GOD IS

We believe that there is only one true God, who eternally exists as a Trinity of equally divine persons: Father, Son, and Holy Spirit.* This does not mean that there are three Gods or that one God merely manifests himself as Father, Son, or Holy Spirit on various occasions. The Trinity is one God who eternally exists as three distinct persons—Father, Son, and Spirit—who are each fully and equally God in eternal relation-

---

* **One God**: see Genesis 1:1; Deuteronomy 4:35, 39; 6:4-5; 32:39; 1 Samuel 2:2; 2 Samuel 7:22; 22:32; 1 Kings 8:59-60; 2 Chronicles 15:3; Psalm 86:8-10; Isaiah 37:20; 43:10; 44:6-8; 45:5, 14, 21-22; 46:9; Jeremiah 10:10; John 5:44; 17:3; Romans 3:30; 16:27; 1 Corinthians 8:4-6; Galatians 3:20; Ephesians 4:6; 1 Thessalonians 1:9; 1 Timothy 1:17; 2:5; James 2:19; 1 John 5:20-21; Jude 1:25. **Father**: see John 6:27; 17:1; 1 Corinthians 8:6; 2 Corinthians 1:3; Ephesians 1:3; 1 Peter 1:3. **Son**: see Matthew 28:9; John 1:1-4, 14; 5:17-18; 8:58-59; 10:30-39; 12:37-41; see also Isaiah 6:9-11; Matthew 26:63-65; John 5:17-23; 19:7; Romans 1:3-4; 9:5; 1 Corinthians 8:4-6; Galatians 4:4; Philippians 2:10-11; Colossians 1:16-17; 2:8-9; 1 Timothy 6:15; Titus 2:13; Hebrews 1:8; 1 John 5:20; Revelation 1:8, 17-18; 17:14; 19:16; 22:13-16. **Holy Spirit**: see Genesis 1:2; Psalm 104:30; Micah 3:8; Hebrews 9:14; see also Acts 1:8; Romans 15:13, 19; Isaiah 40:13-14; see also John 14:16-17; Acts 5:3-4; 1 Corinthians 2:10; 2 Corinthians 3:16-18.

ship with each other. Each member of the Trinity thinks, acts, feels, speaks, and relates, because each is a person and not an impersonal force. Each member of the Trinity is equally God, which means each of them shares all the divine attributes, such as eternality, omniscience, omnipotence, and omnipresence.[*]

This is a defining issue of Christian faith. No other religion or spirituality adheres to the Trinity. But there are some nuanced issues around the Trinity that are secondary border issues. For example, in 1054 there was a Great Schism between the Western and Eastern Church over the issue of whether the Holy Spirit "proceeds" from the Father alone or from the Father and the Son. There is also a historic debate related to Jesus' ministry on earth. During this time, Jesus Christ clearly demonstrated submission to God the Father by saying he came to do the Father's will and by praying, "Your will be done."[†] The question is whether this apparent hierarchy within the Trinity is something eternal and part of its very structure or was something unique during Jesus' time on the earth.

REVELATION: GOD SPEAKS

We believe that God reveals himself to everyone everywhere through general revelation, which includes creation, common grace, and conscience.[‡] In general revelation, God has made known his power, divine nature, wisdom, majesty,

---

[*] **Eternality**: see Psalm 90:2; 93:2; 102:12; Ephesians 3:21. **Omniscience**: see Job 42:2; Psalm 139:1-6; 147:5; Isaiah 40:12-14; 46:10; Hebrews 4:13. **Omnipotence**: see Job 42:2; Psalm 147:5; Matthew 19:26; Ephesians 3:20. **Omnipresence**: see Deuteronomy 31:6; Psalm 139:7-12; Proverbs 15:3; Jeremiah 23:24; Colossians 1:17.

[†] See John 14:31; Mark 14:36, respectively.

[‡] **Creation**: see Psalm 8:3-4; 19:1, 4; 139:13-16; Romans 1:19-20. **Common grace**: see Exodus 31:2-11; 35:30-35; Psalm 65:9; 104:14; Matthew 5:45; Acts 14:17. **Conscience**: see Romans 2:14-15.

justice, and goodness.* We believe it is only by special revelation—God's gracious self-revelation—that anyone comes to
a saving knowledge of God.† We believe God has supremely
revealed himself to fallen humans through Jesus Christ, the
Son of God and his incarnate Word. We believe that while
Jesus is God's final Word to us, all of the divinely inspired,
inerrant, authoritative, and written sixty-six canonical
books of the Bible reveal to us the incarnate Word of God,
Jesus Christ.‡

Secondary border issues abound on the issue of revelation. Does God speak today through such things as dreams,
angels, or prophecy? How are we to "test the spirits" to see
whether a message is from God or a demon? How much
weight should we put on the findings of the hard sciences
and social sciences as they work from general revelation and
common grace? What are good Bible translations, and what
are bad Bible translations? What is the best study Bible?

CREATION: GOD MAKES

We believe that the Trinitarian God of the Bible—Father,
Son, and Holy Spirit—created the heavens and the earth
out of nothing, and lovingly prepared them as a good gift
to humanity and as a home in which to worship and enjoy

---

* **Power and divine nature:** see Romans 1:20. **Wisdom:** see Psalm 104. **Majesty:** see Psalm 8:1. **Justice:** see Romans 2:14-15. **Goodness:** see Acts 14:17.
† See Acts 10:1-7; Romans 2:7, 10; 10:15-18.
‡ **Jesus is God's final Word to us:** see John 1:1; Hebrews 1:1-2. **The Bible is divinely inspired:** see 1 Corinthians 2:13; 2 Timothy 3:16; 2 Peter 1:20-21. **Inerrant:** see Numbers 23:19; 2 Samuel 7:28; Psalm 12:6; 19:7; 119:140, 160; Proverbs 30:5-6; Isaiah 55:11; John 17:17; Titus 1:2; Hebrews 4:12; 6:18. **Authoritative and written:** see Matthew 4:4; 5:18; 1 John 1:1-3. **Reveals Jesus Christ:** see John 1:1. **The entire Bible reveals Jesus Christ:** see Matthew 5:17; Luke 24:27; Romans 15:3-4; 2 Timothy 3:15.

him.* We believe that all of creation comes from God: "In the beginning, God created the heavens and the earth."† The one, true, eternal God is both the author and subject of history. Everything in creation and history is dependent upon God and is only good when functioning according to his intentions for it. God, who inaugurated history, will also bring history to an end and create a new heaven and a new earth.‡

Perhaps no issue is as tribal as the preceding one. Debates rage in every direction on a list of secondary border issues, including the following: Is the earth very young, very old, or something in between? Are the six days of Creation literal twenty-four-hour days or some other period of time? Is Genesis 1–3 to be interpreted literally, or is it mainly poetry, communicating big ideas and not scientific specifics? Was there death of any kind before the Fall, including plant and animal death? What about dinosaurs? How big was Noah's flood—regional or global?

IMAGE: GOD LOVES

We believe that God created the first human beings, Adam and Eve, as male and female, in God's own image and likeness, equal in dignity, value, and worth, in order to mirror and reflect God as an act of worship and obedience. We

---

* God the Father's role in Creation: see Genesis 1:1; Psalm 33:6, 9; Hebrews 11:3. God the Son's role in Creation: see John 1:1-3; 1 Corinthians 8:6; Colossians 1:13-16. God the Holy Spirit's role in Creation: see Genesis 1:2; Job 33:4; Psalm 104:30. The earth was created out of nothing: see Hebrews 11:3. The earth was lovingly created: see Genesis 1:3, 6, 9, 11, 14, 20, 24, 26. The earth is a good gift to humanity: see Genesis 1:4, 10, 12, 18, 21, 25, 31. The earth is a home in which people can worship and enjoy God: see Psalm 19:1-2; Isaiah 43:7; Jeremiah 10:12; Revelation 4:11.
† Genesis 1:1.
‡ See Isaiah 65:17; 2 Peter 3:13; Revelation 21:1.

believe that human beings alone are God's image bearers. We believe that human beings, as God's image bearers, are under God and over lower creation, and that great error arises when humans are pulled up toward God or pushed down toward animals.* We believe that human life begins at conception and that an unborn baby is an image bearer of God.† We believe that God created marriage for one man and one woman, and created sex only for married couples.‡

Innumerable secondary tribal border issues surround this issue of human anthropology, particularly in the area of gender. Was there a hierarchy between Adam and Eve prior to the Fall? Does the entire idea of a hierarchy within marriage undermine true equality between men and women? Does Jesus' salvation eradicate the hierarchy that existed between husbands and wives because of the Fall? How does this all affect the government of the home today? Should husbands be family leaders, is there an entirely mutual sharing of leadership, or is it okay for the wife to lead the family if she is stronger than her husband? How does this affect the government of the church—may a woman be a pastor?

FALL: GOD JUDGES

We believe that God created this world in a perfect state and that upon the creation of the man and woman, God declared his entire creation "very good."§ This intended state of perfect

---

* See Genesis 1:26-27; 2:7; 5:1-3; 9:6; Romans 1:25; 1 Corinthians 11:7; James 3:9.
† See Psalm 51:5-6; 139:13-16; Isaiah 49:1; Jeremiah 1:5; Luke 1:15.
‡ See Genesis 2:18-25; Proverbs 5:18-19; Matthew 5:32; 19:9, 18; Mark 7:21-23; Galatians 5:16-24.
§ See Genesis 1:31.

beauty in all things is described in the Old Testament as *shalom.** Satan, in the form of a serpent, tempted Eve in Eden to mistrust God's word, and she was subsequently deceived by his crafty arguments.† The sin committed by Adam, also called "original sin," has been imputed to all human beings, except for Jesus.‡ Because of original sin, all human beings are sinners by both nature and choice.§ As a result of this sin nature, all fallen humans are by nature sinners, children of wrath, and destined to death.¶

On the issue of sin, there are numerous secondary tribal border issues, including the following: Do unborn babies who die in the womb, children who die at a young age before they can understand the gospel, or those without the mental capacity to understand the gospel have any chance at salvation, since they are sinners? Are people depraved, as most Arminians teach, or *totally* depraved, as most Reformed types teach? Are some people genetically predisposed to certain kinds of sins, and if so, does that affect their guilt?

COVENANT: GOD PURSUES

We believe a covenant is an agreement between two parties, and in Scripture covenants are particularly depicted as life-or-death relationships with God on his terms.** As a bond, a covenant

* See Isaiah 2:2-4; 11:1-9; 32:14-20; 43:1-12; 60:1-22; 65:17-25; Joel 2:24-29; 3:17-18.
† See John 8:42-47; 2 Corinthians 11:3; 1 Timothy 2:14.
‡ See Romans 5:19.
§ See Psalm 51:5; 58:3; Isaiah 53:6; 64:6; Romans 3:23; 1 John 1:8.
¶ See Romans 5:12, 19; Ephesians 2:3; 1 Corinthians 15:21-22, respectively.
** See Genesis 26:28. **The covenants of Abraham:** see Genesis 15:18. **Moses:** see Exodus 24:8; Deuteronomy 5:2. **David:** see 2 Chronicles 21:7; Psalm 89:3. **The New Covenant:** see Jeremiah 31:31; Ezekiel 37:26.

is a relationship that commits people to one another, God to God's people, and people to God. Oaths, promises, and signs accompany the bond or commitment. God made five major covenants in the Bible: with Noah and his family, with Abraham and his descendants, with Moses and the Israelites, with David and the kingdom of Israel, and the New Covenant of Jesus and the church.* God's covenants reveal his loving grace and mercy, because although people deserve nothing but condemnation, God gives gracious, covenantal salvation.

Regarding covenants, there are many secondary border issues between tribes. Can you be born into the covenant as part of a covenant family, or is what really matters personal faith regardless of your family? If people born into believing covenant families deny the faith, were they unbelievers all along, are they apostate, or did they lose their salvation and covenant membership? What is the sign of the covenant: the Holy Spirit internally, baptism externally, or both? If baptism is a sign of the covenant, should babies be baptized or only those old enough to profess faith in Christ? How should a Christian family educate their covenant children—home, public, private, Christian, or other schooling?

INCARNATION: GOD COMES

We believe that the eternal Son of God, the second person of the Trinity, became flesh—that is, assumed an additional

---

* **Noah:** see Genesis 6:18; 9:8-17. **Abraham:** see Genesis 12:1-3; 15:18; 17:1-14; 22:16-18. **Moses:** see Exodus 3:4-10; 6:7; 19:5-6; 24:8. **David:** see 2 Samuel 7:8-19; Psalm 89:3. **The New Covenant:** see Matthew 16:17-19; 26:28; Luke 22:20.

human nature—and entered into human history as the God-man Jesus Christ.[*] Jesus alone is one person with two natures, fully God and fully man. Jesus Christ is the Word, or *Logos*, of God because he is the personal, eternally existing Creator of the universe, distinct from yet equal with God the Father. The Son of God came in the flesh to demonstrate his glory in grace and truth and to reveal life and light to men.[†] Jesus Christ was conceived by the miraculous power of the Holy Spirit and born of the Virgin Mary in Bethlehem in order to redeem man and become the one mediator between God and man.[‡] We believe that Jesus Christ, during the Incarnation, laid aside the continual exercise of his divine attributes and lived his perfect life by the power of the Holy Spirit.[§]

Tribal border issues surrounding Jesus include the following: When Jesus was tempted to sin, was he really tempted, and if so, how could this be, since God is not tempted to sin? Did Jesus consume alcohol, and may we as well, or is all alcohol consumption a sin? What did Jesus do during his late teens and twenties that we have virtually no record of?

CROSS: GOD DIES

We believe that Jesus Christ lived a perfectly righteous and sinless life and died in the place of sinners, fully absorbing the wrath of God, in order to pay the just penalty for their sins

[*] See Matthew 1:18-25; Luke 1:30-38.
[†] See John 1:1-14; 1 John 1:1; Revelation 19:12-13.
[‡] See Isaiah 7:14; Micah 5:2; Matthew 1:18-23; 1 Timothy 2:5.
[§] See Matthew 3:16; 4:1-10; Mark 2:1-7; Luke 4:1-2, 14-21; 10:21; Hebrews 4:14-16.

and to reconcile them to God.* This doctrine is called *penal substitutionary atonement*. Jesus Christ on the cross substituted himself for sinners and suffered and died in our place to forgive us, love us, cleanse us, and embrace us—not in spite of our sins, but because the punishment for our sins was diverted from us to Jesus. Jesus did this not by demanding our blood but by giving his own.†

Secondary tribal border issues regarding the Cross include the following: Which side is right in the debate between Calvinists and Arminians on whether Jesus' atonement was limited to the elect or unlimited for all people? What happened to the Trinity when Jesus cried out that he had been forsaken by God the Father? Where did Jesus' soul go in the time between his death and resurrection? Is physical healing guaranteed by Jesus' atonement?

RESURRECTION: GOD SAVES

We believe that Jesus Christ, after dying on the cross, arose bodily from the grave on the third day, appearing to many witnesses and proving that he was physically alive three days after his death.‡ Innumerable blessings are conferred on believers who are by faith united with the risen Christ, raised with Christ, and granted the same powerful Holy Spirit that

---

* See Isaiah 53:5, 12; Romans 3:23-25; 4:25; 5:8; 2 Corinthians 5:21; Galatians 3:13; Hebrews 4:15; 1 Peter 3:18; 1 John 2:2.

† **Jesus substituted himself for sinners:** see Isaiah 53:6; John 1:29; 3:16-17; 2 Corinthians 5:14-15; 1 Timothy 2:1-6; 4:10; Titus 2:11; Hebrews 2:9; 2 Peter 3:9; 1 John 2:2; 4:14; Revelation 5:9. **Punishment for sins diverted to Jesus:** see Romans 3:23-25; Hebrews 2:17; 1 John 2:2; 4:10. **Jesus accomplished this by giving his blood:** see Isaiah 59:2; Hosea 5:6; John 3:16; 15:13; Romans 5:8; 1 Timothy 1:15-16; Titus 3:4-5; 1 John 4:9-10.

‡ See Isaiah 53:8-12; Matthew 12:38-40; 27:57-60; 28:9; Mark 8:31; 9:31; 10:33-34; Luke 24:36-43; John 2:18-22; 19:34-35; 20:17, 20-28; 21:7, 12; Acts 1:3; 1 Corinthians 15:3-6.

raised Christ.* These benefits include the forgiveness of sins, justification, sanctification, and ultimately glorification.† We believe that justification through the work of Jesus Christ is possible by grace alone, through faith alone, in Jesus Christ alone. To be justified means to trust only in the person and work of Jesus and in no one and nothing else as the object of our faith, righteousness, and justification before God.‡ The righteousness of Jesus is imparted to us at the time of faith, simultaneous with our justification, and brings us new life by the Holy Spirit, who begins the process of making us more and more like Jesus.§

Since salvation is made possible through Jesus' resurrection, a number of secondary tribal border issues arise, including the following: Who is right in the debate between Reformed and Arminian tribes regarding whether our salvation was predestined in eternity past? Once someone is saved, is it possible to lose that salvation? Since Jesus' resurrection is the pattern for ours, what will our resurrected bodies be like?

CHURCH: GOD SENDS

We believe that the local church is a community of regenerated believers who confess Jesus Christ as Lord, and that the universal church is all of God's people in all times and places.¶ In obedience to Scripture, believers organize under quali-

* See Romans 6:5; 1 Corinthians 6:14; 2 Corinthians 5:15; Colossians 2:12; 3:1.
† See 1 Corinthians 15:3-58; Romans 4:25; 1 Corinthians 15:20, respectively.
‡ See Acts 13:38; Romans 4:3-5; 5:1, 16-17; Titus 3:7.
§ See 2 Corinthians 5:21.
¶ See Acts 2:36-41; Matthew 16:18, respectively.

fied leadership, gather regularly for preaching and worship, observe baptism and Communion, are unified by the Spirit, are disciplined for holiness, and scatter to fulfill the great commandment and the great commission as missionaries to the world for God's glory and their joy.*

Secondary tribal border issues are numerous and include the following: How should the church be governed—by elders, the congregation, or someone else? Are there any limitations on the ministry of women within the church, such as the office of pastor/elder? Should a church be aligned with a denomination, a network, both, or remain autonomous? What is the role of parachurch organizations in relationship to the church? What about multisite churches and preaching delivered via video?

WORSHIP: GOD TRANSFORMS

We believe that human beings, created in the image of God the Trinity (who is himself a worshiping community in the Godhead), are unceasing worshipers who continually outpour all they are, all they do, and all they can ever become in Christ.[2] Worship includes praise, proclamation, service,

---

* Believers organize under qualified leadership, gather for preaching, and observe baptism and Communion: see Acts 2:42. **Gather for worship:** see Matthew 2:11; 4:9; 8:2; 28:9; Acts 2:47; Romans 1:9; 12:1; Revelation 7:15; 19:10. **Are unified by the Spirit:** see Ephesians 4:4. **Are disciplined for holiness:** see Proverbs 19:11; Matthew 18:15-22; Acts 20:25-31; Romans 13:1-7; 1 Corinthians 5:1-13; 6:1-8; 2 Corinthians 2:5-11; 11:3-4, 13-15; Galatians 1:6-9; 5:7-15; 6:1-5; Philippians 3:2-3; Colossians 3:16; 1 Thessalonians 5:12-13; 2 Thessalonians 3:6, 11, 14-15; 1 Timothy 1:4-7, 18-20; 4:1-8; 5:19-21; 2 Timothy 2:14-26; 4:1-5; Titus 3:10-11; Hebrews 10:24-25; 13:17; James 3:1; 1 John 2:19; 3 John 1:9-10. **Fulfill the great commandment:** see Matthew 5:43-45; 6:24; 22:39; Luke 6:32; 10:30-37; Romans 13:9-10; Galatians 5:14; Ephesians 5:25; 6:1-4; 1 Timothy 5:17; Titus 2:4; Hebrews 13:2, 17; James 2:8; 1 John 3:14. **Fulfill the great commission:** see Matthew 28; Acts 1:8; 2:47; Acts 13:43; 17:4, 17; 18:4; 19:4, 26; 26:1-28; 28:23-24; 2 Corinthians 5:11, 20; Colossians 1:28–29. **Act as missionaries for God's glory and their joy:** see Acts 2:41-47.

participation, sacrifice, and submission.* We believe that the corporate worship of a local church is to be God centered.† We believe that the required elements of corporate worship are preaching, the sacraments of baptism and Communion, prayer, reading Scripture, financial giving, and singing and music.‡

There is a long list of secondary tribal border issues, including the following: What is the order of service or liturgy? What is the worship style that dominates congregational singing, including which, if any, instruments? How often and in what mode should Communion be practiced in corporate worship gatherings? Should sermons be expository or topical?

STEWARDSHIP: GOD GIVES

We believe that all followers of Christ are to be stewards who gladly acknowledge that they belong to the Lord, that everything they have and are belongs to the Lord, and that everything ultimately belongs to the Lord. Christians seek to faithfully oversee all that God has entrusted to their care.§ We believe that a steward seeks to accomplish meaningful and purposeful things for God while on the earth.¶ Stewards must always seek God's priorities for life and remain devoted to them, balancing work and Sabbath so that their time is

---

* See Hebrews 13:15-17.
† See Matthew 4:8-10.
‡ See Matthew 28:19; 1 Corinthians 11:17-34; 2 Corinthians 8–9; Colossians 3:16; 1 Timothy 2:1; 4:13; 2 Timothy 4:2.
§ See Haggai 2:8; Malachi 3:8; Romans 1:6; 1 Corinthians 4:7.
¶ See Ephesians 2:10.

managed well and God is glorified.* We believe that spiritual gifts are a special grace of the Holy Spirit, given to us at our new birth to serve the mission of Jesus.†

Secondary tribal border issues on stewardship include the following: Should Christians tithe an actual 10 percent, or more, or less? Should we give from our gross or net income? Are the continuationists or the cessationists right in arguing that all the miraculous gifts continue or have ceased? Should Christians keep a hard-and-fast day each week for Sabbath rest, and if so, should it be Saturday, Sunday, or another day?

KINGDOM: GOD REIGNS

We believe that God created humans as thinking, feeling, moral persons made up of spirit and body tightly joined together.‡ Death is not normal or natural, but an enemy, the consequence of sin.§ Death is the tearing apart of these two intertwined parts and the cessation of life on this earth. The body goes to the grave and the spirit goes into an afterlife to face judgment.¶ The Bible is clear that there will one day be a bodily resurrection for everyone, to either eternal life with God or eternal condemnation apart from him.** We believe that Jesus' resurrection gives us confidence in his other promises that we are waiting to see fulfilled, such as his returning

---

* See Genesis 2:2, 15; Exodus 20:8-11; Proverbs 18:9; 21:25; Ecclesiastes 3:22; 1 Corinthians 15:10; Colossians 3:23-24; 2 Thessalonians 3:10.
† See Romans 12:6-8; 1 Corinthians 12:8-10, 28-30; Ephesians 4:11; 1 Peter 4:11.
‡ See Genesis 2:7.
§ See Genesis 2:17; Romans 5:12.
¶ See Ecclesiastes 3:20-21; 12:7; Psalm 104:29; 146:4; Hebrews 9:27; James 2:26.
** See Daniel 12:2; Matthew 25:46.

one day to judge sinners and reward saints.* We believe that the full effects of Jesus' resurrection will be seen one day following Jesus' return. The time between Jesus' resurrection and our resurrection is a lengthy season of love, grace, and mercy as news of the gospel goes forth, inviting sinners to repent of sin and enjoy the present and future salvation of Jesus Christ.†

Secondary tribal border issues on matters of eschatology are among the most numerous of all. Are you premillennial, postmillennial, amillennial, or something else? Will Jesus' return be soon or far into the future? *Can* we have some sense of when Jesus will return? Will there be a Rapture, and if so, when? Is Jesus' thousand-year reign literal or figurative? What is the mark of the beast? Who is the Antichrist? What is "Babylon" in Revelation? How exactly is the book of Revelation to be interpreted—figuratively, literally, or a combination of both?

STICKING TOGETHER

I am not saying that these secondary border issues don't matter or that we should not hold convictions on them. I have a studied conviction on every issue. I believe the Holy Spirit proceeds from the Father and Son; the English Standard Version is the best English word-for-word Bible translation, and the *ESV Study Bible* is tops; the six days in Genesis 1–2 are literal, twenty-four-hour days; the earth may or may not

* See John 14:3.
† See John 14:3; Acts 17:30-31.

be very old, but human life on the earth is young; men should lovingly lead their families; apart from Christ people are totally depraved, but Jesus can save a baby from the womb; the inward sign of the New Covenant is faith through the Holy Spirit, with believer's baptism being the outward sign; Jesus lived by the power of the Holy Spirit, as we should; Jesus died for all people and in a saving way for the elect; the Reformed tribes are correct on issues such as predestination and election; pastors/elders should only be qualified men; video preaching and multisite churches are great; we should give of our gross income, with 10 percent being a floor and not a ceiling; and the thousand years in Revelation 20 are literal, which means I lean historic premillennial but would not die on that issue, let alone suffer a paper cut for it.

If you attend the church where I preach or if you listen online, you will hear me teach on these issues without apology and in detail as we work through books of the Bible verse by verse most Sundays. But there are differing borders for how my family does things, what our church believes, what our tribe believes, and what is required to be a faithful Christian. My family and church family need more than just the national borders, but I would be acting in a way that was unnecessarily divisive if I were to enforce the boundaries of my family, or church family, on all of Jesus' people. In this way, the big Christian family is kind of like my extended biological family. In my house we do things a certain way for reasons we find compelling. But when we spend time with other families, we also learn some things they do better than we do and vice versa, which helps both families. Unless there is a clear sin, I would not press my family's way of doing things on another family, though in love I might respectfully discuss some things if I thought they would help serve that family. Otherwise I'd not make a fuss and would simply enjoy the other families we know. If, however, there was something obviously wrong, such as adultery, I would not hesitate to speak up and get involved because engaging in sin is crossing a very different kind of line than something like determining when the kids go to bed.

Borders are about drawing lines. All lines are important, but not all lines are equally important. Some things are more important than others. This is why Paul called the gospel "of first importance."* This is why Jesus also speaks of "weightier matters" in a heated sermon on the religious leaders in Matthew 23:23-24. Jesus mocked them for making sure they tithed out of their spice rack (secondary issue) while forgetting to love and help others (primary issue). Commenting on this exchange, fourth-century bishop Hilary of Poitiers said, "God laughs at the superficial diligence of those who measure cucumbers."[3] While it's easy to laugh at the Pharisees, we must remember that we are each like them in some way, as we are each prone to major on the minors and minor on the majors. Yesterday is the same as today. Their silliness will always be more obvious and more troubling than our own. Jesus called this ever-popular game "plank" and "speck."

Being distinctive without being divisive is increasingly

---

* See 1 Corinthians 15:3.

vital for all Christian tribes. Much of the tribal infighting among Christians is a luxury we no longer have as a minority. One thing minority groups of all sorts quickly learn is that despite their differences, they cannot afford division. They stick together for their survival.

This struck me most clearly in Turkey. In the back of your Bible you will find a map or two showing Paul's missionary church-planting journeys and the seven churches of Revelation led by John. Most of those places are in modern Turkey. Operation World has identified Turkey as one of the least-churched nations on earth, with only 2 percent of the population identifying as Christian (including Catholic and Orthodox).[4] Out of some seventy-five million people, there are fewer than eight thousand evangelical Christians. That is not a typo. The entire Christian population of Turkey is barely large enough to qualify as one of the one hundred largest churches in the United States. I was leading a group of American and Canadian Christians through the archaeological sites, preaching in places such as Ephesus, Pergamum, Laodicea, and Sardis. On a Sunday, I was honored to preach at a church filled with Turkish Christians, thanks to the help of a translator. The pastor was gone that day, possibly for safety reasons, as he had been arrested numerous times for preaching the gospel. I was told that military police would be on hand to hear my sermon and that if I insulted Islam in any way or said anything political, I would likely be arrested. I had my wife, Grace, and our five kids sit in the back of the church near an exit and instructed them not to engage with me in any way so that if I were arrested, my family would not be involved. Things went without incident, and hundreds of believers packed the church. I don't know which ones were continuationists or cessationists, which ones were paedobaptists or credobaptists, or which ones liked hymns and which ones liked rock bands leading worship. But it didn't really matter. When there's only one church around and the pastor keeps getting arrested and the police are beating the Baptists and the Lutherans, Jesus' people stick together and figure out how to be the church on mission.

As an aside, you will often hear that persecution only makes a church stronger. But that's not always true. The church body is like the human body—a bit of weight to carry makes it stronger, but too much can break it. History reveals that sustained, intense persecution can wipe out, or nearly wipe out, Christian faith in an area. That is precisely what has happened in Turkey, as believers fled the nation from which the gospel went out to the nations.

I am not predicting that things in the West will get that dire anytime soon, if ever. But things are not trending in the direction of Bible-believing, Jesus-loving, sin-repenting, mission-serving Christianity. We are a minority in an increasingly hostile host culture, and the sooner we accept that reality, the better off we will be. We have to stick together around the national border issues, stop wasting our energies on infighting, and start investing our energies in evangelizing.

As the opposition from outside the church increases, so does the surrender inside the church. It's amazing how quickly evangelicals turn into evangellyfish with no spiritual vertebrae when they start to lose money, job security, cultural clout, or public support. We don't know which border issues we'll see supposedly Christian leaders waving the white flag on next, but we are already seeing it on issues related to gender, sexuality, hell, and repentance. The trouble always begins with a low view of the Bible as a word from mankind about God rather than the Word of God to mankind.

All of these obstacles we face today actually provide great opportunities. In an age when a lot of preaching is virtually indistinguishable from psychology-laden self-help, motivational speaking, and bootstrap-pulling life coaching, a little pressure to get God centered and doctrinally clarified is long overdue. Some of the greatest theological and practical biblical reflection to serve the mission of Jesus has historically come in response to the kinds of problems we are facing from without and within today. Jannes and Jambres helped keep Moses sharp. Sanballat and Tobias kept Nehemiah sharp. Hymenaeus and Alexander kept Paul sharp. Nestorius kept Cyril of Alexandria sharp. Marcion kept Tertullian and Irenaeus sharp. Arius kept Athanasius sharp. Pelagius kept Augustine sharp. You get the idea. Once a heretic shows up at your Bible study, it's amazing how much more intently the group members start studying.

It is increasingly important for Jesus' people to be Bible people. To see Jesus clearly, we need to open the Bible humbly.

THE HERO OF THE BIBLE

It may seem obvious to some, but people in general and Christians in particular need to do a lot more Bible reading and study. The most recent research funded by the American Bible Society reveals,

- 88 percent of Americans own a printed Bible (and of course, anyone with the Internet has access to a seemingly unlimited supply of Bibles, Bible teaching, and Bible study tools).
- 80 percent of Americans say they think the Bible is sacred.
- 61 percent of Americans say they wish they read the Bible more than they do.[5]

Reading the Bible is apparently like eating our vegetables—we know it's good for us, but we just don't do it. What is perhaps most interesting in the American Bible Society's findings is that eighteen- to twenty-nine-year-olds are the least likely group to read the Bible, but they are among the most likely to think it has a lot of wisdom to offer for the practical matters of life such as dating, marriage, sex, relationships, and family. Fully 66 percent of that age group purported to believe that the Bible they do not read contains everything a person needs to live a meaningful life. In our day of ample opportunity for Bible reading and instruction, we are like fools starving to death at the grocery store.

More Bible reading is critical. But to get the most from the Bible, we must also have *better* Bible reading. Better Bible reading requires knowing what the story of the Bible is and who the hero of the Bible is. The Bible is *for* us, but it is not *about* us.

The opening line of Scripture introduces us to its hero, God. Throughout the pages of Scripture, God is revealed. And in the closing line of the New Testament, we are reminded that the God who is the hero of the true story of Scripture is Jesus Christ.

Simply, when Scripture is rightly interpreted, it is ultimately about Jesus as God, our Savior, King, Lord, the object of our faith, forgiver of our sins, giver of eternal life, and Judge of the living and the dead. Therefore, to correctly interpret Scripture, we must connect its verses, concepts, and events to Jesus. The Bible is not a book of principles to live by but rather a Person to live for.

Unless we recognize Jesus as the central message of the Scriptures, many errors abound. Perhaps the most common error is moralizing. Moralizing is reading the Bible not to learn about Jesus but only to learn principles for how to live as a good person, by following the examples of some people and avoiding the examples of others. That kind of approach to the Scriptures is not Christian, because it treats the Bible like any other book and treats Jesus like any other leader. Only by the Spirit's power can we obey the Spirit's commands in the Scriptures the Spirit has written.

Under the problem of moralizing is a failure to distinguish

between the law and the gospel. The law is what we should do but have not done. The law shows us our sin. The gospel is about what Jesus has done, in perfect obedience to the law, in our place. And the gospel is about Jesus working in and through us by the power of the Holy Spirit.

A moralizing reading of the Bible most common with devout religious people is that the law can save. When read this way, the Bible is a list of dos and don'ts. If we want God to be happy with us, we simply obey him and earn his favor and blessing through our own efforts. When Jesus walked the earth, he had numerous arguments with religious people who had moralized the Bible. So he pressed the law upon them to show them that they, too, were sinners and needed him as their Savior. For example, Jesus said we should avoid not only adultery but also lust—surely no one could say he or she had never broken this law of God. On another occasion, a woman was caught in adultery, and the religious leaders brought her to Jesus to be executed. Looking at the religious leaders present, Jesus invited the one without sin to cast the first stone. Of course no one did. None of us have loved God with our whole hearts and minds. None of us have loved every one of our enemies all the time. If we're honest and are looking for stones to throw at sinners, we should throw the first one at ourselves.

As a pastor I have seen the very dark side of moralizing the Bible. If God blesses only those who earn his favor through obedience, then if you're experiencing suffering, it's your fault. Somehow, you've failed God. You've failed to trust or obey him, and your suffering is evidence he's punishing you rather than blessing you. Having counseled people who suffer under the crushing weight of this kind of bad Bible teaching, I find it cruel. Imagine for a moment if as a father I told my children they could not have my love and blessing unless they earned it. Essentially, they would be starting with a deficit in relationship with me, and every time they sinned or failed, they would make another withdrawal. But if they worked hard to obey me, then over time they might have enough in their relational account to compel me to love and bless them.

Imagine the crushing weight of performance this places on a child, and then ask yourself, *What would the child do if he or she experienced suffering?* The last person the child would run to is a father like that. A picture like this of God the Father means that people whose lives are blessed become arrogant kids who think they earned it. And kids who are suffering are devastated and criticized rather than comforted, because the arrogant kids wrongly believe that their Father is harming the ones suffering as punishment for some failure. That kind of "fathering" would be a spiritual form of abuse.

The Bible must not be read as a job description for motivated, self-disciplined, devoutly religious people to be their own heroes and saviors of their souls. It must be read as the story of guilty sinners and self-righteous hypocrites, visited by a perfect God who lived the life they haven't, died the death they should have, and rose to give the gift they could not earn. The Bible is good news about what Jesus has done before it is good advice about what we should do. The Bible tells us how God serves us before it asks us to serve him.

The two great enemies of the gospel are always sin and religion. Sinners want the Bible to say less than it does. Religious people want the Bible to say more than it does. Sinners want to make the Bible thinner by taking out the parts that condemn them. Religious people want to make the Bible thicker by adding extra rules about their pet peeves to condemn others.

What is the antidote to sin and religion? Every resurgence starts with and is sustained by more and better Bible reading.

ARE YOU EXCITED ABOUT JESUS?

Bible-believing, Jesus-loving, sin-repenting, mission-serving Christianity is not just about what we believe but also about who we get excited for and what we emphasize.

Jesus! Jesus! Jesus!

I cannot think of any Christian person, family, church, ministry, or tribe that would not benefit from more Jesus!

It's easy for families, theologies, churches, ministries, and tribes to become cause centered—and not Christ centered—because it's easy to get excited about evangelism, missions, study, social justice, or some other *cause*. These are all good things that churches ought to be involved in. But the center of our excitement and our focus should always be Jesus—what he has done and what he is doing. As we seek first his Kingdom, all these things will be added to us.

Gospel-centered resurgence is not just a set of convictions.

It's our being excited about Jesus! Ultimately, being gospel centered means that our Bibles are open, God's Word—all of which is Christ saturated and Cross centered—is read and proclaimed, and out of that, justice, mercy, love, compassion, and mission come.

Jesus is *everything*:

He is the image of the invisible God, the firstborn of all creation. For by him all things were created, in heaven and on earth, visible and invisible, whether thrones or dominions or rulers or authorities—all things were created through him and for him. And he is before all things, and in him all things hold together.[*]

It is from Jesus that "we have all received, grace upon grace."[†] That is the heartbeat of gospel-centered resurgence.

Timeless truth is always timely. Truthless times need timeless truths. In the Greatest Generation, many believed the national-border truths of Christianity. In their children's generation, many wrongly assumed these national-border truths were outdated and moved on from theology to therapy. And their grandchildren and great-grandchildren's generations are now outright denying these truths because they do not believe they are sinners who need a Savior. What we need is not new beliefs, but a new passion for timeless truth.

---

[*] Colossians 1:15-17.
[†] John 1:16.

You are not here by chance, but by providence. God has chosen you to be alive now! This is an amazing and exciting time to be alive. We've got truth to tell, work to do, and a King who is coming. Praise God we are alive at the turning point of the Western world and have been sent on Jesus' mission with the Holy Spirit's power. Our lives, our prayers, our dollars, our words, and our efforts really matter in a way they likely did not just a generation ago. We should feel honored instead of hopeless. God always sends the best soldiers on the toughest missions to liberate the weariest captives. Reporting from the front line, I assure you it is a complicated, exhausting, frustrating, and gloriously encouraging, energizing, and transforming place to live.

Some of you reading this are links in a chain of faith that extends back through generations of your family. I urge you not to be the weak or broken link in that chain. Some of you are the first link in that chain, and I encourage you to think in terms of legacy, laboring in the faith that your children and grandchildren and great-grandchildren might serve the cause of Christ faithfully and be with you eternally.

Lastly, for the young guys who spend most of their time watching television, eating chips, and playing video games—we need you to undergo a cranial-rectal extraction immediately. As you sit around with your buddies trying to battle an enemy, liberate a people, and usher in a kingdom in yet another video game, I need you to know that you are wasting your lives. Those deep desires you have to be part of a tribe on mission to defeat evil and set captives free for the glory of a great king and kingdom are there for the cause of the gospel of Jesus Christ, and we need you on the front lines. The faithful grandmas and homeschooling moms are getting tired of holding the line.

Chapter 5

THE HOLY SPIRIT
EMPOWERING THE CHURCH
FOR MISSION

FOR SPRING BREAK ONE YEAR, I took my family to the beach. Unfortunately, it was a beach in Washington. We arrived at our rented cottage in time to enjoy rain that made me wonder if God had revoked his promise to Noah to never flood the earth again.

Finally, there was a very brief sun break. We got dressed in our wool hats, winter coats, and boots to enjoy an arctic walk on the beach. There was no sand on the beach—because it was all in my mouth and eyes.

What was most impressive was the gale-force wind. At one point I literally held on to our youngest child in fear that he would be blown over. Before long, we scurried back to our cottage to thaw out, play board games, and bemoan the fact that we did not live in Southern California. Since this was the first day of what was supposed to be an entire week's vacation, things seemed hopeless.

Looking out the window some hours later, I came up with an idea that I thought might salvage our spring break: kites. I went to find a kite shop so we could try to use the weather to our advantage.

Thankfully, there was an epic kite store not far away. I bought some big, nice, serious kites—the kind that could handle a flight attendant on board. Eventually the rain stopped, so we went out for the maiden voyage of our kites.

We'd never really flown kites much, and the younger kids were excited to see how they worked. I told them to hold the roll of string, letting out just a bit at a time. With the movie *Up* in my mind, I also told them that if the gale-force winds started to cause not only their kites but also their bodies to leave the ground, they needed to let go of the string.

What happened was amazing. The dead kites sprang to life. Filled by the wind, they were empowered. They began to soar and dance because of a power they did not possess in themselves. It was a beautiful sight and caused my youngest daughter to laugh and dance with joy.

The Christian life is supposed to be like that. When the Bible says that Jesus was filled with the Holy Spirit and that Jesus' people are to be filled with the Holy Spirit, this is what is meant. But various tribes approach the Holy Spirit differently because each emphasizes a different aspect of his work. In a cessationist tribe, the functional Trinity is sometimes the Father, Son, and Holy Bible: the Holy Spirit wrote the Scriptures through human authors, and then it's like he's been on vacation ever since. In a Pentecostal church, you know you have the Holy Spirit if you speak in tongues, the primary evidence to Pentecostals that a believer has the Spirit. In a prosperity tribe, the Holy Spirit's ministry is largely to make you healthy and wealthy; he's presented as the source of blessing to those who have faith. In more fundamental tribes, the Holy Spirit has two primary ministries: to write the Bible and convict us of sin. Basically, you are a nail, the Bible is a hammer, and the Holy Spirit's job is to pound you. In charismatic tribes, the fruit of the Spirit is emphasized: the Holy Spirit is the one who causes our character to become more like Jesus' as we pray and worship passionately. In missional tribes, the gifts of the Spirit are emphasized, thereby helping believers discover the ministry God has for them as part of his mission. In Reformed churches, you won't hear a lot about the Spirit, as they tend to attribute much of his work to the gospel and the sovereignty of God. So when lives are changed, the explanation is that what happened was because of the gospel without much reference to the Spirit's application of it. And when God works out circumstances to some favorable end, Calvinists are prone to attribute it to God's sovereignty, while continuationists are prone to attribute it to God's Spirit. Often it's little more than a matter of semantics since the Spirit *is* the sovereign God.

Sadly, much of the debate and division among tribes is in

regard to the person and work of the Holy Spirit. I am firmly convinced that for Christianity to have a future instead of a funeral, various tribes must strive to obey Ephesians 4:3, where Paul commands us to be "eager to maintain the unity of the Spirit." The remainder of this chapter is dedicated to that end, as our unity in the Spirit requires agreement about the Spirit.

THE HOLY SPIRIT IS A PERSON

The Holy Spirit appears in the opening lines of Genesis, where he is the Creator God bringing the world into existence along with God the Father and God the Son.* He breathed life into our first parents, allowing them to live and enjoy the world he created for them. The Holy Spirit is a person and not merely an impersonal force. This explains why the entire Bible, including the words of Jesus, consistently refer to the Holy Spirit as *he* and not *it*. Promising the coming of the Holy Spirit in John 14, Jesus refers to the Holy Spirit as "he" and "him" no fewer than five times. The Holy Spirit can be grieved, resisted, and insulted.† An impersonal force can't experience these things; only a person can.

This point is important, since spirituality today generally reflects belief in a spiritual force that is impersonal and indwells nature. According to research by *USA Today*, even professing, churchgoing Christians are confused: "Going to church this Sunday? Look around. The chances are that

---

* Genesis 1:1-3; see John 1:1-3.
† See Ephesians 4:30; Acts 7:51; Hebrews 10:29, respectively.

one in five of the people there find 'spiritual energy' in mountains or trees."[1]

As the third person in the Trinity, the Holy Spirit is a Helper given to us to help us do and be what God has called us to. Without the Holy Spirit, we wouldn't know anything about God. The Spirit reveals God through the Bible. Tim Smith, one of my fellow pastors at Mars Hill Church, has articulated this concept well for the benefit of our congregation:

> The Spirit worked through the words of men carrying them along to record the words of God: from Moses and Genesis to John and Revelation, the Spirit is the Author behind the authors. However, the Spirit does much more than just inspire words. From creation onward, the Holy Spirit has been active in the lives of God's people. The Holy Spirit is the empowering presence of God, seeking to fill all believers for his mission to make Jesus known. In Old Testament times, the Spirit empowered specific people for service to God. . . . This special and occasional filling was just a shadow of the work of the Spirit to come. The Old Testament clearly points to a time when the Spirit will fill all God's people. The prophet Ezekiel looked to a time when God would take our hearts of stone and give us new hearts and a new Spirit. All this would come together in the Messiah in whom the Spirit of God would perfectly dwell.[2]

In his first sermon, the apostle Peter declared the fulfillment of God's promise to send the Holy Spirit. As a result, about three thousand people were converted. The Holy Spirit shows up when Jesus is preached.*

We are to know, love, and befriend God the Holy Spirit just as we do Jesus and the Father. Do you? It is common to hear Christians say they love Jesus but less common to hear them say they love the Holy Spirit. It is common to hear Christians say they have a personal relationship with Jesus but less common to hear them say they have a personal relationship with the Holy Spirit.

THE HOLY SPIRIT WORKS IN THE WORLD AND IN OUR LIVES

What exactly does the Holy Spirit do? Why does Jesus say, "It is to your advantage that I go away, for . . . if I go, I will send [the Holy Spirit] to you"?†

We know that Jesus accomplished redemption and forgiveness through his life, death, and resurrection. The Holy Spirit applies that redemption and forgiveness to us. His ministry is missional: he continues and expands the ministry of Jesus through the lives of believers. Without the Spirit we can do nothing that is faithful and fruitful in God's eyes.

In 1 Timothy 6:4, Paul tells us not to quibble over words. Yet that is exactly what we do when it comes to terms surrounding the Holy Spirit such as *Spirit filled*, *anointed*, and

---

* See Isaiah 11:2-3; Ezekiel 11:19; Acts 2:14-41.
† John 16:7. John Murray's book *Redemption Accomplished and Applied* (Grand Rapids, MI: Eerdmans, 1955) gives us a great answer to these questions.

charismatic. Admittedly, the Bible uses phrases such as *Spirit filled, Spirit anointed,* and *Spirit powered* quite interchangeably. So in an effort to sidestep debates about tongues and whether church services should mimic karaoke night at a dive bar happy hour, I prefer to use the term *Spirit empowered.* This term carries less baggage than a word such as *charismatic* and allows us to keep our focus on the person and work of the Holy Spirit.

When we become Christians, the Spirit of God enters us, and that changes everything. The Spirit exists to glorify Jesus, and through the Spirit we can do the same. As we behold the glory of Jesus, we are transformed to be more like him through the power of the Spirit. Apart from the work of the Spirit, we would not recognize the glory of God. It's only by the Spirit that we can even say, "Jesus is Lord."*

The Holy Spirit does not simply come alongside our efforts and make us more effective. Rather, through the Spirit, we live a new and different life. To become a Christian is to experience true death and resurrection—not gradual change through our own efforts. We must die to ourselves and be born again by the Spirit.†

The Holy Spirit, the third person of the Trinity, gives life, and that life is in Jesus Christ. Scripture is clear that there are signs of this new life: through the Spirit we receive a new mind, desires that are set on pleasing God, and the life and peace that come with that pursuit. Whereas our lives used to

---

* See John 16:14; 1 Corinthians 12:3; 2 Corinthians 3:18; 4:4.
† See John 3:5-8; 6:63.

be characterized by such fruit as pride, selfishness, idolatry, and sexual immorality, with the Spirit we begin to bear new fruit: love, joy, peace, patience, kindness, goodness, faithfulness, gentleness, and self-control.*

The Holy Spirit's active work in history and in the lives of individuals takes many different forms, and Christians have historically either underemphasized or overemphasized one specific aspect of the Holy Spirit's work. Underemphasizing the Spirit's work has resulted in believers acting like functional deists and suggesting, if not by their words then by their actions, that God no longer works in the history of the world at all, but rather works his ways from the lofty heavens. (This is hard cessationism.) Overemphasizing the Spirit's work has resulted in believers operating as overspiritualized and undereducated functional New Age mystics, seeing every wind that blows, leaf that falls, and storm that brews as the movement of the Spirit. (This is hard charismatic.) The functional deist emphasizes divine transcendence and fails to see what God is doing right now through the Holy Spirit, and the functional mystic emphasizes feeling, unclear signs, and "moves of the Spirit" over the already divine revelation of God through the Scriptures.

SPIRIT EMPOWERED LIKE JESUS

What does it mean to be Spirit empowered in the truest sense of the word? It means to be like Jesus! Most of the Christian

---

* See John 6:63; Romans 8:5-8; Galatians 5:22-23; 1 John 5:11-12.

creeds we repeat miss out on Jesus' life. They say he was born and he died. But what else did he do? We must focus on what is missing from the creeds—the Spirit-empowered life of Jesus.

How did Jesus live his sinless life and die on the cross for our sin? Most Christians would answer simply, "He was God." And yes, there is a sense in which this is true. Jesus is eternally God—past, present, and future. However, in the greatest act of humility the world has ever known, Jesus joined his divinity to humanity, taking the form of a servant, and temporarily set aside the continual use of his divine attributes.* Simply put, this means that Jesus did not cheat while on the earth and lean into his deity to make his hard times easy. Hebrews 4:15 says, "We do not have a high priest who is unable to sympathize with our weaknesses, but one who in every respect has been tempted as we are, yet without sin."

So if Jesus chose to lay down the use of his divine rights, how was he able to live the life he lived? How did Jesus resist temptation? How did Jesus forgive his enemies? How did Jesus remain obedient even to the point of death on the cross? How did Jesus perform miracles? How did Jesus preach? How did Jesus endure suffering? How did Jesus obey? How did Jesus heal? How did Jesus cast out demons? It was all by the power of the Holy Spirit. He was Spirit filled, Spirit anointed, and Spirit led. As Peter said, "God anointed Jesus of Nazareth with the Holy Spirit and with power. He went

---

* See Philippians 2:7.

about doing good and healing all who were oppressed by the devil, for God was with him.'"*

Jesus' life was lived, fully human, by the power of the Holy Spirit. Too often when we think about the role of the Holy Spirit, we turn just to the book of Acts to see how the Holy Spirit empowers believers. But Acts is a *sequel* to the book of Luke.

For Luke, the words *power* and *Holy Spirit* are almost always interchangeable, both in his Gospel and in Acts.† The book of Luke is the account of the Spirit-empowered ministry of Jesus on the earth, and Acts is the account of the Spirit-empowered ministry of Jesus' people on the earth, the extension of Jesus' ministry through his people by the Spirit's power.

Jesus' life by the Spirit's empowerment is repeatedly stressed in Luke's Gospel. We find, for example, that Jesus was conceived by the Holy Spirit and given the title *Christ*, which means "anointed [by the Holy Spirit]." Jesus baptized people with the Holy Spirit, and the Holy Spirit descended upon Jesus at his own baptism. Furthermore, Jesus was "full of the Holy Spirit" and "led by the Spirit"; he came "in the power of the Spirit" and declared that "the Spirit of the Lord is upon me." He also "rejoiced in the Holy Spirit." Regarding the Holy Spirit's ministry to and through Christians, Jesus also promised that God the Father would "give the Holy Spirit to those who ask him" and that the Holy Spirit would teach us once he was sent.‡

---

* Acts 10:38.

† We can see this by looking at the words of Jesus in Luke 24 and then in Acts 1:8. In light of that, Luke 5:17; 6:19; and 8:46 also speak loudly.

‡ See Luke 1–2; 3:16, 21-22; 4:1-2, 14, 18; 10:21; 11:13; 12:12; cf. Isaiah 61:1.

Jesus said it was "to our advantage" that he would no longer be with us on the earth, because in his absence he would send a "Helper," the Spirit of truth, to be with us and to lead us into all truth. He said the Father would send the Spirit in Jesus' name to teach us all things and bring into remembrance all that Jesus said. Jesus said the Spirit would convict the world concerning sin, righteousness, and judgment. In possibly the greatest promise of the coming work of the Spirit, Jesus said the Spirit would take everything that is Jesus' and make it known to us. All these promises were fulfilled when the Holy Spirit was poured out on all believers in Jesus Christ at the Pentecost (Acts 2) and the subsequent outpourings of the Spirit recorded in the book of Acts.*

Being Spirit empowered does not mean we are equal to Jesus, but it does mean we can do some of what he did by the Spirit's power. Let me make this very clear and simple: by the power of the Holy Spirit you can overcome the temptation to sin, you can become more like Jesus Christ, you can understand and apply Scripture, you can pray over the sick and not be shocked if/when some are healed, you can pray with those experiencing demonic torment and see them delivered, you can have a joy that does not come from the circumstances around you but from the Spirit within you, and you can expect to see lost people saved, saved people grow, and inbreakings and outpourings of the Kingdom of God scattered throughout the otherwise mundane days of your life.

Being Spirit empowered like Jesus means living on mission

* See John 14:15-27; 16:7-14; Acts 2, 8, 10–11, 19.

in culture to establish the church and expand the Kingdom as Jesus did. It's not about your speaking in tongues. It's not about fulfilling your potential or finding your destiny. It's not about expanding your own kingdom. It's not about you experiencing prosperity. It's not about your healing. It's not about your breakthrough. It's not about *you* at all. It's all about Jesus. It's all about Jesus' mission. That's what it means to be Spirit empowered—saved by Jesus and sent on mission, empowered by the Spirit.

Practically, this means that if you are not serving the local church, you are grieving the Spirit. If you are not open about your faith and sharing it with others, you are grieving the Spirit. If you are not being generous with your time, talent, and treasure to expand the Kingdom of God, you are grieving the Spirit. If you and your church are not giving to global missions, you are grieving the Spirit. If you and your church are not giving to national and international church planting, you are grieving the Spirit. If you are not seeking to grow in holiness by putting sin to death, you are grieving the Spirit. If you are not spending time in Scripture seeking the mind of Christ, you are grieving the Spirit. If you are not connecting with God through worship and prayer, you are grieving the Spirit. If you are living life as if you were the center instead of Jesus, you are grieving the Spirit. The primary and overarching ministry of the Holy Spirit on the earth today is glorifying Jesus by saving people and empowering them for Jesus' mission for the fame of Jesus' name.

SPIRIT-EMPOWERED CHURCH

What we see in Acts is that Jesus' people—the church—continue his ministry by the power of the Holy Spirit and through the outpouring and filling of the Spirit. Much of the Spirit's work is missional: making disciples and planting churches. This is not because that is the church's mission; rather, it is the *Spirit's* mission, and the church is merely part of it.

Acts records what happens when the church follows the Spirit. Acts is often wrongly called the Acts of the Apostles. The truth is, it is the Acts of the Holy Spirit, as *he* is the driving force of the mission of the church and does extraordinary things through ordinary people. This gives us hope that he can use us to advance the mission of Jesus.

In the book of Luke, it's obvious that Luke sees the Spirit as living and active. As Justin Holcomb points out in his commentary on the book of Acts, Luke organized his Gospel's sequel according to the four major outpourings of the Holy Spirit (in Acts 2, 8, 10–11, and 19) in which the Spirit came to different groups of people in a spectacular manner, empowering them for mission.[3] Luke's goal is to describe the expansion of the gospel to more and more people and types of people.

Echoing Jesus' baptism, Acts 2 depicts the Spirit's descent on Jesus' people to anoint and empower them to continue Jesus' ministry. One hundred twenty Jewish believers are filled with and empowered by the Holy Spirit for Jesus' mission. Then, Holcomb writes,

Acts 8 describes how the Samaritans—considered racial half-breeds by Jews—were filled and empowered with the Spirit after they believed the gospel preached by Philip. In Acts 10 and 11, Peter preached to Gentiles, who believed and were empowered with the Spirit. [In Acts 19] Paul meets some followers of John the Baptist who didn't even know what Jesus did and taught. So they believe and are filled. In this progression we see the ever-expanding scope of the gospel. The Spirit's ministry is expansive, just as Jesus' ministry was—including those who previously were excluded. The gospel-centered focus of Acts can be pictured by expanding concentric circles—the Holy Spirit brings Jesus' good news to a small group of disciples, to one hundred twenty Jews, to the Samarians, to Gentiles, and to the entire world.[4]

The Holy Spirit has the same mission for every local church—to be on mission locally, regionally, nationally, and internationally. Reaching more people, more kinds of people, in more places and more cultures is the mission of the Holy Spirit. Practically, this means that mission starts across the street and extends around the world.

THE GIFT OF TONGUES

Let's pause for a moment to discuss a specific Holy Spirit–related issue that often results in tribalism. Seemingly every discussion of Acts quickly degenerates into the tongues debate. This is one issue that quickly and tragically divides tribes who could otherwise be working together for God's mission. This must be a secondary border issue if we are to reduce infighting and increase evangelizing.

The spiritual gift of tongues—along with all other spiritual gifts and enablements of the Spirit—is given in order to make more disciples and plant more churches. The issue is complex, and I will deal with it briefly to keep our little journey out of the ditch.

The Greek word sometimes translated "tongues" is best translated as "languages." The confusion regarding tongues is because Scripture mentions at least three different uses of the gift.

First, "tongues" is used to describe a private prayer language, which Paul speaks of in 1 Corinthians 14:14, saying, "If I pray in a tongue . . ." He also says in 1 Corinthians 13:1, "If I speak in the tongues of men and of angels . . . ," and some think the prayer language he mentions may actually be the language of the angels in heaven. And in 1 Corinthians 14:2 and 4 we read, "One who speaks in a tongue speaks not to men but to God; for no one understands him, but he utters mysteries in the Spirit. . . . The one who speaks in a tongue builds up himself." This kind of tongues, often called a prayer language, is to be done in private for personal edification and not in church meetings. As Paul later says in verse 19, "In church I would rather speak five words with my mind in order to instruct others, than ten thousand words in a tongue."

Second, the word "tongues" refers to a public missionary gift that enables someone to share the gospel of Jesus with foreigners in their native language that the speaker does not know. Acts 2:1-13 records just such an occasion, when three thousand people were saved in one day as the gospel was preached through the early Christians in languages the speakers did not know.

Third, "tongues" can be a revelatory language whereby a message from God is spoken in a language unknown to the speaker and must be translated for the people in the church. This use of tongues requires the assistance of someone with the gift of interpretation.

Great confusion and conflict happen when people misunderstand these different kinds of tongues.

First, problems arise when a private prayer language is exercised publicly. This misuse of the gift can cause lost people in church to be completely confused, hampering evangelism and mission. Paul speaks of this in 1 Corinthians 14:23: "If, therefore, the whole church comes together and all speak in tongues, and outsiders or unbelievers enter, will they not say that you are out of your minds?" I was once talking to a realtor who was very recently saved. He was excited to share Jesus with his friends, and one of his unsaved friends showed interest in Christianity. Not knowing that churches were different, the realtor found a church near his friend's house and took him there. Everyone was yelling in tongues and flopping like fish on a dock, and the new Christian and the non-Christian had no idea what was happening or why.

The non-Christian was so spooked, they had to leave church early, and he now has no interest in Christianity because he thinks Christians are people who have lost their minds.

Second, problems arise when someone is speaking in a foreign language/tongue in a church service and the congregation does not understand what is being spoken. Paul explains this, saying that five words of instruction are more beneficial to the listeners than ten thousand unintelligible words. Paul expects that church gatherings will be edifying to the people in attendance.*

Third, problems arise when those who have the revelatory language gift of tongues do not use an interpreter to confirm what is said so that it can be tested by church leadership and understood by church members. This is what Paul means in 1 Corinthians 14:27: "If any speak in a tongue, let there be only two or at most three, and each in turn, and let someone interpret."

The point of all spiritual gifts, including tongues, is not one person's personal edification, personal experience, or personal satisfaction—especially if it is at the expense of people getting saved, disciples getting made, and churches getting planted. That kind of thinking is childish, selfish, and immature, which is why Paul commands those with that mind-set to "not be children in [their] thinking."† Rather, the Holy Spirit empowers the church for mission. What we see in Acts and 1 Corinthians is not a model for personal

---

* See 1 Corinthians 14:18-23.
† 1 Corinthians 14:20.

or individual experience but a description of the gospel's missional expansion—geographically, racially, and theologically—by the Spirit's power.

For the gospel to expand, God's people must distinguish between private and public spirituality. We get into great trouble when something that should be private is done in public. I was sitting at a coffee shop, and a woman took her shoes off while sitting in a big, comfy chair. She then proceeded to trim her toenails, sending nail clippings flying through the air. That kind of thing is well and good, but best done privately instead of publicly. This principle is true spiritually as well. Maybe speaking in a private prayer language edifies you, and if so, you should do it—in private. Practically, this is why we also encourage some people with good hearts and bad voices (like me) to sing their hearts out to Jesus at home or in their cars, but we don't give them microphones in church on Sunday. Not every use of every gift works best in front of the entire church, including some forms of tongues.

On this issue of tongues, cessationists are often overreacting to an imbalanced and unbiblical use of tongues that makes God look like a bartender who overserves at church. They rightly are concerned about the wrong use of spiritual gifts. But the answer is not to forbid the use of some gifts, but rather to use them biblically, maturely, and wisely, with the big idea of mission in mind. For example, perhaps no spiritual gift has been more abused than teaching, but the answer is not to remove teaching from the church. Rather, the solution is to have better teaching—and more of it. This is why Paul tells us "not [to] forbid speaking in tongues."*

To justify what is in effect quenching the Spirit, cessationists are fond of quoting 1 Corinthians 13:8-12:

> Love never ends. As for prophecies, they will pass away; as for tongues, they will cease; as for knowledge, it will pass away. For we know in part and we prophesy in part, but when the perfect comes, the partial will pass away. When I was a child, I spoke like a child, I thought like a child, I reasoned like a child. When I became a man, I gave up childish ways. For now we see in a mirror dimly, but then face to face. Now I know in part; then I shall know fully, even as I have been fully known.

They then like to say that the "perfect" described in this passage was the closing of the canon of Scripture, and once the final pages of the Bible were written, certain supernatural spiritual gifts ceased. The cessationists are right that at least some spiritual gifts will cease. For example, in God's future Kingdom we won't need the gift of evangelism or healing—everyone will be saved and no one will be sick. But until then we need all the gifts. Certainly, the Word of God is perfect, but what Paul is referring to is the second coming of Jesus Christ, when we shall see him "face to face." Jesus is perfect

---
* 1 Corinthians 14:39.

and will bring perfection with him at his Second Coming. At that time we won't need some of the imperfect things we have today, such as your ministry and mine.

So while cessationists are correct that some gifts cease, they are incorrect that the time of their ceasing is in the past rather than the future. Church history proves this fact. The supernatural gifts, including tongues, are reported in the church's history following the final inclusion of the books of the Bible.[5] D. A. Carson says, "There is enough evidence that some form of 'charismatic' gifts continued sporadically across the centuries of church history that it is futile to insist on doctrinaire grounds that every report is spurious or the fruit of demonic activity."[6] Simply put, the Spirit of God empowers the people of God to continue the mission of God until Jesus returns, and at that time everything will be made perfect.

We need to remember that this life is not about us. It's all about Jesus. It's all about Jesus' message, Jesus' mission, and Jesus' glory. Some will say that everyone should speak in tongues, others will say that no one should speak in tongues, and perhaps most will say that some people should speak in tongues. As one who has never spoken in tongues but has continually defended the ongoing use of the gift while leading a church staff where the majority of senior leaders pray privately in tongues, I am certain this has to be a secondary border issue. What has to remain the primary border issue is mission—by the power of the Spirit, we seek to overcome any and every barrier, including language barriers, to bring the Good News of Jesus Christ to as many people as possible. We should organize our church services not so they are seeker sensitive but rather seeker sensible so that lost people can hear about Jesus and get saved. Immature Christians think the mission of the church is their experience and satisfaction. Mature Christians know the mission of the church is bigger than just them. They think like the parents of a large family seeking to adopt more kids, rather than like a spoiled only child.

A final word on tongues. As you read the book of Acts, you'll notice that roughly half the time the Scripture says a person or group received the Holy Spirit in some way, it then says something to the effect of they "spoke in tongues." And the other half of the time it says they "spoke the word of God boldly." What people do pretty much every time they receive the Holy Spirit in Acts is *speak*. They speak about Jesus. Sometimes in a language they know, sometimes in a language they don't. What matters is not the language spoken, but who is spoken about. The evidence of the Holy Spirit is an internal love for Jesus that compels external speaking about Jesus so that others will be saved. Tongues is a secondary issue; the primary issue is that people hear about Jesus and that any barrier is overcome to make that possible. This is also why Christians believe in translating the Bible and other resources into various languages; it is simply another form of the gift of tongues, overcoming the language barrier so that people hear about Jesus.

THE EARLY CHURCH AND MISSION

Before his return to his heavenly throne, the Lord Jesus promised, "You will receive power when the Holy Spirit has come upon you, and you will be my witnesses in Jerusalem and in all Judea and Samaria, and to the end of the earth."* This is the promise of Spirit-empowered mission.

Luke shows us how Acts 1:8 is fulfilled in the lives of the apostles—by the power of the Holy Spirit. The book of Acts is a narrative organized geographically, as follows: "in Jerusalem" (Acts 1–7), "in all Judea and Samaria" (Acts 8–12), and "to the end of the earth" (Acts 13–28).

Much like we see in our Western culture today, Acts describes stiff opposition to the gospel message and mission during the days of the early church. "Demonic forces, worldly powers and authorities, governmental opposition, language and cultural barriers, intense suffering and bloody persecution, unjust imprisonment, unbelief, internal disunity, and even shipwrecks and snakes" all rise up in an attempt to stop the gospel from spreading to all the nations of the earth.[7] But these attempts are in vain. God has promised to bless all the nations in Christ—and his word never returns empty.

The book of Acts records this great harvest. And although the apostles are long gone, the Spirit is not done; he continues to act in our cities, doing the kinds of things he always has for the mission of Jesus. Acts continually reminds us that any truly Spirit-empowered ministry is not marked primarily

* Acts 1:8.

by private spiritual experience but rather by the public proclamation of the gospel that leads to the salvation of sinners. This point cannot be overstated. People need to be saved, and there is no such thing as faithful Christian mission without effective evangelism:

- Acts 2:47: "The Lord added to their number day by day those who were being saved."
- Acts 5:14: "More than ever believers were added to the Lord, multitudes of both men and women."
- Acts 6:7: "The word of God continued to increase, and the number of the disciples multiplied greatly in Jerusalem, and a great many of the priests became obedient to the faith."
- Acts 9:31: "The church throughout all Judea and Galilee and Samaria had peace and was being built up. And walking in the fear of the Lord and in the comfort of the Holy Spirit, it multiplied."
- Acts 12:24: "The word of God increased and multiplied."
- Acts 13:49: "The word of the Lord was spreading throughout the whole region."
- Acts 16:5: "The churches were strengthened in the faith, and they increased in numbers daily."
- Acts 19:20: "The word of the Lord continued to increase and prevail mightily."
- Acts 28:30-31: "He lived there two whole years at his own expense, and welcomed all who came to him,

proclaiming the kingdom of God and teaching about the Lord Jesus Christ with all boldness and without hindrance."[8]

These verses should give us hope as we smell the growing cultural stench, because they reveal a harvest that grows best amid manure.

SPIRIT-EMPOWERED MISSION TODAY

Maybe a decade ago, I had the honor of cofounding a church-planting network whose mission was to help young leaders plant missional churches, particularly in major cities filled with unsaved young people and a lot of manure. So far, more than four hundred churches have been planted in the United States alone, with many more planted globally. We work across denominational lines as a tribe. We call this network Acts 29. The reason? Though the writing of the Bible is finished and Acts has twenty-eight chapters, the acts of the Holy Spirit are ongoing. The Holy Spirit is still at work across every nation of the earth and is still available to Jesus' people. The truth of the gospel is timeless, and there are still sermons to be preached, sinners to be reached, churches to be planted, afflicted people to be comforted, and comfortable people to be afflicted. Our means is the Spirit's power through the church, our message is the gospel, and our mission is eternal.

As Christopher Wright notes, "God's mission is what fills

the gap between the scattering of the nations in Genesis 11 and the healing of the nations in Revelation 22. It is God's mission in relation to the nations, arguably more than any other single theme, that provides the key that unlocks the biblical grand narrative."[9]

We cannot be on God's mission without God's power. Without the Holy Spirit, nothing is possible. With the Holy Spirit, anything is possible.

Do you have hope for a real harvest in this culture? Perhaps an admittedly peculiar illustration will be helpful:

Some years ago, we needed to have a yard put in at our home. The professionals showed up, prepped the ground, and then laid a thick coat of something they called "steer coat." It smelled horrible. We could not open the windows to our home, because the stench was unbearable. Why? Because *steer coat* is a fancy phrase for manure. Manure is, as you know, highly unpleasant. The sod shipment to our house got delayed, which meant that for many days all we had was a yard filled with . . . you guessed it. There was nothing lovely, enjoyable, or desirable in our yard. Eventually, the sod got planted. Before long it rooted. And then it flourished and really started growing—thanks to the manure.

The primary difference between manure and fertilizer is what you do with it. Manure rightly used is actually quite valuable. It can be made into good fertilizer.

Our culture is admittedly filled with a lot of manure. If you turn on the TV, listen to the radio, log on to the Internet, read the newspaper, or head to the mall, pretty much all you will find is steaming piles of unpleasantry. It's everywhere. And it all stinks.

The good news is that ancient Rome, like our modern cities, included a lot of proverbial manure. And the first Christians, following the Spirit, rightly saw fertilizer. Subsequently, the church was planted, took root, and became fruitful. Acts records this process to give us hope. The Holy Spirit has an amazing track record of turning a mountain of manure into fertilizer in which we scatter gospel seed for a great harvest.

Chapter 6

REPENTANCE
A BIBLICAL RESPONSE

As a father of five kids, two of my main goals in life are that my children have fun and that they stay safe. In fact, my three rules for almost any situation are to be safe, have fun, and love others. But one frightful day, despite my desire for my children's safety, things quickly went from delightful to deadly.

For our summer vacation we loaded up the family Suburban the kids affectionately call "Hank the Tank" and drove to eastern Washington. There the summers are hot and dry. We stayed at a country home on a river with a big yard for the kids to play Wiffle ball and catch frogs. Meandering through the backyard was a slow and shallow river that was really more of a creek. You could walk across it safely, and the ice-cold water from the melting snowpack upstream felt amazing during the heat of the day.

Excited to have fun with my kids, I put life jackets on the younger two (Gideon was around five, and Alexie was around seven), and we jumped on the new, big inner tube I'd just bought to use as a raft. We slowly made our way down the creek, sometimes bumping the river bottom in areas that were shallow. We stopped at a sandbar, and the kids played in the middle of the creek for a while. We then climbed back on board to slowly float some more.

Then everything changed. Suddenly, the water got deep, and the current picked up quickly. We came to a point where our creek intersected with another creek, and both dumped into a large river with a strong current. This river was very deep, moved very fast, and was very wide. The kids started laughing; for them it was simply a fast and fun water ride like the kinds they had been on at the state fair. But I knew we were no longer having a fun family float.

The current was moving so fast and was so strong that it carried us all the way to the other side of the river. I could not steer the raft and was afraid one of my kids would fall off and float away. Foolishly, I did not have a life jacket on, and although I can swim, I'm not a strong swimmer. Even with the life jackets, there was no way the kids could possibly swim against this current.

Looking down the river, I was trying to put together an escape plan to get us to the bank. Suddenly, our raft got caught on a branch barely sticking above the water. We sprang a leak and started losing air. Now I was getting panicked. I got into the river, clung to the deflating raft tightly, and started kicking as hard as I could in an effort to push us across what was now an intense, fast-moving river. I was making little progress but kept trying. The longer we floated, the deeper and faster the river got. A sign on the bank informed us that there was one place downriver that had a sloped bank where we could exit, but if we missed it, we would float downriver a long time into even more dangerous conditions. I knew we had to make that bank and could see it approaching fast. We needed to push across the current for what seemed like fifty to seventy yards. Eventually, I made a little progress, but we had a long way to go, and I was gassing out. I tried to hide my fear so as not to scare the children. I closed my eyes and asked Jesus to forgive me for not acting as wisely as I should have and to empower me to bring my kids across the river to the safety of the bank without losing either of them.

Jesus answered that prayer. Somehow, by God's grace, we made it. The inner tube was nearly deflated by the time we reached the bank. I was completely exhausted and had to sit down for a while—I did not have the energy to even walk up the short hill.

Sin is like that float down the river. Repentance—turning away from sin—is often like that swim to the bank.

Sin usually starts off as fun, slow, leisurely, and something we can control. Soon, however, things change. A strong current starts moving us into places we did not intend, until we feel out of control and in danger. Few people really see this as a problem, since most are in that river floating along, not concerned about what awaits them the farther they go.

Repentance means acknowledging our foolishness, turning to Jesus for help, and leaning into God's grace to do whatever it takes to get out of our situation. Only then can we walk away from the life we were living and the path we were following and start on a new path with Jesus. This new and narrow path, to use Jesus' illustration, is walked by few but mocked by many floating by.

A CHRISTIAN'S LIFE IS REPENTANCE

From beginning to end, the Bible calls sinners to repent while there is still time.

Famed preacher Charles Haddon Spurgeon said, "The same sun which melts wax hardens clay. And the same Gospel which melts some persons to repentance hardens others in their sins."[1] This is why the prophets who preached repentance lived lives of exile and were familiar with grief. Hebrews 11:35-38 explains their fate, saying,

> Some were tortured, refusing to accept release, so
> that they might rise again to a better life. Others
> suffered mocking and flogging, and even chains and
> imprisonment. They were stoned, they were sawn
> in two, they were killed with the sword. They went

about in skins of sheep and goats, destitute, afflicted, mistreated—of whom the world was not worthy—wandering about in deserts and mountains, and in dens and caves of the earth.

John the Baptizer got his head chopped off for preaching repentance. Jesus Christ was stripped nearly naked, beaten beyond recognition, and nailed to wood for preaching repentance.

The Bible recognizes those who only and always preach peace, tolerance, love, and acceptance toward sin as false prophets and prophets for hire. The Old Testament and Revelation are littered with references to whoredom, describing false prophets who prostitute their message for profits.

False prophets love to tell us that God is only and forever tolerant. But the Bible teaches that God is not tolerant of sin but rather patient with sinners. Second Peter 3:9 says, "The Lord is not slow to fulfill his promise as some count slowness, but is patient toward you, not wishing that any should perish, but that all should reach repentance." God hasn't held off lighting the match for eternal fire because he finds our sins tolerable but rather because he is patient in giving sinners an opportunity for repentance before the burning begins.

The false prophets tell us that God is not exclusive, but inclusive, and is equally approving of all lifestyle choices. God *is* inclusive in one sense, in that he welcomes all people to repent of their sin. This is what Paul declared in Athens, a city marked by its arrogance, perversion, and Spiritless spirituality. He said, "God . . . commands all people everywhere to repent."* God is inclusive in his invitation to repent. God is exclusive in that only those who do so will enjoy his Kingdom forever.

Renowned theologian J. I. Packer is one of the elder statesmen of evangelicalism. He left the Anglican Church of Canada (ACC) because he believed the ACC was denying the teachings of the Bible by endorsing same-sex unions. I once had an opportunity to spend some time with Dr. Packer, and when I asked him why he had left his denomination, he said in effect that he did not leave his denomination as much as his denomination left him.

When I asked him why he opposed the ACC's stance, Packer said that blessing and affirming same-sex unions was a heresy. Now, when J. I. Packer says the word *heresy*, it carries much more weight than when bloggers use the term to describe the views of those who simply disagree with them. Even so, I asked Dr. Packer to explain why he considered this particular error to be a theological crime against God. His answer was insightful.

Packer pointed out that at the very top of Martin Luther's Ninety-Five Theses nailed to the Wittenberg door was this statement: "All of a Christian's life is one of repentance." That statement was not only the heart cry of the Protestant Reformation but was also the herald of every prophet God has ever sent. Packer explained that the essence of the gospel

---

* Acts 17:30.

of Jesus Christ is repentance, and any theology that does not call people to repent is heresy.

The real issue is not homosexuality. The issue is not fornication. The issue is not same-sex attraction. The issue is not sexual identity. The issue is not sexual preference. The issue is not diversity. The issue is not love. The issue is not tolerance. The issue is not equality. The issue is not acceptance.

The issue is repentance.

The issue is always repentance.

Whatever the issue is, the issue under the issue is always repentance.

We can never repent of repentance.

Does God have a right to tell people no? Does God have a right to be God?

Yes, Jesus loved people, including those in sexual sin. But we read of his public ministry that "Jesus began to preach, saying, 'Repent, for the kingdom of heaven is at hand.'"* In his private ministry, we also see Jesus sitting down with the woman at the well, who had a minivan full of ex-husbands, and lovingly telling her that he was God and that she needed to start worshiping him in spirit and truth—which would require her to stop sleeping with the guy she was shacking up with.†

Biblical Christianity calls us to repent of both unrighteous sin and self-righteous religion. If at any point God's people fail to echo God and do not repent of sin and invite others to do the same, then we are in fact guilty of heresy.

---

* Matthew 4:17.
† See John 4:4-42.

But before we preach repentance, we must practice repentance. The world does not need more hypocrites playing the ever-popular religious game of "plank" and "speck." Before we can boldly call a sin a sin, we must humbly call *our* sin a sin. G. K. Chesterton modeled this winsomely. In response to an inquiry in a British newspaper asking what was wrong with the world, he replied in a letter to the editor, saying simply, "Dear Sir: I am."

Non-Christians find the call to repentance unloving, just as a child might who gets upset with his parents who forbid some dangerous behavior for the child's own good. But Christians should know better. Those who have repented of sin and experienced the forgiveness of Jesus Christ and the new life of the Holy Spirit know that repentance is an invitation to experience the deepest and most satisfying love of all—the love of God poured out in Jesus Christ. Far better than us loving ourselves and demanding that others do the same is God giving us his love freely. In love, the God of the Bible invites us to come to him just as we are. And it is God's love that changes us to gladly repent and become more and more like Jesus Christ by the transforming power of his love. God loves us enough to welcome us as we come to him with our sin. But God loves us too much to allow us to stay in our sin. More than just tolerating us, God's love actually *changes* us. Again, as a good Father, God is a parent who embraces a child no matter what state the child's life is in, but then he also expects his love to help mature that child.

In chapter 2 we examined some cultural issues that have

rung our bell. In the remainder of this chapter we will revisit those issues and examine how they are ultimately opportunities for us to practice and preach repentance.

THE CHURCH AND NEW PAGANISM

As I am writing this book, research is well under way for my next book. I wanted to know the specific reasons why younger people are not attending church or practicing Christian faith, and I wanted to learn more about their actual spiritual beliefs. So we hired a non-Christian research firm with expertise in political polling and corporate market research as well as a PhD professor of sociology to ensure credible results. Over 913,000 calls were made for our research, until a thousand people matching our demographic target answered our questions. The findings clearly show that, among other things, people are increasingly unwilling to accept any divisions when it comes to spiritual beliefs. They simply add Christian beliefs on top of UFOs, karma, and alternative sexual lifestyles. Here is what the non-Christians say they believe. As you can see, it's very in-line with new paganism.

- 88 percent believe Jesus existed.
- 78 percent believe God exists.
- 73 percent believe in evolution.
- 71 percent believe in karma.
- 68 percent believe in heaven and hell.
- 67 percent believe spirituality exists in nature.

- 65 percent believe in angels and demons.
- 59 percent believe Jesus rose from the dead.
- 53 percent believe in the devil.
- 46 percent believe in extraterrestrials, aliens, or UFOs.

In addition to these findings, our research shows that the number one reason non-Christians oppose Christianity is that "Christians are too intolerant." Simply stated, Christians don't believe everything and are discriminating in their beliefs.

If people with these beliefs show up at a church or ministry where the teaching is mainly psychology-based self-help baptized with a few out-of-context Bible verses, they will simply add whatever is taught to their already long list of disconnected and even contradictory beliefs. In this culture of new paganism, we must assume that people know little to nothing about what the Bible actually says. They will not come to the truth apart from solid teaching.

The opening pages of the Bible reveal to us that our God creates distinctions and divisions. He separates Creator from created, the skies above from the land and seas below, day from night, humans from God, animals from God, humans from animals, and so on. The Bible separates angels and demons, salvation and damnation, false teachers and God's teachers, truth and lies, heaven and hell, Christians and non-Christians, Jesus and everyone else.

The fact that God is separate from mankind, however, does not mean he is distant. In fact, Christian Scripture teaches that God interlocks heaven and his creation. We see evidence throughout the Old Testament: Jacob saw a ladder coming down from heaven; a pillar of cloud by day and a pillar of fire by night led God's people in the wilderness; the Tent of Meeting traveled with God's people as a portable meeting place between heaven and earth until they built the Temple, where the Ark of the Covenant was kept in the Holy of Holies; and the Holy of Holies itself was a sort of interlocking place between heaven and earth. For the Christian, "the creation of the world was the free outpouring of God's powerful love," says N. T. Wright. "And, having made such a world, he has remained in a close, dynamic, and intimate relationship with it, without in any way being contained within it or having it contained within himself."[2]

The New Testament describes how Jesus entered this world. The Creator entered his creation. He remained holy and set apart from sin. He died in the place of sinners to reconcile rebels with their Maker. He rose from the grave to conquer sin and death. He is the connection between created men and their Creator God. Atheists are wrong; Jesus is God. Pantheists are wrong; Jesus is God and is separate from his creation. Deists are wrong; Jesus did not stay distant from the world. He was killed for saying he was Creator and God. He is alive and well today, and that is the truth. Everything else is a lie—the same old lie the serpent told our first parents, trying to convince them to abandon the created order and be gods themselves rather than worship their Creator.

When confused pagans interact with Christian belief, they will understandably consider it intolerant, because it is.

The answer here is not tolerance but teaching, and one of the church's primary ministries must be teaching. Without teaching, we do not know that the way we naturally are is not wonderful but sinful. Without teaching, we do not know that we need to be changed at the deepest level because the way we are is fundamentally flawed by sin. Without teaching, we do not know that once who we are is changed, how we think, what we desire, and what we do changes by the Spirit's power at work within us. Without teaching, we assume that who we are, how we think, what we desire, and what we do are good, and that anyone who says otherwise is bad. Teaching is essential for seeing ourselves as we really are.

The original lie of one-ism—that there is no distinction between the Creator and his creation—is not limited to new paganism. There are many other trends undermining the biblical truth of two-ism. For example, gender confusion and sexual sin are sure signs that pagan idolatry has taken root in our culture, as Romans 1:18-32 explains:

> The wrath of God is revealed from heaven against all ungodliness and unrighteousness of men, who by their unrighteousness suppress the truth. . . . They are without excuse. . . . Claiming to be wise, they became fools. . . .
>
> Therefore God gave them up in the lusts of their hearts to impurity, to the dishonoring of their bodies among themselves, because they exchanged the truth about God for a lie and worshiped and served

the creature rather than the Creator, who is blessed forever! Amen.

For this reason God gave them up to dishonorable passions. For their women exchanged natural relations for those that are contrary to nature; and the men likewise gave up natural relations with women and were consumed with passion for one another, men committing shameless acts with men and receiving in themselves the due penalty for their error. . . . They not only do [these things] but give approval to those who practice them.

Sex is the pagan sacrament of one-ism. In two-ism we worship the Creator by enjoying and stewarding his creation, including our bodies, gender, and sexuality. In one-ism we worship the created by offering our bodies as sexual sacrifices and refashioning our gender roles in rebellion against God's created order. The human body is the most amazing, beautiful, fascinating, and enjoyable thing that God created. Like the past pagans who were devoted to Chemosh and Molech—demonic gods who invited illicit sex as a worship act and demanded child sacrifice—today we are equally perverted pagans, and we simply call our method of infanticide "choice."

THE CHURCH AND HOMOSEXUALITY

In the providence of God, the same week I'm typing these words, I also preached at our church in downtown Seattle, surrounded by hundreds of thousands of supporters of homosexuality out on a Sunday for the annual Pride Parade. The streets surrounding our church building were packed with people and floats. There were a lot of typical-looking folks. And there were a lot of atypical folks, including grown men dressed up like Catholic nuns, men wearing nothing but leather chaps, topless women, and numerous men wearing rainbow tutus and little to nothing else. The parade was led by the Boy Scouts, who acted as the color guard, the mayor, and the chief of police. The gay pride flag flew over the iconic Space Needle and over the Mariners game for the first time in Major League Baseball history. The rainbow, which God showed Noah in a covenantal promise to never again flood the earth because of sin, was repurposed as the most visible symbol for the event, and a large rainbow cross was carried by gay clergy out in support of gay marriage. The air was incredibly festive; participants had seen victory after victory for their cause, and many others had jumped on the proverbial bandwagon, much as a winning sports team suddenly gathers a lot of new fans. And the city smelled like pot: the drug's recent legalization contributed to this day without restraint, despite the presence of many young children. At least two street preachers showed up. One held a sign saying, "Repent." (He was knocked to the ground, his sign taken and ripped up.) The other preached repentance until he was punched in the mouth and his face bled.

This is the city Jesus has called me to, and I've been ministering here for about two decades. I can assure you, it's complicated. (On the day gay marriage legislation was passed, couples were calling our churches asking to rent our buildings for their ceremonies.) As the parade went by, I was preaching through Acts on the themes of having courage and preaching repentance. My preaching schedule is laid out far in advance, so I had no idea this text would fall on the day of the Pride Parade.

The broader church is unprepared for the pastoral complexities that will come with the acceptance of gay marriage in our society. For example, if a gay couple is married in the eyes of the government, are they also married in the eyes of God? If at least one person in a gay marriage gets saved, do they need to divorce? And if so, how does that work, since the Bible says God hates divorce? Can they simply live together in a loving relationship if they promise to abstain from sex, and if so, how in the world do we confirm that? If a married gay couple has children and we expect them to divorce upon conversion, what happens to their children? These and many more issues are enormous pastoral complexities on the horizon. We need to avoid the ditch on the left, where we don't call sin a sin, as well as the ditch on the right, where we are angry culture warriors battling unbelievers instead of evangelizing them.

In the days to come, we also have to be careful that we are not constantly dragged into skirmishes over homosexuality. Since Christians and non-Christians disagree on a long list of issues, it should not surprise us when we disagree on a long list of sexual issues. Both homosexuals and Christians are, curiously enough, organized minority groups. If Christians war with homosexuals, what we're ignoring is the majority—all the people between the two groups at some point on a continuum. And as a general rule, those people in the middle are the very people we've been called to evangelize. If they see us as being mean spirited, they will be less likely to want to hear about Jesus from us.

Admittedly, when it feels like you're being punched, the natural instinct is to punch back, forgetting the crowd that has gathered to watch the brawl. But Jesus tells us to turn the other cheek, not because he likes it when we lose a fight, but because he likes it when we win people who are watching the fight. This becomes increasingly complex when former evangelicals such as Rob Bell go astray and say things such as, "I am for marriage. I am for fidelity. I am for love, whether it's a man and a woman, a woman and a woman, a man and a man. I think the ship has sailed and I think that the church needs to just . . . this is the world that we are living in and we need to affirm people wherever they are."[3] (I played basketball for a few years, was never very good at it, had no success in it, and stopped playing years ago, so I should not be an NBA coach. Likewise, when a guy shrinks his church, leaves his church, and is no longer participating in any church, the last thing we should consider him is an expert on anything related to the church.)

Christians will lose the battle for a biblical definition of marriage; of that I have no doubt. This issue will join a long list of things that are legal according to the laws of government but not according to the laws of God. Remember, parents cannot call the cops when their kids fornicate, get drunk, download porn, cohabit, commit adultery, file for divorce without biblical grounds, or date someone of the same gender. So regardless of which tribe we are in, our efforts have to be focused on retaining our biblical beliefs while working for our religious freedom and evangelizing lost people. For the Christian, changing God's laws in Scripture by popular opinion makes as much sense as changing God's laws in nature—including gravity and the temperature at which substances freeze and boil. Non-Christians don't need to accept these laws but to tolerate them, if indeed they believe in tolerance, diversity, and inclusion, as they boast. We won't agree because we don't agree.

Lastly, four things will help guide us.

One, the church needs to lovingly welcome in attendance but not leadership anyone and everyone, because the same Bible that talks about sin is equally clear about love. The church I serve as pastor includes people who are practicing homosexuals, as well as others who are struggling with same-sex attraction to varying degrees. They sit in service next to single people cohabiting, people who watch porn, adulterers, and religious people who look down on all of them. The church was custom built by Jesus, and we are all works in progress. We do not expect people to get their sin in order before attending church any more than a hospital expects people to get healed before they show up.

Two, temptation and sin are quite different. The Bible

is clear that Jesus was tempted and did not sin. Just because someone is tempted does not mean that person is in sin. Temptation is an opportunity for sin or for victory. We must not shame or condemn people who experience various kinds of temptation—including sexual temptations such as same-sex attraction or heterosexual fornication or even pornography—if they desire repentance. We must not endorse or encourage caving in to sinful desires either. Instead, we need to walk lovingly with people, telling them that part of the Spirit's work in their lives is self-control, and that so long as they want to fight for holiness, we want to fight not against them but for them. And as they gain victory, we ought to celebrate and encourage them all the more.

Three, Christians who practice repentance should be the only ones allowed into church membership and leadership. This does not mean in any way that they are perfect, but that they agree with the Bible and that when they are in sin, they are willing to fight to overcome sin by God's grace. We're not asking for perfection but rather for a desire for progress in victory over sin.

Four, the best defense is a good offense. The best thing the church can do for marriage is encourage and assist good marriages. This includes lots of teaching on sex and marriage, great premarital counseling, a supportive community for married couples, and efforts to nurture marriages that are enduring and endearing so that God's people are getting divorced only on rare occasion because of extreme circumstances.

THE CHURCH AND PORNOGRAPHY AND OTHER SEXUAL SINS

The fallout caused by pornography and sexual sin includes both perpetrators and victims. Churches have developed entire programs to help those who are suffering from such things as drug and alcohol addictions, but as yet most have failed to deal with the grip of pornography, the incredibly complex issue of sexual assault, and other matters related to human sexuality.

It doesn't help that one-third of evangelical pastors admit to viewing Internet pornography on a semi-regular basis,[4] or that 50 percent of Christian men and 20 percent of Christian women say they are addicted to pornography.[5] To add insult to injury, the most popular day of the week for viewing porn is Sunday, the day of Jesus' resurrection and the Christian Sabbath.[6] This may explain why few Christians talk about pornography; people with dirty hands tend to feel bad telling others to go wash up.

The Bible describes the curse of sin as slavery. Sin committed against us and sin we commit has the power to oppress our lives. As sinners living in a sinful world, we not only need Jesus' sacrifice in our place (he died to pay the price for your porn addiction), we also need him to redeem us from our bondage to sin. Colossians 1:13-14 describes precisely that: "He has delivered us from the domain of darkness and transferred us to the kingdom of his beloved Son, in whom we have redemption, the forgiveness of sins."

At Mars Hill Church, Redemption Groups are weekly small groups that gather for one quarter at a time to unpack the truth of Jesus' work on our behalf and the many ways that this great display of love affects our lives on a practical level. For addicts, victims, idolaters, and others, this gospel-centered approach provides hope, help, and healing through Jesus and his people in community. We've seen great things happen in people's lives. And when my wife, Grace, bravely shared her own story of sexual assault,[7] this removed some of the stigma for victims in our church, invited them to be honest about the sin committed against them, and encouraged others to love and serve them in the painful places in their souls.

Whatever the method, it is imperative for the future health and well-being of the Christian faith that churches confront the realities of pornography and also deal forthrightly and lovingly with the issue of sexual assault. The two go together, as one fuels the other.

THE CHURCH AND BAD DADS

The essence of masculinity is taking responsibility for yourself, then a wife, then children. These are the kinds of things the Bible says qualify a man to be a church leader.* Guys who don't do this act irresponsibly, take rather than give, and dump their responsibilities on others by virtue of their childish ways. This is why Jeremiah wrote, "It is good for a

---

* See 1 Timothy 3.

man to bear the yoke while he is young."* Men are like trucks: they drive straighter when carrying a load.

Men need to know that they are to be creators and cultivators. God is a creator and a cultivator, and we were made to reflect him. Create a family and cultivate your wife and children. Create a ministry and cultivate other people. Create a business and cultivate it. Be a giver, not a taker; a producer, not just a consumer. Stop looking for the path of least resistance and start running down the path of greatest glory to God and good to others, because that's what Jesus, the real Man, did. Unless this message gets jackhammered into the hearts of young men, the Christian faith is doomed.

"Single-parent families tend to emerge in places where the men already are a mess," says Christopher Jencks, a professor of social policy at Harvard University. "You have to ask yourself, 'Suppose the available men were getting married to the available women? Would that be an improvement?'" Instead of making marriage more attractive, he says, it might be better for society to help make men more attractive.[8]

Now more than ever, for Christianity to flourish, discipleship is parenting. Many young adults have not been parented. They know virtually nothing about biblical dating, sex, financial stewardship, parenting, and other practical life issues—the kind of stuff every line of Proverbs is dripping with wisdom about.

Christian women are more likely than Christian men to attend church. While women and children attend church,

* Lamentations 3:27, NIV.

dad is often at home watching football, downloading porn, and texting his girlfriend. So churches tend, with good intentions, to build programs for women and children. Meanwhile, the bad dad is not the functional pastor of his family; he is not leading them spiritually and loving them daily. Pretty soon, the bad dad's sons get older and decide that real men, like their dad, don't attend church or step up in roles of spiritual leadership. Make no mistake—there is a spiritual war, and if we get the men, we can win. If we lose the men, we will lose.

Maybe an illustration from an experience I had with my daughter Ashley will help. As a young girl she was swimming in a pool during summer break, and I was in the water playing with her. A teenage girl wearing a barely-there swimsuit showed up with two boys. She jumped in the pool and swam to one boy, whom she flirted with and kissed, and then swam to flirt with and kiss the second boy as well. With a puzzled look on her face, Ashley swam up to me. She wanted to talk about what we had just witnessed. "Did you see that, Daddy? She kissed both boys!"

I replied, "I saw. What do you think about it?"

Ashley's answer revealed a lot about how she sees the world: "I think she has a bad dad."

The bad dad epidemic is having a profound impact on how newer Christians and younger people are seeing God and church. In a day when families are broken and scattered by people constantly moving, nowhere feels like home, and no one feels like family. This provides an amazing gospel opportunity for the Christian faith to simply work from biblical imagery and teaching about five truths.

First, God is Father. I believe there is a correlation between the rising tide of bad dads and the correlating rise in moralistic, therapeutic deism among younger generations, as verified by the noted sociologist Christian Smith.[9] Young people's views of God reflect their perceptions of their earthly fathers—distant and uninvolved, essentially having abandoned them to figure out life on their own. The father wound is deep, but the love of God the Father is deeper still. In the Old Testament, God is referred to as Father roughly a dozen times, and always in relationship to the nation of Israel and not to an individual person. But everything changes with the coming of Jesus Christ. Jesus taught us to pray to God as Father and refers to God as our Father some sixty times in the four Gospels, much like what my kids mean when they call me "Poppa Daddy." When people hear that God is a Father who has given them new life, loves them, seeks them, cares for them, listens to them, protects them, provides for them, and will never leave or harm them, then faith, hope, and love well up within them. This is doubly true of those who have had bad dads, since God is a "father to the fatherless."*

Second, church is family. Bad dads and broken families mean that a lot of people have never had a family and have had to in essence raise themselves, which results in immaturity, pain, and loneliness. Yet a healthy church is a family. This explains why the Bible speaks about us having brothers

* Psalm 68:5, NIV.

and sisters in Christ. Practically, this means that older godly married couples function like moms and dads, helping to encourage, support, instruct, and correct younger believers in major life decisions about such things as education, career, budgeting, dating, marrying, and parenting. This means that young adults in particular don't want to be placed in some life-stage ministry only for singles. Instead, they want to know people of all generations in the church, as the church helps to replace what they've missed in their birth family.

Third, church buildings are living rooms. Younger generations tend to prefer older church buildings. This is because in an age of bad dads, most do not have intact families with still-married parents living in homes that serve as gathering places for the extended family for meals and holidays. They find comfort in seeing older church buildings built before they were born. They like the idea of being part of an extended family of God's people, of gathering in a place as a family, with God as their Father. This explains why as generations fled the cities and the old buildings for the suburbs and the warehouses there, children and grandchildren are planting churches in those old buildings back in the cities, where they now live. There is some sense of generations having lived in these spiritual homes.

Fourth, family traditions are rituals not routines. The difference between rituals and routines is inward not outward. Two people can be doing the same thing outwardly, while only one finds deep meaning inwardly. One thing I have learned as a dad is that children cherish rituals. For my family, this includes such things as family dinners together around the table; trips to the coffee shop after school to talk and play board games; and Saturday movie nights, when we all get our pajamas on and pile on the couch to snuggle up, eat popcorn and licorice, and watch a movie. In the era of bad dads, lots of people wish they had a family to make memories with through rituals. This helps explain why emerging generations are increasingly likely to include Communion, testimonies from new Christians, enthusiastic celebratory baptisms, and redone hymns set to new music alongside newer songs in their weekly worship gatherings. It also explains why when the church scatters during the week, members like to meet together in homes, condos, dorms, or apartments as small groups to eat a meal together, apply God's Word together, and pray for one another as friends. As one single man in his late twenties said, "Until I came to our church, I had not had a home-cooked meal in years. When a family in the church invited me to their house for their small group, it was the first time in my life I ever sat at a table with an intact family (mom, dad, kids) and ate a meal. Deep down I've always wanted that but was scared as I'd never seen it."

Fifth, church history is family history. The trend of bad dads also helps to explain why church history has become increasingly interesting to emerging adults. This includes the rise of "New Calvinism" and Christian hip-hop led by my friend Lecrae. Younger people are intrigued by dead guys like John Calvin, Jonathan Edwards, and Charles Spurgeon, even sprinkling them in rap songs and displaying them on T-shirts. When you don't know your family history and you get born again into the family of God, then church history becomes your family history. You start to adopt living old preachers and dead old mentors and learn from their life lessons, much as you would have learned from your great-great-grandparents.

The bad news is that there are very few tribes actually seeing men converted to Christian faith and raised up to be godly fathers. The good news is that the longings created by bad dads have opened the door to biblical Christianity, where God is Father and the church is family brought together by Jesus our big Brother. Our experience shows that this is a massive opportunity for generation-altering ministry.

THE CHURCH AND CHEAP CHRISTIANS

Next time you are in a store, imagine that, instead of a cash register, there was a bucket and a sign that read, "Pay Whatever You Want, and If You Don't Want to Pay Anything, That's Fine Too." How long do you think that store would remain in business?

That is the business model of the church. Unlike the government, which simply takes money from you, or an actual business, which will have you arrested if you do not pay for a good or service you receive, the church depends entirely on generosity. But the statistics reveal that most professing Christians are not generous givers:

- More than one out of four professing American Protestants give away $0.
- The median annual giving for a Christian is $200—just over half a percent of after-tax income.
- About 5 percent of Christians provide 60 percent of the money to churches and religious groups.
- Twenty percent of Christians account for 86 percent of all giving.
- Among Protestants, 10 percent of evangelicals, 28 percent of mainline folk, 33 percent of fundamentalists, and 40 percent of liberal Protestants give nothing.[10]

Jesus devoted roughly 25 percent of his words in the Gospels to the resources God has entrusted to our stewardship. This includes some twenty-eight passages. In the Old and New Testaments combined, there are over eight hundred verses on the subject, addressing topics ranging from planning and budgeting to saving and investing, to debt and tithing. Furthermore, money, wealth, and possessions are the greatest idols in our culture. There is simply no way to be a disciple of Jesus and not learn to worship God with stewardship.

Jesus stressed that we either worship our wealth or worship *with* our wealth. He said, "No one can serve two masters, for either he will hate the one and love the other, or he will be devoted to the one and despise the other. You cannot serve God and money."*

* Matthew 6:24.

Sadly, much of the teaching about stewarding one's treasure is prone to either poverty or prosperity theology. *Poverty theology* considers those who are poor to be more righteous than those who are rich; it honors those who choose to live in poverty as particularly devoted to God. Conversely, *prosperity theology* considers those who are rich to be more righteous than those who are poor; it honors those who are affluent as being rewarded by God because of their faith. In fact, both poverty and prosperity theology are half-truths; the Bible speaks of four ways treasure can be stewarded:

1. Righteous rich stewards gain their treasure by righteous means, such as working hard and investing wisely. Righteous rich stewards also manage their treasure righteously by living within a reasonable budget, paying their taxes and bills, and giving generously. Biblical examples of righteous rich stewards include Abraham, Isaac, Jacob, Joseph, Job (both before and after his tragedy and season of poverty), Joseph of Arimathea (who gave Jesus his personal tomb), Lydia (who funded much of Paul's ministry), and Dorcas (who often helped the poor).

2. Unrighteous rich stewards gain their treasure through sinful means, such as stealing and dishonest business practices, because their monetary idolatry drives them toward greed. Unrighteous rich stewards poorly manage their treasure because they do not budget prudently, spend reasonably,

invest cautiously, or give generously. In fact, one thorough study reported, "Earning higher incomes does not make American Christians more generous with their money. It actually appears to make them more stingy, protective, and distrustful."[11] The study also said, "Higher income earning American Christians—like Americans generally—give *little to no more money* as a percentage of household income than lower income earning Christians."[12] That study also reported,

> Generally, between 1959 and 2000, while the financial giving by American Christians was *declining*, the personal consumption expenditures of Americans *increased* for eating out in restaurants, toys, sports supplies, live entertainments, foreign and domestic travel by U.S. residents, lottery tickets, casino gambling, photography, sports and recreation camps, and other entertainment expenses.[13]

Biblical examples of unrighteous rich stewards include Laban, Esau, Nabal, Haman, the rich young ruler, and Judas Iscariot.

3. Righteous poor stewards work hard, act honestly in business dealings, live within their means, stay out of debt, and live in contentment with the treasure God has appointed for them to manage. There are

apparently many righteous poor stewards, since the poorest Christians give away more dollars than all but the wealthiest Christians.[14] Biblical examples of righteous poor stewards include Ruth and Naomi, Jesus Christ, the widow who gave her mite, the Macedonian church, and Paul, who often knew want and hunger.

4. Unrighteous poor stewards, like unrighteous rich stewards, seek to gain their treasure through sinful means, such as freeloading and stealing, but fail to succeed. Unrighteous poor stewards do not invest their treasure wisely; are prone to foolish spending (such as eating and drinking too much), gambling, and chasing get-rich-quick schemes to obtain wealth without wisdom or effort; and/or are lazy and do as little work as possible. Biblical examples of unrighteous poor stewards include the sluggard and the fool, who are repeatedly renounced throughout the book of Proverbs.

The Scriptures give us a far richer understanding of stewarding our treasure than poverty and prosperity theology do. In Scripture the issue is not primarily whether someone is rich or poor, but whether someone is a righteous or unrighteous steward in obtaining and managing wealth. The way out of the ongoing war between prosperity tribes and poverty tribes is generosity. Whatever you have, steward it wisely and give it generously.

The church is in trouble. With more needs emerging from a broken society, more oppression from an increasingly hostile culture, and fewer resources to work with, it will take every one of God's people giving and serving in order to reach lost people, help victims, make disciples, and plant churches. It's not about the money; it's about the people. Jesus gave his life. The least we can do is give our wealth.

TOUGHEN UP AND LOVE

In order to do ministry in the odd world of intolerant tolerance, Bible-believing Christians will need to toughen up and turn the other cheek—rather than crumple in a heap—when slapped with words like *hateful*, *bigoted*, *intolerant*, *shameful*, *cruel*, *unloving*, *homophobic*, *prejudiced*, *discriminatory*, and more. Jesus told us to love our enemies; his assumption was that we would have enemies to love.

It should not be shocking that Christians and non-Christians think differently. Romans 8:7 says, "The mind that is set on the flesh is hostile to God, for it does not submit to God's law; indeed, it cannot." And 1 Corinthians 1:18 and 25 say, "The word of the cross is folly to those who are perishing, but to us who are being saved it is the power of God. . . . For the foolishness of God is wiser than men, and the weakness of God is stronger than men." The Bible says that God is a potter and we are clay.* Heretics always see it the other way around: God becomes clay to be fashioned and

* See Isaiah 64:8; Romans 9:20-21.

molded into whatever we want and later recast as something else when the cultural mood changes.

Today, the tolerant god is fashionable. Ironically, a tolerant god that simply permits whatever we want to do is far less loving than the true God. Thankfully, as D. A. Carson points out:

> [God] does not merely put up with our sin and anarchy; rather, he is unimaginably kind and loving, demonstrated most overwhelmingly in the fact that he has sent his Son to pay the price for our sinfulness and restore us to himself. To talk about the tolerance of God apart from this richer biblical portrayal of God is to do him an injustice. His love is better than tolerance; his wrath guarantees justice that mere tolerance can never imagine.[15]

The tolerant god did not write the Bible, is not troubled by sin, is incapable of wrath, does not damn anyone, and will save everyone. The tolerant god does not care what name you call him/her/it/they or what religion you adhere to. However, the tolerant god is real, and really powerful. The tolerant god is curiously tolerant of everyone and everything except the real God—because the tolerant god is the same serpent who appeared in the Garden so long ago.

How strange it is that our current pagan culture continues to drive around the same old cul-de-sac and doesn't notice the view hasn't changed. Just like every generation before, this one touts the amazing progress we've made. What I see, however, is millions of murdered babies, a bunch of people who want an excuse to get naked, and a mean-spirited intolerance of anyone who maintains "primitive" notions that babies are for kissing instead of killing, sex is for marriage, and God is to be obeyed.

When sins become civil rights, there is a temptation for Christians to keep our mouths shut and turn what is supposed to be a public faith into a private faith, but we are commanded to not be ashamed of the gospel. We may feel social pressure to accept the new norms, or at least approach sensitive issues in a way that attempts to make the truth palatable and socially acceptable. But the world has enough politicians; it needs more prophets. We can't expect that we'll be more palatable and socially acceptable than Jesus was. He was the only sinless human being who ever lived. He did nothing wrong and everything right. He articulated the gospel perfectly, obeyed God flawlessly, loved people completely, and yet still died bloody. "If they have called the master of the house Beelzebul," Jesus said, "how much more will they malign those of his household."* Jesus' opponents compared him to the devil and then killed him. With all of our shortcomings and failures, we can't expect to fare much better.

Some Christians are called to suffer overt persecution, which may include dying for Christ. All Christians are called to suffer covert persecution, which is part of living for Christ. Most persecution in the Western world is covert. You're

* Matthew 10:25.

probably not going to get executed for your faith, but you may get fired. If you're a professor at a state university, you may get censored in the classroom or ostracized among your peers. If you're in a business, you may sacrifice a promotion, an income, or a job offer in order to operate with Christian integrity.

In addition, some Christians experience covert persecution within their families. Some have been abandoned by spouses, family members, or friends. A man at our church said that when he met Jesus, he shared the news with his family. "You better not be one of those born-again Bible thumpers," was the response. "We don't want to hear any of this Jesus stuff. Keep it to yourself." In other words, don't celebrate Jesus, don't say anything about Jesus, don't pray to Jesus in our presence, or else we'll persecute you.

Covert forms of persecution include emotional, relational, social, and familial opposition, but as the continuum progresses and opposition escalates, overt persecution begins to emerge. It often arises when the governing authorities identify Christianity as a threat to the establishment. In some countries, this results in laws that prohibit Christian assembly, preaching, and evangelism. In more extreme cases, Christians are attacked, murdered, or displaced. Overt persecution is a daily threat to millions of Christians around the world. Visit Persecution.org to read about current examples of such cases and pray for our brothers and sisters around the world.

If we say what Scripture says, we should expect to suffer

as Scripture promises. In fact, Jesus promises that we'll see trouble, experience hardship, and be hated. Rather than run away or fight back, however, he invites us to endure and persevere:

> They will lay their hands on you and persecute you,
> delivering you up to the synagogues and prisons,
> and you will be brought before kings and governors
> for my name's sake. This will be your opportunity
> to bear witness. Settle it therefore in your minds not
> to meditate beforehand how to answer, for I will
> give you a mouth and wisdom, which none of your
> adversaries will be able to withstand or contradict. You
> will be delivered up even by parents and brothers and
> relatives and friends [covert persecution], and some
> of you they will put to death [overt persecution]. You
> will be hated by all for my name's sake. But not a hair
> of your head will perish. By your endurance you will
> gain your lives.*

This will be your opportunity! Not your tragedy but your opportunity. Not your end but your beginning. Not the worst thing that could have happened but the biggest opportunity you've been given. For what? *To bear witness.* We have a message of help, healing, and hope: Jesus Christ is alive. He is King of kings and Lord of lords. Jesus makes life, death, suffering, and persecution meaningful.

---

* See Luke 21:12-19.

Jesus asks us to endure what he endured for us. And if you know that Jesus loves you and you love him, you will be willing to do this, though it is hard. Jesus says there are five ways you may be mistreated as he was:

1. *Tribulation.* This means it will be harder to live in this culture as a Christian.
2. *Poverty.* Being a Christian will cost you money. Some will lose jobs and inheritances, and this loss will not be repaid until the future Kingdom of God.
3. *Slander.* Being a Christian means that your reputation might be destroyed. People will say things that are untrue, perhaps, about you or your church or your faith. They will misunderstand or misrepresent what you believe.
4. *Suffering.* Being a Christian will make your life far more difficult.
5. *Death.* For some in the church's history, all the way to the present, this has been the price. We do not aspire to die or to cause any conflict. But we believe the words of the Bible: "To live is Christ, and to die is gain."*

Whatever the price, we belong to the Lord, and he promises that after death there will be no second death. There will be no hell, condemnation, or wrath. For Christians, this life is as close to hell as we will get. For non-Christians, this life

---

* Philippians 1:21.

is as close to heaven as they will get. Because Jesus died for us and rose for us, if we die for him, we will rise with him. To persevere, we have to keep repenting of our sins and our fears in hopes that others will also repent of their sins and meet Jesus now—because the worst day with Jesus is better than the best day without him.

Chapter 7

MISSION
SEVEN PRINCIPLES FOR RESURGENCE

IF THE BIBLE WERE an old-time Western, the Gentiles would be the guys wearing the black hats. Egyptians, Canaanites, Babylonians, Romans—they are all presented in Scripture as vile, lost, pagan sinners, aka the "bad guys." The Gentiles worshiped the wrong gods, practiced unspeakable sexual sin, and lived without any real knowledge of, repentance toward, or love for the God of Israel.

Then something quite unexpected happened. After Jesus' resurrection and ascension, a lot of formerly pagan Gentiles became Christians. The confused Jews, who were now their brothers and sisters in Christ, then started getting asked the kinds of questions they had perhaps never had to deal with in their Hebrew homeschool co-op: Can we be gay Christians? Can a Christian guy have sex with his dad's (we sure hope second) wife? Can we have sex with prostitutes on our way to church? Can we divide our time between the Christian church and pagan temple to embrace a more inclusive spirituality? Can a Christian boyfriend and girlfriend live and sleep together if they don't get married? Can a Christian man dress up as a woman? If we're running low on funds, can we generate some extra cash by suing fellow church members? And where in the Bible is that verse that says it's okay to get drunk, since our small group really likes to get hammered and party hard?

Do you think I'm kidding? Just read the book of 1 Corinthians. This letter is Paul's attempt to answer these very kinds of questions. In fact, it could persuasively be argued that the New Testament letters are in large part a missiological response to the questions that newly converted pagans have when they meet Jesus. Each letter addresses questions that people from sinful backgrounds and diverse cultures have when they become believers. This also helps explain why Paul is referred to as the apostle to the Gentiles. He was the one God primarily chose to help untangle all the Gentile knots.

In some ways, Christendom for us has been similar to life in ancient Israel. There was one dominant religion, most people assumed they were born into a nation favored by and in good relationship with God, and following the basic moral guidelines of Scripture was generally thought to be what was best for society.

And now, with the rapid decline of Christendom, the church in the twenty-first century finds itself in a place that's similar to Israel in the first century. As we seek to encourage the preaching of the gospel for, the planting of churches by, and the discipling of the Gentiles of our day, there are some missiological principles that have proved helpful in Seattle. I have seen these same principles bear fruit in other parts of America, as well as in other nations.

I'm not proposing methods as much as I'm encouraging principles. Methods are timely and ever changing, but principles are timeless and never change. The Bible commands us to follow God's timeless principles, but encourages us to follow our conscience, our context, godly leaders, wisdom, and the Holy Spirit to figure out our methods. That's methodology.

Methodolatry occurs when we lose sight of the principle and remain committed to the method, even when it's no longer the most effective or even the most connected to biblical principle. This manifests itself in arguing for tradition: "This is not how we do it here" or "We've never done it that way." Tradition is not always bad, but sometimes tradition gets in the way of mission. And when tradition gets in the way of mission, we have to go back to the principle and reconsider our method. Therefore, be careful of methodolatry.

By clinging to biblical principles, we have been able to reach out to a large population of college-educated, urban "Gentiles" and have seen much fruit in our church over the past few years. I understand that not everyone who reads this book will be a church leader, but I believe every one of God's people can be part of the resurgence to grow our churches and ministries so that we bear good fruit for years to come by God's grace.

When I was growing up, my dad owned a lot of tools for working on our house and car. Once I left home and started living on my own, he gave me a basic set of tools—the ones you need for most situations. Without a basic set of tools, you cannot really build or fix anything. And while you may at times require a specialized tool for a particular task, the basic tools are always necessary, whatever the job. In the same spirit, the rest of this chapter is a basic set of ministry tools— principles that cover a wide range of situations and that can be used to build or fix a church or ministry.

1. PREACH THE WORD

Paul commands that a qualified leader "preach the word."* However this is done, it still works today if the Bible is opened so God's truth can be spoken, sinners are called to repentance, the grace of Jesus through his death and resurrection is offered, the people are loved, and God is glorified. In saying "it still works," what I mean is not pragmatism but power.

The same Holy Spirit who inspired the writing of Scripture is glad to empower the preacher to proclaim that same Word and is glad to illuminate the understanding of

* 2 Timothy 4:2.

the hearer to receive and obey that Word. When the Word of God is accompanied by the Spirit of God in power, the results are more Christians and better Christians. Lost people get found, and found people get closer to Jesus.

This explains why even video preaching works—because the power is in the Word of God, not the method of delivery. So long as the Word of God is in a room along with the people of God and the Spirit of God, it does not matter if the servant of God is there.

In this day of scandalous stories about the moral and ethical failings of our Christian leaders, many people no longer have respect or trust for Christian leadership in general. Today more than ever, we must understand that authority is not innate but derivative. It is foolish to assume that because people occupy leadership offices or are even formally trained and ordained, they have any innate authority. Instead, authority is derived from being under the authority of Scripture. As leaders repent of sin, demonstrate humility, and remain teachable while still courageously leading God's people in God's truth, people will increasingly trust them, because these leaders are not only in authority but under authority.

As culture grows more and more hostile toward Christian faith, there will be a corollary hostility toward Bible-saturated, Jesus-centered, sin-hating, grace-giving truth telling. Terms like *hate speech* will be used to malign and marginalize the message of those who preach the Word of God. Do not get distracted; there is more at stake on this issue than your little reputation.

God spoke creation into existence with a word. God continues to speak his truth, often through prophetic preachers teaching the Bible, to a world that increasingly hates to hear it. Words are weighty. *Pride* is not *self-esteem*. *Adultery* is not *falling out of love*. *Fornication* is not *love*. God chooses specific words to convey specific truths, and to change the words is to lose the truth.

The prophets of old were often exiled, and most did not have to worry about a retirement plan, since they knew they would not live long enough to cash it in. Jesus himself was put to death not because he hugged children, fed the poor, was nice to women, loved his mom, healed the sick, or befriended the outcast—rather, death was the only way to shut him up. Following in this death march, every apostle but John was murdered, and John was boiled alive, though he somehow survived, only to then be exiled. The modern notion that if we sand the rough edges off the truth and cover it with enough varnish, it will be easier to market is curious. To echo the world is to mock the Lord.

For the record, I'm not against relationship evangelism. Maybe buying muffins and hugging people will eventually convert them to saving faith in Jesus Christ, and if so, feel free to make more muffins and give more hugs. I, however, am also a fan of riot evangelism. As we read the book of Acts, we see that the church comes into being through a Spirit-empowered sermon by Peter on the day of Pentecost and not through some guy spending six months playing checkers with people, hoping to somehow earn the right to share the gospel. And the New Testament church continued growing in large part through preaching Jesus to groups large and small.* Virtually the only chapters of Acts that do not include preaching record seasons when the preachers are in prison for preaching and therefore temporarily unable to preach.

What we do *not* see in Acts is Paul taking years or decades to befriend people before he feels he has the right to tell them about sin and Jesus. In short, he does not have a lot of relationships. In fact, he has more enemies than friends and seems to initiate far more riots than group hugs. But he does win a lot of converts because he preaches and God blesses. His plan seems to be (a) pull into town and say something controversial and offensive; (b) wait for a crowd to show up; (c) preach the gospel and call people to repent of sin and trust in Jesus; (d) get out of town before being murdered; (e) send in people like Timothy and Titus to straighten things out and establish a local church by gathering the converts; and (f) repeat the process. At our church, I do riot evangelism while our people do relational evangelism.

To the preachers who read this, I say this: You need to preach. Don't be a coward; preach! Don't be a motivational speaker; preach! Don't cave in to your critics; preach! Don't share your feelings; preach! And if you won't preach, then have the humility to find someone who will, and go find a job where the eternal fate of people is not at stake.

* See Acts 2–4, 9–11, 13–14, 17–26, 28. See also Acts 5:42; 6:2-4, 7; 8:3-5, 25, 40; 15:35; 16:10.

2. LOVE THE CHURCH

If Jesus does not return in the next five hundred years, there's a good chance all the current companies, organizations, and businesses will no longer be even a memory, let alone a reality. But there will still be the church of Jesus Christ.

Despite its failures, faults, and flaws, the church of Jesus Christ is the longest-lasting, most impactful, most diverse, and largest entity the world has ever known.

Why?

The church is the only organization Jesus Christ founded. Jesus Christ loves the church like a groom loves his bride. Jesus loves it when new churches are planted. Jesus loves it when old churches get new life. Jesus loves it when churches reach lost people. Jesus loves it when churches help hurting people. Jesus loves it when children born in the church grow up to be born-again members of the church. Jesus loves it when churches raise up young leaders. Jesus loves it when the church sends out gifted missionaries.

Jesus is grieved when people use the church, criticize the church, abandon the church, and attack the church.

We need to love the church, serve the church, give to the church, and pray for the church, because Jesus does all of these things.

And we need to do all that we can to help urban church planting. Churches planted in rural areas will likely never reach the cities. But churches planted in the cities will also often reach the suburban and rural areas. In our culture, everything hinges on the well-being of our cities. Cities are strategic for two reasons: first, there are more people there, and second, culture emanates and flows from the city. The city is upstream, and suburban and rural areas are downstream. The river flows one way. Culture does not come from the rural areas into the city. The way to change culture is with culture-making, gospel-saturated, city-serving churches.

Both Christian and non-Christian movements have nearly always started in cities. It's not the number of people who live in a city that matters—it's the type of people. Today, most cities are non-Christian, and the suburban and rural areas are more Christian. So when Christians become frustrated with culture—films, music, books, art, politics—they need to consider ways to be in the city. The key to actual change is to start upstream. We need to lead politicians, artists, judges, musicians, and the like to Jesus. If we want to stop complaining about culture and start making culture, our degree of influence is not about how many people we convert. It's about their place upstream.

3. CONTEND AND CONTEXTUALIZE

Every expression of Christianity is culturally contextualized. The only differences are what culture and what year.

There is no such thing as a Christian faith apart from time, place, language, customs, holidays, traditions, and the like. Next time you are in church, remember that seating, electricity, speakers, Bible translations, and the printing press are all historically recent innovations and cultural contextualizations.

In fact, our God Jesus Christ came into a specific culture. He spoke a specific language (not every language), he lived in a specific place (not every place), he was a citizen of a specific nation (not every nation), and he celebrated specifically Jewish holidays (not every holiday).

A key component of being a missional Christian is engaging culture. For the missional church, living in relationship with the people of its community carries with it a burden to understand the needs, desires, hopes, dreams, and fears of the people in that particular culture. This is what we mean when we talk about mission.

Over the years I have enjoyed numerous conversations about missiology with Dr. Ed Stetzer. He is perhaps the leading missiological researcher alive today. On more than one occasion, he has explained that now that we in the West find ourselves in an increasingly non-Christian culture, we have to simultaneously contend and contextualize.[1]

Jude 1:3 commands us to "*contend* for the faith that was once for all delivered to the saints" (emphasis added). Quite frankly, there are certain things that we need to just adhere to and fight for with deep passion and conviction—the national border issues, as we discussed in chapter 4.

But while we contend for the faith and hold firm to its core doctrines, we must also contextualize, using what Paul calls the "means": "I have become all things to all people, that by all means I might save some."*

Paul is the biblical author who speaks of predestination, sovereign grace, and election. Those who hold more Reformed theological beliefs are the most likely to be criticized by other tribes for lacking in overall evangelistic zeal and Christian converts. And while this Reformed group likes to say they are most true to Paul's teachings, to be truly Pauline is not merely to believe what Paul believed, but also to do what Paul did. He traveled upward of twenty miles a day on foot, preached the gospel to anyone and everyone, suffered repeatedly, was imprisoned, and was nearly unstoppable when it came to evangelism.

Contextualization is not about being seeker sensitive but about being seeker sensible. In 1 Corinthians 14 Paul says that when the church gathers, believers should interpret and translate for any unbelievers present so the unbelievers can understand what is being said. Preachers often spend hours each week reading scholars. But our job should not be to parrot them. Rather, we need to interpret and translate them. As an example, the New Testament was written in the common, Koine version of Greek used by the average worker and mom, not the academic form of Greek available in its day. We have to define and explain theological terms. And we cannot simply tell people to get "saved" and to be in "fellowship," since they don't know what those words mean unless we take the time to explain them. The truth is,

* 1 Corinthians 9:22.

even many Christians don't know what those words mean, and in our day of growing biblical illiteracy, we cannot take anything for granted. This dawned on me most clearly years ago when a seminary professor's daughter asked me what a concordance was. Assume nothing, and you will be right most of the time.

Contextualization is *not*

- forsaking the gospel
- softening the offense of the gospel
- redefining the gospel
- co-opting the gospel
- ignoring the gospel or
- doing anything that moves Jesus and his work on the cross and his resurrection from the center stage

Contextualization is about showing the relevance of the gospel, not making the gospel relevant. That's the essence of contextualization. Those who want to make the gospel relevant begin with a false assumption that it isn't, so they'll find something interesting, like a smartphone, and build a whole sermon series around it, rather than starting with the Word of God. At the end of every sermon they'll say something like, "God's like a smartphone. He's always connected, and faith is like a button you push to turn it on. And there are lots of spiritual gifts that, like apps, make life better." This may seem cool and hip, but this approach assumes that the Bible, Jesus, and the gospel are irrelevant.

Because the gospel of Jesus Christ is timeless, it is always timely.

As one brutal example, if everybody left Mars Hill except the men, women, and children who have been sexually abused, assaulted, raped, or molested, we'd still have a megachurch. What is the Good News for them? What does a contextualized gospel look like for them? The gospel is that Jesus is God, and he was assaulted, abused, beaten, and killed. It's Hebrews 4:15: "We do not have a high priest who is unable to sympathize with our weaknesses." The Good News for those victims is that we worship a God who himself fully identifies with not just a specific suffering, but with *their* suffering. No other religion, self-help book, or philosophy offers a God like that. Furthermore, the Bible says that God covers their shame and cleanses their sin so that they are clean and righteous in his sight with a new identity that is not determined by what their abusers did to them but by what Jesus has accomplished through his own abuse on the cross. That's the essence of the missional church and contextualization. We assume the gospel is relevant and seek to show that fact lovingly.

4. BE ATTRACTIONAL AND MISSIONAL

Another implication for churches that are both sending and sent is that the church should be both attractional and missional. Attractional churches are those that bring people through the doors for preaching and teaching, large-scale programming, and special events like concerts and conferences. Every church should have attractional ministries. A lot of people knock attractional churches because they think being attractional means watering down the pop until it no longer has any fizz. But Jesus had an attractional ministry and drew large crowds. There is nothing wrong with large crowds coming to hear the gospel preached. The only time attractional ministry goes wrong is when the crowds are drawn but the gospel is not preached.

So being attractional—gathering people together under the preaching and authority of a qualified Christian leader who is under the authority of God's Word—is a very good and biblical thing to be. Our churches should be attractional on whatever scale and with whatever resources they have. But attractional churches also need to be missional churches. In other words, being the church is not just bringing people into the church building for meetings, but also sending people out in groups that meet in homes, condos, dorms, apartments, coffee shops, and parks to talk to people about the person and work of Jesus.

In the 1980s, evangelicals used the attractional church model of ministry by hosting big events, making them excellent, and watching seekers pour in. Now that the cultural itch has changed, this kind of scratch is not as desired. Today, we live in a culture that is less concerned with excellence and more concerned with authenticity. That's why there are more than two hundred reality TV shows. The programming is less than excellent, because everyone wants not what's perfect but what's "real"—despite the irony that authenticity is often contrived in reality TV. And while the culture struggles to find authenticity in things like reality TV, the church should be doing better than anybody else at providing true community and authenticity.

Think about it this way: the most real, authentic witness is the person who's not on staff at a church; hasn't been to seminary; is actually in relationship with other real people; has experienced real wins and losses; and has felt joys and struggles, aches, pains, healing, peace, and triumphs. Those around them can actually peek into their lives, their marriages, their kids' lives, their work, their hope, and their faith. You see them battle with cancer. You see them struggle through unemployment. And you get to observe firsthand that their theology informs their lives and that they respond to the challenges of life with joy and grace because their view of God is healthy, robust, and biblical. Their God is sovereign and good. Even if circumstances are painful, they can be sanctifying. So the "real" person receives every circumstance ultimately as a gift.

These Christian missionaries have credibility through their authenticity with lost people. Non-Christians may come to our churches and hear our sermons, but they don't necessarily see pastors' lives, so they may wonder about our sincerity. This is why it's so important to have authentic Christian witnesses inhabiting the places where unbelievers naturally convene. Not to blow the Mars Hill horn but to share something we rejoice in, we have averaged more than one thousand baptisms per year over the last few years. These represent people who have professed faith while at our church. Yet we have never taught an evangelism class. We don't have an evangelism department. We don't have anyone on staff who oversees evangelism. What we do have are Christians on mission. That's the key for a missional church or ministry. Missional people are used by the Holy Spirit to convert more people to Christianity. They see missions not as a department of the church, but as the purpose of the whole church as a people sent by God.

Missionaries are people who live life with Jesus, under God's mercy, clinging to the Good News out in the world where people don't know the gospel and don't have a saving relationship with Jesus. This is what Peter was getting at when he said that every Christian ought to be ready to give a reason for the hope we have—to be ready to share the gospel with everyone who asks. This "everyone" carries the assumption that the people who ask you about your faith are people who know you, see your life, and want to find out more about you by asking questions.

5. RECEIVE, REJECT, REDEEM

We've established that cultural engagement is not only important but is also the call of God for the church—we are to go to those who need to hear the gospel and proclaim it in ways they will comprehend, with boldness, gentleness, and humility. We don't compromise the gospel in our proclamation; we contend for truth and communicate to people the relevance of the gospel for all times, all people, and all places. How do we do that? What does it look like to enter into culture, with all the brokenness and junk that might come with it, and live as effective missionaries?

I believe that when it comes to cultural engagement, we have three options: receive, reject, or redeem. Let's break these down in turn.

Receive

There are certain things in culture we can receive because they're part of the *imago Dei* (image of God), common grace, and general revelation. For example, the Internet is not biblically off limits. Missionaries can spread the gospel and testimonies of God's goodness, healing, and mercy on the Internet. Praise God for this opportunity! What's interesting is that most reformation and revival movements occur around an innovation in technology like this. So we receive the Internet as an opportunity to distribute the teaching of the Bible and the preaching of Jesus.

Reject

Other things in our culture need to be rejected outright. Despite what culture might suggest or promote to us, we must know our Bibles and be able to identify and recall where the Bible is clear about what is permissible and what is not.

Take sex, for example. Huge discrepancies exist between

the Bible's boundaries around sex and culture's virtually boundaryless approach to the subject. The Bible says that out-of-bounds sex (outside the heterosexual marriage covenant) is a sin against God and whomever you're having sex with. No matter how strongly culture derides the biblical boundaries, faithful Christians must reject what God rejects.

Christians who reject culture's notions about issues such as sex—and in particular homosexuality—are guaranteed to face rejection themselves by people who have rejected God. So the question is not, "Will you be rejected?" It is, "Who are you rejecting: unrepentant sinners or God?"

Redeem

There are things we can receive, there are things we must reject, and there is much that we can redeem. Some things in our culture started out as good but have been corrupted.

Augustine builds the foundation for us here when he says that evil is not a "thing" God created but the act of choosing less than what is from God. Neither does Satan create sin or evil; he corrupts what God creates and makes it less than it ought to be. We do the same.

Let's stay with the theme of sex here. God created sex, and we corrupted it. The choice, then, for Christians is to receive sex as is, even though it has been corrupted; reject it as corrupted; or redeem it, precisely because it has been corrupted. I believe that Christians are to redeem sex within the context of biblical marriages that are lived to the glory of God.

Sex—like many things such as food, drink, and power—can easily be used in a way that dishonors God, or it can be redeemed in a way that honors him.

We need to have discernment about such things so that we don't miss out on God-given ways to glorify him and testify to his goodness and mercy. Sectarians who actively separate from culture define themselves by who and what they're against. Syncretists who embrace whatever culture produces are known for what they endorse, which is anything and everything, regardless of whether God allows or forbids it. Good, gospel-centered missionaries will seek to redeem what has been corrupted so that people might see the goodness of God in a form they understand.

6. CONSIDER THE COMMON GOOD

Many years before he became as widely known and broadly respected as he is today, Dr. Tim Keller was kind enough to talk with me about evangelism and church planting. This started when I was in my late twenties, and each time I got an hour with him, I felt as though I had enough to think about for the next six months because he was so insightful. On more than one occasion he quoted Jeremiah 29:4-9, which was something of a go-to passage for him as he worked in the sometimes hostile context of Manhattan, New York. Several principles can be drawn from this passage for all Christians living in a difficult cultural climate.

First, Christians are to see themselves as missionaries to

the cities in which they live. This is because where we live is part of God's calling on our lives, even if we're brought there by negative circumstances. Where we live is not dictated by chance, happenstance, or circumstance, but rather providence. It might even be a place we do not like and would rather not be. This was the case with God's Old Covenant people, of whom God says, "I have sent [them] into exile from Jerusalem to Babylon."* Babylon was founded by the godless man Nimrod, and symbolically it came to be associated with the counterfeit kingdom of Satan and the haven for all sin.†

Admittedly, there are many days when living in Seattle is tough. I have five kids but live in the US city with the second lowest concentration of children. The cost of living is very high. Real estate is tough to come by, thanks to the trifecta of water, hills, and political liberals. It rains most of the year, and we are so far north that it is dark and wet for weeks and sometimes months at a time. In recent years we actually went nearly two consecutive months without one sunny day—though it rained every single day. It's easy to get depressed in a place like Seattle.

I've seen numerous young, well-meaning, yet naive Christians move into urban areas expecting to do good works and be loved by the whole city. I always warn them to pack a helmet. You can love your neighbors, but not everyone will love you back.

---

* Jeremiah 29:4.
† See Genesis 10:10; Revelation 18:2, 10, 21.

Our church recently moved into the oldest church building in downtown Seattle. When we did, we got a lot of positive attention from the media, which was seen as a negative thing by a number of local bloggers. About that same time, the feces and the fan intersected when some of the younger, well-meaning Christians in our church began recruiting volunteers to serve in non-Christian community organizations. Admittedly, we tripped over our feet a bit in the way we worded our intentions. But things really got heated when one community leader stated about us on the nightly news, "Flat out, they're unwelcome. The neighborhood belongs to equality-minded folk, not anyone who would preach separatist theories."[2] Although we truly want to love our neighbors, the feelings have clearly not yet been reciprocated.

Second, Christians must become stakeholders in their cities. God's people are commanded to "build houses and live in them; plant gardens and eat their produce."* Christians with missional minds need to treat their cities as homes, not hotels. We must put down roots, get invested, and learn to know the city. Accordingly, buying a home is not just an economic investment; it's also a spiritual one. And planting a garden is a prophetic statement that God will make the sun rise tomorrow, and we will be here on mission with him when it does.

Third, Christians must live as a city within the city. Jesus said, "You are the light of the world. A city set on a hill cannot

---

* Jeremiah 29:5.

be hidden."* Jesus taught that the church was supposed to be a small city of God's Kingdom within the big cities of the world. Speaking to Jeremiah, God says that marriage, children, and grace are to be the hallmarks of the city within the city: "Take wives and have sons and daughters; take wives for your sons, and give your daughters in marriage, that they may bear sons and daughters; multiply there, and do not decrease."†

In this age of dating, relating, and fornicating, part of missional work is parental work as we teach our kids and those in the church who are without godly parents what a godly family looks like. God's people are to be holy, or different, meaning they do sex, marriage, and family differently. Christian parents and the church need to ensure that women do not get used and abused, but rather married and cherished. Men are to grow up and take responsibility for their wives and children. And children are to be seen as treasured blessings who will one day love and serve their own cities. This is what the Bible refers to when we read that God is "seeking . . . Godly offspring."‡

Across many European cities we are seeing Muslims run this very play from our playbook. As historically Christian Europeans have fewer and fewer children, Muslims are moving into the cities, having large families, and within a few generations are arguing for the implementation of aspects of Sharia law. Marriage and family are an important part of our missiology because we think to a thousand generations.

Fourth, Christians must serve the common good. This

* Matthew 5:14.
† Jeremiah 29:6.
‡ Malachi 2:15.

means that Christians can be first concerned about helping one another but must also be concerned about everyone in their cities, as every person bears God's image and is worthy of justice. Consider Jeremiah's words: "Seek the welfare of the city where I have sent you into exile, and pray to the LORD on its behalf, for in its welfare you will find your welfare."* Paul echoes this idea in Galatians 6:10: "As we have opportunity, let us do good to everyone, and especially to those who are of the household of faith."

Practically speaking, this is where issues of justice and mercy enter in. This includes contending for just laws for all people, including our enemies. And it includes mercy and generosity to all people, including our enemies. Justice and mercy are not themselves the gospel, but they are a demonstration of how God justly dealt with us at the Cross and generously gives grace to us. These good works accompany the Good News.

In the United States today, the issue of just laws and the common good has to include consideration of the Latino population. Latinos are statistically more likely to be Christian, which makes this demographic one of the greatest hopes for a vibrant and growing evangelical Christianity. *Time* dedicated a cover story to this phenomenon in April 2013. "More than two-thirds of the 52-million-plus Latinos in the US are Catholic; by 2030, that percentage could be closer to half," the magazine reported. "Many are joining evangelical Protestant [congregations]." Moreover, "the longer their

---

* Jeremiah 29:7.

families have been in the U.S., the more likely Latinos are to be Protestant."[3] Latino Protestants generally trend toward charismatic and Pentecostal theology. According to a 2012 report by the Barna Group, 49 percent of Latinos "hold on to the belief that the charismatic gifts, such as speaking in tongues and healing, are an active part of our world today."[4]

As our church has opened locations in Southern California and New Mexico, the opportunity has become even more evident. I personally resonate with many from Latino immigrant backgrounds: I grew up in a diverse, working-class neighborhood in a large Catholic family where my father was a construction worker and my charismatic Catholic mom stayed home to raise the children. She went to Catholic mass on Sundays and Protestant women's prayer meetings during the week. My family was conservative on social issues related to sex, marriage, and family. But my dad often supported Democratic politicians because they better supported the unions and worker laws. I don't want to oversimplify an incredibly complex set of economic and demographic trends, and I realize that there's a great deal of diversity within the native and immigrant Latino community. Nevertheless, my point is that anyone who loves Jesus and loves people has to be thinking hard about immigration, justice, and mercy, in particular as it relates to the Latino population. After all, Jesus' father was a churchgoing, God-fearing, hardworking carpenter who had a large family and immigrated to another nation for some years to provide a better life for his family.

Fifth, Christians must not fear the city. When we live in

a context that is opposed if not hostile to our faith, we have reasons to fear. We can fear for our safety, the well-being of our children, our employment, our social standing, and even our lives. This requires courage and discernment. There are real reasons for fear, but we need to look not only at the purveyors of doom and gloom but also up to the God who rules over it all: "This is what the LORD Almighty, the God of Israel, says: 'Do not let the prophets and diviners among you deceive you. Do not listen to the dreams you encourage them to have. They are prophesying lies to you in my name. I have not sent them,' declares the LORD."*

"Christianity served as a revitalization movement that arose in response to the misery, chaos, fear, and brutality of life in the urban Greco-Roman world," writes sociologist Rodney Stark. He continues:

> To cities filled with the homeless and impoverished, Christianity offered charity as well as hope. To cities filled with newcomers and strangers, Christianity offered an immediate basis for attachments. To cities filled with orphans and widows, Christianity provided a new and expanded sense of family. To cities torn by violent ethnic strife, Christianity offered a new basis for social solidarity. . . . And to cities faced with epidemics, fires, and earthquakes, Christianity offered effective nursing services.[5]

---

* Jeremiah 29:8-9, NIV.

Christianity's fearless stand in the face of various forms of urban adversity—physical, social, economic, natural, political—played a significant role in its rapid rise in influence within the Roman Empire. Our ancient brothers and sisters provide a worthy example of what it looks like to not just endure but also bear fruit within an oppressive society.

7. EVANGELIZE THROUGH SUFFERING

Pastor Doug Wilson once quipped that "a great reformation and revival . . . will happen the same way the early Christians conquered Rome. Their program of conquest consisted largely of two elements—gospel preaching and being eaten by lions—a strategy that has not yet captured the imagination of the contemporary church."[6]

Good luck building any tribe on an invitation to suffer. Western Christians are, generally speaking, bad at suffering. You can't major or minor in it in Bible college or seminary. Preachers are reticent to speak on it because people don't want to hear it. Instead, we'd rather believe that faith is a stick and God is a piñata, and if we swing hard enough, health and wealth will come pouring down upon us. We don't want to hear that we have to "walk through the valley of the shadow of death,"* and so we keep buying books and listening to teachers who promise to give us a map showing us how to walk *around* the valley of the shadow of death. We don't want to embrace suffering. We want to avoid it.

---

* Psalm 23:4.

Why do we avoid calling people to repentance? Often the answer is fear of suffering. Who or what we fear determines what we do and how we live.

What are you fearful of—rejection, criticism, mockery, conflict, hatred, loneliness, unemployment, poverty, a loss of status?

Often we try to organize our lives to avoid suffering. This is especially true in the age of social media, when it's easy to become utterly consumed by how others are responding to and speaking of us. This reflects a fear of man; in counseling circles, it's referred to as peer pressure, people pleasing, codependency, or low self-esteem.

But rather than having an unhealthy fear of man, according to the Bible we are to have a healthy fear of God—meaning that we need to care more about what he says than what others say, and we must be willing to endure whatever we have to, knowing that he will reward us eternally for being faithful even if life is painful. Through Christ, God identified with us and suffered for us in order to save us. In turn, we identify with him and suffer for him in hopes of glorifying him and sharing his salvation with others.

Acts 5:41-42 reports that early church leaders, after being arrested and beaten for preaching Jesus, "left the presence of the council, rejoicing that they were counted worthy to suffer dishonor for the name. And every day, in the temple and from house to house, they did not cease teaching and preaching that the Christ is Jesus." The early church leaders simply accepted the truth we have rejected: "It has been granted to you that for the sake of Christ you should not only believe in him but also suffer for his sake."*

Somehow the myth has gotten around that if something is difficult or if we encounter opposition, it must not be God's will. God's will, we are wrongly told, involves blessing. Yet we fail to accept that suffering for Jesus *is* a blessing.

When we planted Mars Hill Portland, we met very stiff resistance early on. Once the news broke that we were starting a church there, the biggest newspapers in the city of Portland and the state of Oregon had articles calling me the "anti-gay preacher." On one of our first Sundays, an angry mob gathered outside the church building. The protesters wore all black, including black ski masks like bank robbers. Pastor Tim Smith was there and reports, "They were yelling sexual obscenities at the kids and telling them that their parents were brainwashing them. There was one gal dressed up like a devil pacing back and forth on the sidewalk, cracking a whip."

Not long after that, the church building was vandalized. Our executive pastor was the first to arrive at the church and inspect the damage. Nine windows had been busted by rocks, including many of the one-hundred-year-old stained glass ones.

By 9:00 a.m., local TV stations and reporters from local newspapers began showing up at the church and calling our PR director in Seattle. The local FOX station notified us that an e-mail had been sent to them from a sexual activist group who claimed responsibility for the vandalism. They

* Philippians 1:29.

disagreed with our biblical views on sex and decided that vandalism was the best way to show their disapproval. Upon hearing this, and to respond to the many media requests, we issued a press release articulating our love for the city and desire to live at peace. The story was covered by every local news program, radio station, and newspaper and was also picked up nationally by the *Huffington Post*, *Washington Post*, and *Christian Post*, among others, for a total of some twenty stories locally and nationally.

Later in the afternoon, a group from a local center for the LGBT community came to the church to help pick up glass, repair windows, and share their sympathy and disappointment over how others in the gay community acted toward Mars Hill. The next day Pastor Tim and a local leader in the LGBT community went on the air with the local NPR radio station to discuss the events and to show their gratitude for each other. At the close of the show, the host asked the LGBT leader, "Despite all of your differences, do you feel like Tim loves you?" He replied, "Yes."

Pastor Tim explains this season of the church-planting process, saying,

> Both the protest and the vandalism opened doors
> for relationships that would not have likely come in
> any other way. I met prominent leaders and activists
> from the gay community, and we were able to find
> points of common ground and build relationships.
> I met mayoral candidates in the middle of an

election and was able to share the story of our church. I met numerous leaders of Portland churches who extended hands of friendship and support. Our neighbors in the immediate neighborhood came out in force to show support and let us know that while they may not agree with us, they support our right to be here and that the protesters and vandals do not speak for them. Many of these relationships are still developing. Many people visited the church based on this publicity and heard the gospel for themselves. At least one person read about the vandalism in the paper and visited the church and became a Christian. He had not been in a church in over fifteen years, his marriage was falling apart, and he was desperate to find some kind of hope. He had read about us in the *Oregonian*, was challenged by what I said about Jesus, and came to visit. He was baptized a few weeks later, and God has done great things in his life and marriage. And a leading gay-rights activist has also gotten saved and is now walking with Jesus at our church because he connected with us by opposing us before joining us.

I am proud of Pastor Tim and our people. As a new church, they could have given up or fought back, inciting online wars with critics. Instead, they kept their wits about them, persevered in a season of suffering, and kept talking about Jesus. Within one year they were a church of nearly eight hundred people with many new Christians in the urban core of a city that was first made aware of the church by a painful controversy. This kind of thing needs to happen over and over and over and over by God's grace and the Spirit's power for Jesus' fame.

RESURGENCE

Throughout Western history, Christianity has endured seasons when our faith should have been forever defeated, if not obliterated. The church of Jesus Christ should have had a funeral with the fall of the Roman Empire, the spread of Islamic armies, the Enlightenment, political upheaval in Europe, or the philosophical attacks led by Marx, Darwin, Hume, Nietzsche, and Freud.

But God brings dead things to life, and at the heart of our faith is belief in resurrection. In each instance when Christianity seemed to be dying, it was renewed in strength, leaning on Jesus' promise that almost sounds like a battle cry: "I will build my church, and the gates of hell shall not prevail against it."[*] Eventually, the world as we know it, including the United States of America, will fade away. But the church will endure until Jesus comes to take his bride home.

The truth is, the world we live in today is a lot like the first-century context in which Christianity flourished. The Romans worshiped their nation and political leader; Pontius Pilate asked, "What is truth?"[†]; Paul encountered

---

[*] Matthew 16:18.
[†] John 18:38.

an "unknown god"*; the Greeks were openly pro-gay; the Ephesians were converted from witchcraft and demonic spirituality; and the Corinthian Christians needed to stop their cross-dressing and cancel their memberships at the pagan temples. But the gospel—the same gospel that's alive and well today—transformed lives and spread despite all the conflict.

We have been chosen by God to live at this time and in this culture with all its faults and flaws, as part of the church of Jesus Christ with all her faults and flaws, as people with our own faults and flaws. Today we have an unprecedented opportunity for mission. Christendom may have died, but in that death there is a real opportunity for a resurgence of biblically faithful, personally humble, evangelistically fruitful, missional Christianity.

It will be costly for us to stop making a dent and start making a difference. But if we do, we will have some amazing stories to tell our grandkids.

You didn't think you were here just to kill time listening to Christian music until Jesus returned or you died, did you?

Get to work.

---

* Acts 17:23.

Appendix A

A WORD TO THE TRIBES

1. TRIBAL HISTORY: A SURVEY OF MISSIONAL MOVEMENTS

Just as I tell my children our family history, I tell them stories about church history and the members of God's big family who have gone before us, paved a way for us, and left a deposit in us. As we consider what's working in our day, I believe it is also helpful to examine particularly fruitful seasons of rebirth throughout church history. This will, I trust, be helpful for three reasons:

1. *Most Protestant Christians know very little of church history.* Yet we are part of a spiritual family, as we

have been adopted by our Father through the payment of our big Brother, Jesus, into a global and historical family called the church. Those who have gone before us do impact and affect us in positive and negative ways, whether we are aware of this or not. Knowing the spiritual history of our entire family and all the tribes is important for us.

2. *In examining our spiritual family history, we will learn why our tribe does some things and not others and believes some things and not others.* Often we are born or born again into a Christian tribe and just assume that all the other tribes are pretty much like ours—or, smugly, that ours is the most godly, holy, and biblical one. Yet as we learn about our family history, we can more fully appreciate our spiritual heritage and also not be blind to its weaknesses and shortcomings, thereby allowing us to continue to mature and grow in God's grace.

3. *Learning about other Christian tribes and their family histories helps us to better understandand and appreciate our brothers and sisters in Christ.* This does not mean we will always agree with them on everything, but it does improve our odds of understanding them, learning from them, and loving them by seeing them in the context of their histories. In this way, our tribe can be a home and not a prison. We can fully enjoy, value, and commit to our tribe. But we can also visit with, learn from, and invest in brothers and sisters

from other tribes as an act of love, knowing that the family of God is made up of many tribes much like any extended family is made up of many families. As you read, look for the tribal commitments, means of tribal communications, and some of their practices that were innovative at the time but have been adopted and are now assumed.

The Reformation

The Protestant Reformation emerged in pockets throughout Europe. Three particularly influential leaders of the Reformation were Martin Luther in Germany, Thomas Cranmer in England, and John Calvin in France and Switzerland.

MARTIN LUTHER

German theologian and pastor Martin Luther (1483–1546) towers over church history as the seminal figure of the Protestant Reformation, which transformed Western society and launched the Protestant stream of Christianity. Luther was teaching theology at the University of Wittenberg at a time when the Roman Catholic Church dominated religion in Europe and was struggling with corruption, superstition, and biblical illiteracy. At the time, church leaders were trying to fund the construction of a new cathedral in Rome, and in Germany they began selling "indulgences," special letters that purported to release buyers or designated loved ones from punishment in purgatory for their sins. Luther's famous

Ninety-Five Theses protested the abuse of pastoral authority in the way indulgences were promoted, but more important, the theses challenged the authority of the pope and urged a return to the authority of Scripture.

Luther's challenge launched a firestorm of controversy and tapped into latent frustration with church authority, corruption, and abuse. He was officially condemned by the highest levels of the church and the Holy Roman Empire but was protected by the local German princes, who supported more political independence, allowing him to continue to preach, teach, and write prolifically from Wittenberg. From there, he influenced a generation of leaders who rose up in the Reformation with his fiery writings and his teachings on the authority of Scripture, justification by faith alone, clerical marriage, the priesthood of all believers, and the role of the sacraments in Christian life.

With his keen intellect and prolific pen, Luther produced numerous important works that shaped the rise of Protestantism. Believing in the authority of Scripture and the importance of Christians being allowed to read the Bible for themselves, he produced the first German translation of the Bible, which remains a classic and even influenced the development of the German language. Seeing the need for concise ways to teach essential biblical doctrines, he wrote the Smaller and Larger Catechisms, which are still in use today among Lutherans. He also produced numerous commentaries, lectures, pamphlets, and even hymns, including "A Mighty Fortress Is Our God."

THOMAS CRANMER

Not as well known as many of the big names of the Reformation, Thomas Cranmer (1489–1556) was nonetheless a leader of major significance in the English Reformation. Raised in the traditional faith of the medieval Catholic church, Cranmer studied and taught theology at Cambridge. At the time, Luther's ideas on the authority of Scripture were gaining steam in Germany, and the subject was becoming pressing in England for political reasons. King Henry VIII (1491–1547) had obtained special permission to marry his brother's widow. The pope approved the request, but after the king's new union failed to produce a male heir, the king sought an annulment, and this time the pope refused to cooperate. Since Cranmer's views on scriptural authority were favorable to the scheme, he was recruited to the king's team of scholars and sent on a diplomatic mission to Germany, where he came under the influence of the Lutheran Reformers and became convinced of salvation by grace alone.

Then, unexpectedly, the king called him back to England and appointed him the new Archbishop of Canterbury, the senior leader of the church in England. In this position, Cranmer spent the rest of his life fighting to implement the Reformation in England and bring the church back to a biblical faith centered on the grace of God. During his time as Archbishop of Canterbury, he was responsible for developing three major documents that laid the theological foundation for the Church of England: a set of sermons called *The Book of Homilies* (1547), a liturgical book called *The Book of*

Common Prayer (1549 and 1552), and an official statement of theological beliefs called the *Forty-Two Articles* (1553).

In his teachings, Cranmer emphasized the tragedy of the human condition and the gracious, unmerited favor of God toward the undeserving. He was known for practicing this theology of grace in his personal life, as he was notorious for not only forgiving his enemies who schemed against him but even working to help them. Cranmer died a martyr for his faith in God's unmerited grace under the short-lived reign of the Catholic Mary I—known as "Bloody Mary" for her brutal persecution of Protestants. However, not long after his death the founding documents he had authored were restored as the official theology for the Church of England, and they remain the standard of doctrine for the Anglican branch of Protestantism to this day.

JOHN CALVIN

John Calvin (1509–1564) is one of the most towering Bible teachers in the history of the church, known primarily today for his writings.[1] Many are unaware, however, of his work as a tribal leader and church planter. In the 1550s it was John Calvin who saw the population of his city of Geneva double as Christians fled there from persecution. One of those refugees who came to Geneva was the Englishman John Bale, who wrote, "Geneva seems to me to be the wonderful miracle of the whole world. For so many from all countries come here, as it were, to a sanctuary. Is it not wonderful that Spaniards, Italians, Scots, Englishmen, Frenchmen,

Germans, disagreeing in manners, speech, and apparel, should live so lovingly and friendly, and dwell together like a . . . Christian congregation?"[2]

God in his loving providence forced Geneva to become a short-term training ground in missions, where Christians from varying cultures lived together under the teaching of John Calvin and determined what to receive, reject, and redeem from their cultures to effectively contextualize the gospel and evangelize.

After they had such wonderful theological training and missiological experiences, many of the Christians returned to their cultures once persecution subsided. And the result was an explosion of contending, contextualizing, and church planting, which is the logical result of the previous two works. In France alone there were only five underground Protestant churches in 1555, but by 1562 there had been 2,150 churches planted with some three million people in them. Furthermore, some of the churches were megachurches, with anywhere from four thousand to nine thousand people in attendance.

Additionally, Calvin sent church-planting missionaries to Italy, the Netherlands, Hungary, Poland, and the free imperial city-states in the Rhineland. Church-planting missionaries even crossed the Atlantic Ocean, going to what is today Brazil.

Puritanism

Puritanism was a Kingdom-minded, countercultural movement sparked by many years of conflict in England, where the Church of England vacillated between Catholic and Protestant practices depending on which king or queen was ruling at the time. Despite hardship and persecution, some Puritans were patiently determined to work incrementally for reform within the Church of England. Some Puritans, however, grew impatient with the slow pace of change and wanted to pursue a radical experiment with a church free to obey Scripture without the hindrances of bishops and kings. These revolutionaries were largely young, zealous Christians in their twenties who came to be known as the Pilgrims.

The Pilgrims felt compelled to set sail for the New World, America, and there founded a religious experiment where God and Scripture ruled over all of life. One hundred passengers left Plymouth, England, on September 16, 1620. Two months later the Mayflower landed at Cape Cod, Massachusetts, and Plymouth was settled in the New World. The Mayflower Compact was instituted on November 11, 1620, in an effort to establish law and order.

Puritanism was a tribal movement started as an opposition party within the Church of England during Queen Elizabeth's reign (1558–1603). Their tribal commitments included seeking to rid the church of what they saw as "popish" Catholic elements, such as *The Book of Common Prayer*, and moving toward simpler worship services focused on sermons and personal Bible study. Many Puritans left England for America in the early 1600s and became tribal chiefs, such as John Winthrop, William Bradford, John Eliot, Thomas Mayhew, John Cotton, and Cotton Mather. The American

Puritans saw themselves as furthering the Reformation as an example to the rest of the world, and especially to the Church of England. They wanted to be in the world, working to redeem such things as sex, food, drink, and work in everyday life. Deeply theological, they were experiential and practical Calvinists, emphasizing the supreme authority of Scripture and the sovereignty of God with sermons often lasting one or two hours. They highly valued literacy and education, starting many schools. They also emphasized the home as the center of religious instruction during the week, with each father being the pastor of his family, leading his wife and children in studying Scripture, praying, and worshiping. These revolutionaries were largely twentysomethings dismissed by some because of their youth.

The First Great Awakening

The First Great Awakening was a massive outpouring of the Holy Spirit that led to thousands of conversions, the reconfiguration of the Western Protestant world, and the birth of modern evangelicalism during the middle part of the 1700s. Simply put, many tribes came into being following the First Great Awakening, as is often the case when there is reformation or revival.

This Awakening in America was a part of a transatlantic Awakening, and it combined Puritan convictions with Pietist practices. The Puritans had called for more earnest preaching that emphasized the need for conversion and a more experiential Christianity that was personal and internal, encouraging personal holiness and Bible study. Continental Pietism was a hugely influential movement that began in the late 1600s. It called for renewed personal piety in Christians, in contrast to the dead orthodoxy seen in much of the state church in Germany. Continental Pietism influenced Puritanism and Methodism and still continues to influence American evangelicalism. This tribe emphasized small groups (*collegia pietatis*), practical holiness, ministries of mercy, publishing, and other things that are regular emphases of modern evangelicalism.

The First Great Awakening spread, as revival came to many different regions. In the wake of these revivals, there were disagreements among leaders over various issues, which led to many of the tribes that continue in some form to this day under the broad umbrella of evangelicalism.

The Continental Moravian Revival began when Nikolaus Ludwig Count von Zinzendorf (1700–1760) invited a group of Moravian refugees to live at his estate in Herrnhut in 1722. Their tribal commitments emphasized conversion and justification by faith. The Moravians experienced revival in the 1720s and spread out to England, the American colonies, and many other places. They were the first cross-cultural missionaries as we know them today and were devoted not to spreading their state church system but rather the gospel, using what were considered pioneering and cutting-edge missiological strategies. They lived among Native Americans, eating their food and dressing like them.

Some of them even sold themselves into slavery to reach the slaves. They set up prayer and accountability groups. They also encouraged and promoted a conversion-focused, inter-denominational, international kind of Christianity where various tribes worked together for the sake of evangelism and church planting, much like our modern-day networks comprised of multiple tribes.

Revival also spread to England, where the English Methodist Movement was born out of the ministry of John Wesley (1703–1791). While attending a meeting on Aldersgate Street in London on May 24, 1738, where he heard the reading of Luther's *Preface to Romans*, Wesley came to faith in Christ. The Methodist tribal commitment to heart religion is clear in Wesley's famous words, "I felt my heart strangely warmed." Wesley founded and organized the Methodist movement, which exploded over the next fifty years, so that by 1790 there were 294 Methodist preachers in England and over 71,000 Methodists, in addition to over 43,000 in the United States. There were also revivals occurring in Scotland, Wales, and America at the same time.

The beginnings of the First Great Awakening in America are seen in the ministry of Solomon Stoddard (1643–1729), a pastor in Northampton, Massachusetts, who was the grandfather of Jonathan Edwards. Stoddard urged preachers to preach passionately, to focus on justification by faith, to preach hell and judgment, and to avoid moralistic rules without a redemptive heart. His methods and views influenced both Jonathan Edwards's father, who oversaw four local seasons of revival, and Edwards himself, who used much of the same language and held a similar vision for revival.

Jonathan Edwards (1703–1758) saw a mini-revival in 1734–1735 in Northampton and the surrounding towns when he preached a series of sermons on justification by faith. This revival became famous after Edwards described it in minute detail in his famous essay "A Faithful Narrative of the Surprising Work of God" (1737).

One of the driving forces of this Colonial Awakening was the great preacher George Whitefield (1714–1770). A friend of the Wesley brothers who had studied with them at Oxford, Whitefield was a powerful communicator and a dramatic, passionate preacher. His theology was Reformed, and the constant message of his preaching was "You must be born again." Whitefield went to the people, preaching outdoors and in a plain style they could understand. He also used innovative "marketing" techniques such as advertising in the press to reach more hearers with the gospel. During the course of his ministry he made seven trips to America and preached approximately eighteen thousand times to perhaps ten million people. His farewell sermon on Boston Common drew an audience of twenty-three thousand—more than Boston's entire population at the time, and probably the largest crowd that, to that point, had ever gathered in America.

As often happens with revival, this Awakening in America saw conversions and increased cooperation among churches, but it also led to controversy and division among the tribes of New England Congregationalists. The main groups were the Old Lights, the Radical New Lights (Separatists), and the Moderate New Lights ("New Divinity"). The Old Lights, who claimed to be the conservatives in New England, disliked the emotionalism and supernaturalism of revivals. They pointed out negative effects of revivals, such as churches dividing, disrespect for pastors, upstart preachers, and emotional excesses. The Old Lights feared social disruption and thought religion should be orderly. They were theologically liberal, with an emphasis on reason leading to a moral life; their sermons were educated moral lectures with no emphasis on spiritual rebirth or conversion.

The Radical New Lights, or Separatists, not only preached that everyone must be born again but also challenged the established church and social order. Between 1744 and 1754, over a hundred New England churches separated, believing that the established churches were not pure. The Separatists, many of whom became Baptists, rejected state involvement in the church and affirmed believer's baptism. The most enduring influence of the New England Separatists was the exporting of the Separate Baptist movement to the Middle Colonies and the Southern states. Separatist evangelist Shubal Stearns (1706–1771) and his brother-in-law Daniel Marshall were saved in New England and then went on to lead the enormous growth of Separate Baptists in the Southern backcountry, which contributed to making the South evangelical in the nineteenth century.

The Moderate New Lights, led by Jonathan Edwards,

sought to steer a course between Old Light opposition and what they saw as the excesses of the Radical New Lights. They remained skeptical of emotional, mystical experiences such as visions and avoided the radical impulses that they believed undermined society, such as separating from the established churches.

The First Great Awakening had a powerful effect in shaping America and American Christianity. There was a major renewal of the church, as membership increased somewhere between twenty-five thousand and fifty thousand in a colonial population of three hundred forty thousand in 1750. The church saw a revival of preaching, an increase in prayer and devotional reading of Scripture, and increased evangelism to Native Americans and slaves. This Awakening had a democratizing effect on American Christianity, as conversion and piety became more important than education. Conversely, however, it also inspired more education, as colleges like Princeton, Brown, Rutgers, and Dartmouth were founded to advance education and ministry training. Finally, the First Great Awakening saw the acceleration of disestablishment in America, as Separatists abandoned the established churches, and as the non-established churches, such as the Baptists and Presbyterians, grew most quickly from the 1750s to the 1780s.

The First Great Awakening is responsible for creating the movement that is now called American evangelicalism. The evangelical tribe maintained the theological tribal commitments of earlier Protestants, such as the Five Solas of the Reformation, and continued the commitments of their Puritan and Pietist forebears in emphasizing a vital personal relationship with God. But they put what historian Douglas Sweeney calls "an eighteenth-century twist"[3] on Protestant theology with their tribal commitments to gospel urgency and cooperation. Evangelicals were willing to toss out high-church ministry forms and traditions in order to take the gospel to the streets, preaching in the fields, across parish lines, and over tribal boundaries. Seeing themselves as part of a big work of God that transcended ethnic and denominational lines, evangelicals began cooperating across confessional boundaries for prayer meetings, evangelism, and the gospel, foreshadowing the interdenominational and nondenominational movements we see in the church today.

The Second Great Awakening

The Second Great Awakening was a diverse nationwide revival in the United States that is often misunderstood and contrasted negatively with the First Great Awakening, criticized for manufactured revivalism, camp meetings, spiritual manipulation, and wild excesses.[4] But the story of the Second Great Awakening is much more interesting. There are three unique tribes that arose during this revival.

In New England, there was an "Edwardsian" revival, descended from the ministry of Jonathan Edwards. These were Congregational churches led by pastors trained in "log colleges," learning through informal reading and mentoring programs with local pastors. They were a homogeneous, close-knit group whose similar education and theology helped them to work together to promote revival. The Edwardsians "organized extensive 'concerts of prayer,' led common or 'circular' fasts, and joined in alliances with one another for prayer, mutual encouragement, regular pulpit exchanges, and team preaching on revival tours."[5]

The Edwardsian revivals were emotionally reserved, characterized by intense, muffled silence in reaction to the emotional excesses they remembered from the First Great Awakening. They were theological and Reformed, led by educated pastors. They were church-centered, prompted by prayer and by pastors sharing their pulpits with one another, and they led to missions and social reform. Edwardsians started home and foreign missions groups, Bible societies, temperance societies, education societies, and tract societies.

Another tribal stream arose in New York, spearheaded by the Presbyterian minister and evangelist Charles Finney (1792–1875). Finney did not study theology formally, but he was a gifted communicator, using passionate and lawyer-like arguments to convince and persuade people to convert. He also had a strong belief in moral and social reform, working hard for the abolition of slavery. Finney held a new view of revival: rather than seeing it as a sovereign work of God outside human control, Finney believed revival could be reliably produced if only the right methods were used. Revival, he insisted, "is not a miracle, or dependent on a miracle, in any sense. It is a purely philosophical result of the right use of the constituted means—as much so as any other effect produced by the application of means."[6]

Finney's views on revival flowed from his rejection of traditional Reformed theology. He believed human depravity was a "voluntary attitude of the mind,"[7] rather than a nature we are born with, and that people have the "natural ability" to believe. Conversion, therefore, was simply dependent on persuading people to repent and trust in Christ. Because Jesus Christ had given no specific measures to be used in persuading people to repent, new and innovative measures were useful to wake people up periodically. Some of the "new measures" Finney used in his revivals included protracted meetings nightly for a week or more, praying for people by name in a service, allowing women to pray and testify, and the use of an "anxious bench," where people wrestling with whether to trust Christ could come for prayer and counseling. Finney organized his revivals with some new ministry methods that are now common: he obtained financial support from well-off backers; recruited lay workers to organize prayer meetings in advance; and advertised prolifically with posters, newspapers, and door-to-door flyers. He trained ministers to follow up after services with house-to-house visitations and hired a musical assistant to direct singing. In many cities, Finney held extended meetings for weeks, sometimes in tents, other times in buildings. His "new measures" became the foundation for the techniques of later godly revivalists such as D. L. Moody, Billy Graham, and my friend Greg Laurie.

America saw a massive western migration between 1790 and 1840, mostly to rural areas. The Louisiana Purchase in 1803 effectively doubled the land area of the United States, and from 1790 to 1850 the total population rose from 3.9 million to 23 million. In this new demographic landscape, the tribes of the Congregationalists, Presbyterians, and Anglicans were not well-positioned to reach a rural, highly mobile population—but the Methodists and Baptists were. The growing tribes of the Baptists, Methodists, Disciples of Christ, and black churches such as the African Methodist Episcopal Church empowered and focused on ordinary people. They were experience-based, encouraging emotional spiritual experiences and taking them at face value. Spiritual experience was seen as more vital to leadership than education, which meant that anyone could become a pastor. In these tribes, pastors were not above laypeople; in fact, pastoral authority was challenged. The most effective leaders in the nineteenth century were no longer the educated, bookish people, but those who were flexible, creative, and mobile. Many, but not all, tribes in this movement were anti-Reformed in their theology.

One of the fastest-growing tribes in this time period was the Methodists. A key tribal leader was Francis Asbury (1745–1816), who was born in England, received little formal education, became a Methodist circuit preacher, and was sent to America by John Wesley. In 1788 he became the bishop of Methodists in America. Methodism exploded under Asbury, rocketing from 42 preachers and 8,504 members in 1780 to 904 preachers and 256,881 members in 1820. Methodism reached a spread-out rural population through itinerant preachers. The Methodists did not emphasize education; they chose men who were tough, willing to suffer, spiritually gifted, passionate, and able to connect with common people. Methodist preachers would spend four to six weeks on horseback, on foot, or in a canoe to travel circuits of two hundred to four hundred miles, lodging with families or in the open country. They received very low pay, usually less than a quarter of the average salary of a Congregationalist pastor in New England. Asbury himself crossed the Allegheny Mountains sixty times, traveling over 270,000 miles in his life. He wore out six horses, ordained over four thousand preachers, and preached over sixteen thousand sermons.

The Methodists innovated a highly efficient and organized system for gathering and ministering to people. People would be organized into "classes," and lay exhorters, class leaders, and local preachers would be appointed. Methodist theology was straightforward and simple, dealing with gospel themes and emphasizing the urgent need to respond immediately to the message. The Methodist doctrine of prevenient grace affirmed that everything hinged on listeners' choices to accept or reject God's offer of salvation. Preachers exhorted the people with a strong emphasis on holiness and discipline.

The Prayer Revival of 1857–1858

An important revival centered on prayer began in Manhattan in 1857. A Dutch Reformed Church in the city had hired a businessman named Jeremiah Lanphier to do outreach in Lower Manhattan. After little success knocking on doors and handing out Bibles, he decided to hold a prayer meeting for businessmen. Six people showed up the first week, and twenty the second week. Then the New York stock market crashed. Many went into bankruptcy, and soon the crowds attending the prayer gathering overflowed. Within six months, ten thousand people were gathering daily for prayer at numerous sites throughout New York City, and soon the prayer revival spread nationwide.

The Fulton Street Revival, as it came to be called, was centered on prayer rather than any specific preachers or preaching. It was urban, interdenominational, and led and organized primarily by laypeople rather than pastors. It was orderly, well publicized through newspapers and advertising, and widespread, reaching every region of the United States. At one point, fifty thousand conversions were being reported each week, and over one million new Christians joined churches. The prayer revival helped to shape future urban revivals, as it encouraged laypeople to participate and take leadership, and many leaders from this revival helped lead revivals during the Civil War.

The Ministry of D. L. Moody

D. L. Moody (1837–1899), the most famous and influential evangelical tribal leader of the late nineteenth century, began his ministry in the midst of the prayer revival in Chicago, and his ministry had much in common with those kinds of revivals. After his father died when Moody was four, his mother was left to raise nine children all under the age of thirteen. Moody received only six years of education. He came to faith as a teenager while working in Boston; he traveled to Chicago in 1856 to make his fortune in the boot business. There he got involved in the YMCA, which was evangelical and missional at the time. During a prayer revival, Moody quit his job and started a Sunday school in a rough neighborhood. Before long, fifteen hundred students were attending, and in 1864 he planted a nondenominational church out of the Sunday School—a church which survives to this day as the famous Moody Church in Chicago.

In the early 1870s, Moody went to Britain and carried out evangelistic campaigns that drew unprecedented crowds. For example, he held 285 meetings in London that drew a total attendance of over 2.5 million. Moody preached there two years before returning to America with a reputation as a famous revivalist. He then began holding revival meetings all over the United States, finding the most success in urban settings, in contrast to Charles Finney's successes in smaller towns. Moody's business background served him well, as his revival meetings flourished through careful planning, organization, publicity, and fund-raising. Using volunteers, Moody's team went house to house canvassing residents before a crusade and raised funds from business donors. They enlisted local churches and evangelical leaders to cooperate regardless of denominational affiliations. Revival space was rented in a large, central building, and a gospel soloist often helped draw crowds. To Moody, it made more sense "to advertise and have a full house than to preach to empty pews."[8] Pragmatic and results oriented, Moody believed "it doesn't matter how you get a man to God provided you get him there."[9]

Moody's warmhearted, direct, commonsense preaching focused on conversion. He emphasized three Rs: "Ruin by sin, Redemption by Christ, and Regeneration by the Holy Ghost."[10] Doctrinally, Moody's preaching leaned Arminian, though he sought to avoid getting into deep or controversial theological issues that might distract from conversion and holiness. His premillennial view of history is clear in his statement, "I look upon the world as a wrecked vessel. God has given me a lifeboat and said to me, 'Moody, save all you can.'"[11]

Moody believed leading people to faith in Christ was most important, but he still cared deeply about poverty and other social causes. He started schools for impoverished children; supported temperance, the main progressive cause of his day; and criticized American employers for paying starvation wages.[12] One of the reasons we know so much about Moody today is because of his role as an institution builder.

He founded schools for girls and boys, Moody Bible Institute, Moody Press, and the Northfield Bible Conferences. D. L. Moody probably had a larger role in shaping the uniquely American tribe of evangelicalism in the twentieth century than any other leader; he has been called the "founder of contemporary interdenominational evangelicalism."[13] His focus on conversion did not leave much place for the local church, tradition, detailed theology, or extensive education, and his emphasis on evangelism through mass media helped lead to the rise of evangelical publishing houses and radio.

The Student Volunteer Movement and Evangelical Missions

In 1886 D. L. Moody invited 251 college students to Mount Hermon, the boarding school he had founded in Northfield, Massachusetts, for a month-long Bible conference.[14] The students began showing an increased interest in missions, and Robert Wilder, a recent graduate from Princeton, called all those who were interested in missions to a meeting. About two weeks later, A. T. Pierson, who was Moody's friend and a Presbyterian pastor, gave an address titled "Christ Means That All Shall Go, and Shall Go to All." Moved and inspired to take the gospel to the nations, by the end of the conference one hundred students had signed a pledge to go overseas as missionaries.

With the YMCA's backing, Wilder spent the following academic year touring college campuses, telling the story of the "Mount Hermon One Hundred" and urging students to pledge themselves to become missionaries. Some two thousand students responded. In 1888 YMCA leaders organized the Student Volunteer Movement for Foreign Missions (known as the SVM), which formed organizations on college campuses around the United States. Students signed pledge cards declaring their intention to become missionaries and joined weekly meetings to learn about missions under the slogan "the evangelization of the world in this generation."[15] This movement launched the missionary movement among the American Protestant tribes. Before the formation of the SVM, American Protestants supported fewer than one thousand missionaries around the world. Between 1886 and 1920, the SVM recruited 8,742 missionaries in the United States, and around twice that number were actually sent out as missionaries, many of them influenced by the SVM.

During most of the nineteenth century, the predominant form of missions had been denominational missions. But in the late 1800s the "faith missions" movement began, a new kind of missionary endeavor in which people would set out "by faith," not knowing how they would be funded and not asking for money. Hudson Taylor and the China Inland Mission is an example of this movement. Faith missionaries were uncompromisingly evangelical but interdenominational, accepting support from anyone who wanted to give. They relied on faith, often not even making their financial needs known but depending on God to provide. Their premillennial theology, influenced heavily by the rise of dispensationalism, led to an urgency and a willingness to go to new areas, since they believed Jesus' return was imminent.

In faith missions, zeal and piety were more important than formal education, and the missionaries tried many innovative methods. Many important missions organizations were founded out of this movement, including the Central American Mission (1890), the Africa Inland Mission (1895), the Sudan Interior Mission (1893), the World Radio Missionary Fellowship (1931), and Wycliffe Bible Translators (1934). After 1930 the movement expanded even more, leading to organizations such as the Missionary Aviation Fellowship, Trans World Radio, New Tribes Mission, Frontiers, and others. The faith missions movement marked an evangelical takeover of American missions. Joel Carpenter sums up the shift: "From a total of about 12,000 career foreign missionaries in 1935, the North American Protestant missionary force increased to some 35,000 by 1980. While the mainline Protestant missionary force decreased from 7,000 to 3,000 over these forty-five years, the number of more 'sectarian' evangelical missionaries grew from about 5,000 to 32,000."[16]

The Holiness, Pentecostal, and Charismatic Movements

Taken together, the Holiness, Pentecostal, and Charismatic tribes are extremely significant, currently making up the majority of evangelicals and one-fourth of all Christians worldwide at approximately six hundred million adherents.[17]

THE HOLINESS MOVEMENT

The Holiness movement began in the early 1830s as a large number of Christians from various denominations became concerned that American evangelicalism was getting too worldly, mainstream, comfortable, and lazy, gaining cultural and social influence but losing passion and radical devotion. Many looked to the Wesleyan tradition of perfectionism as a solution, calling for holiness in people's personal and public lives.

The most famous woman of nineteenth-century evangelicalism and a tribal leader of the early Holiness movement was Phoebe Palmer (1807–1874). She authored a book titled *The Way of Holiness* (1843) and urged a theology of Wesleyan perfectionism, believing that if people would consecrate themselves to God, God would bless them. The Holiness movement also looked to Charles Finney as a tribal leader as he developed his holiness theology at Oberlin College, giving rise to what became known as "Oberlin Perfectionism." He taught that people had a limitless capacity to defeat their sin, repent, and obey God perfectly, and that a higher form of Christian spirituality could be achieved by leading a holy life, which included abstaining from things like tobacco, tea, coffee, and most forms of entertainment. A banner hung over his campaigns that read "Holiness unto the Lord."

Hannah Whitall Smith (1832–1911) wrote *The Christian's Secret of a Happy Life* (1875), which also helped popularize holiness teaching. In 1875 Smith and her husband, Robert, spoke at a convention in England where eight thousand people attended and became fired up for holiness. The next year a permanent holiness convention was established called the Keswick Convention. Keswick theology encouraged "victorious Christian living" and taught that if Christians would "let go and let God," the Holy Spirit would fill them with power for service. Keswick theology was very influential in mainstream evangelicalism, influencing the ministry of D. L. Moody and the missions movement.

THE PENTECOSTAL MOVEMENT

The Pentecostal movement emerged out of the Holiness movement around the turn of the century. The early influencer Charles Fox Parham (1873–1929) left his Methodist church in 1895 and became an itinerant evangelist. Parham taught that sanctification was a "second blessing" that Christians experienced at a specific time after conversion and that there was a "third blessing" as well, when the believer would be baptized in the Holy Spirit.

One of Parham's students was William Seymour (1870–1922), blind in one eye, who became the most famous early Pentecostal leader. As an African American, Seymour had to sit outside the classroom. In 1906 he went to a Holiness mission in Los Angeles and preached that speaking in tongues was evidence of baptism in the Holy Spirit. He was kicked out of the meeting but kept preaching to the crowds from a porch. Soon Seymour and his followers moved to a warehouse on Azusa Street in an industrial section of Los Angeles, where Seymour preached three services a day for three years.

The Azusa Street Revival, as it was called, brought thousands of attendees together to hear Seymour preach and to receive the "third blessing" of the Holy Spirit. Significantly in this Jim Crow era, the revival was multiethnic, with African American, Hispanic, and white attendees worshiping together. Holiness leaders from all over the United States came, and the Pentecostal movement spread, sweeping through many holiness denominations.

Pentecostalism eventually grew into thousands of denominations around the world. In Los Angeles the evangelist Aimee Semple McPherson (1890–1944) founded the Angelus Temple in 1923; by 1927 her ministry had developed into the International Church of the Foursquare Gospel, emphasizing four points: Jesus saves, baptizes, heals, and is coming again. McPherson was one of the first radio preachers, using big productions to draw large crowds. Like other Pentecostal groups, the Foursquare Church had many female preachers in its early days. The largest Pentecostal denomination, the Assemblies of God, was founded in 1914, holding a more Reformed view of sanctification. Rather than a "second blessing," they emphasized "the finished work of Calvary," available at conversion and appropriated over the course of a Christian's life.[18]

THE CHARISMATIC MOVEMENT

In the 1960s, Holiness and Pentecostal emphases began to arise in mainstream denominations, in Catholicism, and in mainstream evangelicalism, gaining much influence and causing much controversy. This became known as the Charismatic movement, which had many diverse tribal leaders. Granville "Oral" Roberts (1918–2009) left a Pentecostal denomination to join the United Methodist Church, where he brought faith healing and tongues into the mainline and founded a major Christian college bearing his name. Pat Robertson (born 1930) was ordained in the Southern Baptist Convention before growing his Christian Broadcasting Network (CBN) into a massive television station, which brought charismatic Christianity into millions of homes with words of knowledge, faith healing, and speaking in tongues. Robertson became hugely influential, leading the Christian Coalition and running in the 1988 US presidential election.

The 1960s and 1970s saw the rise of the Jesus movement, which emerged from within the hippie subculture. This sprawling, disorganized youth movement sprang up in communal homes, coffeehouses, and music groups in the San Francisco area before spreading around the United States, emphasizing a return to the teachings of Jesus and an ascetic lifestyle. By 1971 it was recognized by newspapers and made the cover of *Time*.[19] Thousands were converted, a 1972 "Jesus Music Festival" drew an estimated crowd of 150,000, and thousands of converts enrolled in Bible colleges and seminaries and went into ministry. The Jesus movement also led to the rise of the Christian contemporary music industry and caused evangelical Christians to become friendlier toward the youth culture. By 1976 the movement was declining, but it influenced the rise of several new tribes that remain strong today, including Calvary Chapel, Vineyard Churches, and Harvest Crusades.

The Post–World War II Evangelicalism

Twentieth-century evangelicalism, or what was once called neoevangelicalism, grew out of the fundamentalist movement, which was an early twentieth-century coalition of orthodox, Bible-believing Christians who came together to fight the theological modernism that was spreading through the mainline denominations. Fundamentalism grew out of movements within nineteenth-century evangelicalism, such as Holiness, D. L. Moody's interdenominational revivalism, and Bible and prophecy conferences. There was an increasing sense of unity across denominational lines, tied together by an emphasis on revival, missions, and holiness. The movement was tied less to churches or denominations than to institutions such as Bible schools and Bible conferences.

Fundamentalists were united on the inerrancy of Scripture and the core doctrines of the faith, including the deity of Christ, the Resurrection, and the Second Coming. Many fundamentalists were also fighting the rise of scientific naturalism, specifically Darwinian evolution, in the schools. In the 1920s and 1930s the fundamentalists lost every major battle for the fate of the mainline Protestant denominations and lost the cultural fight over teaching evolution in the public schools. Most fundamentalists separated from or were thrown out of liberal mainline Protestant denominations. They lost cultural influence and withdrew from political and intellectual engagement.

Beginning in the 1940s, however, many fundamentalists reentered the public square and began to raise up strong leaders, advance education, develop intellectual and apologetic responses to other views, and pray for revival. The National Association of Evangelicals was formed in 1942 to enable evangelical cooperation and advance the evangelical cause, as evangelicals were spread across a variety of denominations and nondenominational churches. Numerous ministries rose up to reach America's youth and college students by focusing on effective evangelism and the use of innovative methods. In the 1930s evangelist Dawson Trotman (1906–1956) founded the Navigators, focusing on one-on-one discipleship among college students and military personnel. His discipleship teachings influenced many other ministries. InterVarsity Christian Fellowship began an American branch of its college ministry in 1941, aimed at witnessing to students and faculty on college campuses. In 1944 Youth for Christ began as a collection of evangelistic rallies in cities across America, Canada, and England. Billy Graham was the first full-time staff, and the rallies led thousands to Christ. At UCLA, Bill Bright (1921–2003) founded Campus Crusade for Christ in 1951. Fifty years later, Campus Crusade employed twenty-six thousand full-time staff and had a presence in 191 countries.

While some ministries that focused on evangelism and discipleship sprang up, other leaders worked for evangelical engagement with cultural, intellectual, and social issues. One major figure was the theologian Carl F. H. Henry (1913–2003), who wrote the hugely influential book *The Uneasy Conscience of Modern Fundamentalism* (1947), which criticized the anti-intellectualism, divisiveness, and lack of social concern in the fundamentalist movement and urged engagement with modern thought and the social issues of the day. Another major influence was the founding of Fuller Theological Seminary in 1947, which sought to encourage rigorous scholarship and help recover the evangelical mind. It was funded by the famous radio evangelist Charles Fuller (1887–1968) and led by Harold John Ockenga (1905–1985), who called for a "new evangelicalism."[20] In 1956, Ockenga joined Billy Graham and others in founding *Christianity Today* magazine with Carl Henry as editor. Intended to be a leading thought journal from an evangelical perspective, *Christianity Today* was shipped free to hundreds of thousands of pastors. Hugely influential, it helped many move away from liberalism and into evangelicalism.

Billy Graham (born 1918) studied at Wheaton College and became an evangelist with Youth for Christ in the 1940s, at a time when an increasing number of pastors in the United States were meeting to pray for revival. In September 1949 Graham planned a three-week evangelistic crusade in Los Angeles. The newspaper mogul William Randolph Hearst, who had never met Graham, directed his newspaper editors to "puff Graham," and within days Graham's crusade was getting national press coverage.[21] Attendance swelled, and the meetings were extended to eight weeks. By the end, over 350,000 people had attended the seventy-two meetings, and three thousand had professed faith in Christ. Graham now had a national platform.

Graham's 1950 Boston Crusade marked an important milestone of revival. When at a New Year's Eve meeting four hundred people came forward to become Christians, Graham and Ockenga believed they were on the verge of a revival, which Graham believed came only from God and only when certain conditions are met: repentance, prayer, unity of God's people, and obedience to God's Word.[22] Graham visited many New England cities, and by the end of the spring nine thousand people had made professions of faith in Christ.[23] During the rest of 1950, Graham preached in many other cities to over 1.5 million people, and nearly fifty thousand people made professions of faith. This period marked a "midcentury revival," with evangelistic meetings packed all over the country with different preachers and reports of revival flowing in from countries like Belgium, Ireland, New Zealand, and Spain. Citywide campaigns were held through much of the 1950s, with hundreds of thousands in attendance and thousands of people coming to faith in Christ. Additionally, there was great unity between different denominations in putting on these combined evangelistic campaigns.

In 1957, Graham invited Martin Luther King Jr. to join him at his New York City crusade, which drew 2.3 million listeners.[24] After this event the more militant fundamentalists split with Graham, believing he should not cooperate with mainline Protestants or Roman Catholics. This marked a split between separatist fundamentalists, who continued to embrace the term "fundamentalists" for themselves, and the more ecumenical fundamentalists, who became known as evangelicals. Talk of revival cooled after 1957, but between 1940 and 1960, church affiliation in America rose from 49 percent to 69 percent, and dozens of new missions agencies and ministries were founded. Evangelical churches and denominations grew, and intellectual engagement increased, as seen in the growing number of evangelical Christians with PhDs and the number and quality of evangelical theological, educational, and publishing institutions. There was also much growth in evangelical social involvement in politics, education, and mercy ministries.

Some churchgoers in America have come to identify evangelicalism with certain kinds of political activism or cultural opposition, and many self-professed evangelicals have drifted away from concern for biblical theology in favor of a kind of self-help, psychologized, anti-theological, or health-and-wealth message. The movement has become so fragmented that it is now impossible to know what people in America mean if they identify themselves as evangelical. However, a growing number of evangelical churches in America are prioritizing biblical truth; Jesus-centered theology; orthodox doctrine; gospel-centered evangelism, ministry, and missions; and Spirit-empowered living. The gospel continues to be advanced as God raises up new movements, leaders, and tribes, and Jesus unfailingly continues to build his church.

2. THE CYCLE OF TRIBAL MOVEMENTS

Historically, when tribal leaders and their tribal followers submit to the Holy Spirit and walk in the truth of his Word and the power of his gospel, missional resurgence is birthed into a tribal movement. In examining church history, we see that movements tend to go through a life cycle.

The Holy Spirit Sets (Often Young) People on Fire

In the history of the church much has been accomplished by Christians who were young. Perhaps Paul's words to Timothy are the most pertinent: "Don't let anyone look down on you because you are young, but set an example for the believers in speech, in conduct, in love, in faith and in purity."[*]

Curiously, throughout church history God has chosen to use young people like Timothy for significant Kingdom work. Jonathan Edwards is the greatest theologian America has ever produced, and he began his life of ministry at the age of nineteen. Additionally, the First Great Awakening began in 1734 in his Northampton, Massachusetts, congregation with the young people who had drifted away from the church but suddenly wanted to begin meeting with him about his sermons. George Whitefield is one of the greatest preachers America has known. He began his life of ministry at the

---

[*] 1 Timothy 4:12, NIV.

young age of twenty-five. David Brainerd is one of the greatest missionaries America has ever had. Brainerd began his life of ministry at the young age of twenty-four. The Methodist circuit riders were devout evangelists who traveled across the country on horseback to lead people to Christ through preaching the gospel and then establish local congregations of believers. Most of the circuit riders began their ministry while they were in their twenties.

D. L. Moody was one of the greatest evangelists in the history of America. He preached to over one hundred million people in his lifetime. Moody began his life of ministry at the young age of twenty-one and went into full-time ministry at the age of twenty-four. Dietrich Bonhoeffer is one of the most well-known pastors of the twentieth century. Bonhoeffer began his life of ministry at twenty-five. Charles Haddon Spurgeon started preaching at the age of sixteen and is among the finest preachers in the history of the church. Billy Graham is easily the most influential Protestant Christian leader of the twentieth century. He began publicly preaching the gospel at nineteen.

If you are a young person who loves Jesus, do something with a church. If you are not ready to do something, get ready and then do something. If you do something and God does not bless it, then do something else.

What young people lack in wisdom, they make up in zeal. I'm not saying older, wise, mature Christians aren't important to movements, but they have to understand their role. If they can make the transition from player to coach, everyone wins.

If not, there are needless attacks and the mission of God can be hindered as Sauls keep chucking spears at Davids.

New Organizations Form

Tribal movements start as simple organizations that see a need and call a few friends to work together to meet that need. God then raises up a tribal leader whom people recognize as the visible face and the person God has called to lead the organization. The organization then grows and becomes big enough to become a movement. The movement generates big interest. More people come. The crowds grow. There is passion, purpose, mission, and expansion. The growth can be fast and furious. People make mistakes, and theology needs to be clarified. It can be a messy time, and some people don't fit in. The movement has influence across multiple tribes as what the Spirit is doing has turned into a wildfire.

Out of the chaos of the early days of the movement come supporting organizations. This is where networks, denominations, conferences, publishing houses, schools, missions agencies, and the like come into existence to support what the Holy Spirit is doing.

Institutionalism Overtakes Mission

The transition from a tribal movement to an institution is caused by fatigue and/or a focus on needing to avoid failure—protecting assets rather than risking and investing them for a greater harvest. In time, a movement has enough success that it stops taking risks. It is afraid of losing what it has achieved, and there is constant pressure upon senior leaders to stop at a moderate level of success and cease pushing forward for new victories because of the cost to the team and the price of potential failure. The illusion at this phase is that momentum can actually be managed and will not be lost. The truth is, a movement's momentum is gained slowly and lost quickly. There is either movement forward or backward but no sustained management of prior success.

I was once on a car ride with a bishop who explained that at one time he was a raging young buck who started a coup to get his tribe back to the gospel and mission. But years later, as he was facing his retirement, he was fearful of young leaders and new ideas. His tribe had stockpiled a ton of cash, and after the end of his ministry tenure he had planned to rule through policies he had "buried so deep in concrete they will never be able to dig them up." He forgot that churches and people belong to Jesus and that the Holy Spirit can empower someone else to do our jobs, and even do them better—which is why he wants our policies in pencil and not cement.

A Tribal Movement Becomes a Museum

Once a movement becomes an institution, the next step is to become a museum unless a course correction is made to get back on mission. Once the mission of an organization becomes the preservation of the institution, the original mission stops, and the Holy Spirit stops showing up in power.

What people used to give their lives for has somehow become simply another job. The remnant that is left behind exists solely to tell the story—not to keep writing it. In one generation a movement can transition to being an institution and then a museum.

There are a number of issues that can cause a tribal movement to become a museum. Let's consider some of them:

- *Doctrinal issues:* Some tribal movements begin with strong doctrinal convictions but are slowed or even destroyed by becoming too rigid—or too loose—theologically. Movements can also stall by reducing the value of healthy ecclesiology, drifting from biblical models of church to pragmatic and politically correct models of church. And they can obsess over secondary issues (such as eschatological speculation) to the degree that they lose sight of primary issues (such as ensuring that their pastors keep their pants on). A healthy movement does not debate doctrines such as the atonement, the Bible, heaven, and hell, but it should be free to discuss secondary issues. The key is to define what you need agreement on in order to be in the movement and what you can safely differ on.
- *Relationships:* Tribal movements may also stall because of an unhealthy view of and value on relationships. It's possible for people to love their circle of friends so much that they are unwilling to break up their circles

to make more room. In other words, it's no longer a community on mission but rather the mission is community. When relationships with people are valued more than making disciples and planting churches, the movement is nearing an end.

- *Organizational failure:* When a tribal movement is organizing, everything is done initially through relationships and verbal conversations. As time goes on, things must be written down, articulated, and defined. They move from the spoken to the written. If those in a movement are unwilling to make those adjustments, they can become an institution. If the reason they don't want policies is that they don't want to become an institution, what they will become is just a poorly organized institution.

- *Organizational pride:* What does organizational pride look like? Some tribes will not sing songs unless they have been written by people within their tribe. They won't read books that have not been written by authors from within their own tribe, nor will they listen with humility and a teachable spirit to those from outside their tribe. There are times when every tribal movement will outgrow the counsel of their leadership and need wisdom from outside. Organizational pride makes it much less likely that movement leaders will seek "outside" wisdom. When that happens, the movement suffers from "Not Invented Here" syndrome.

- *Chasing potential rather than calling:* Tribal movements can chase too many things at once. For example, the YMCA was founded as the Young Men's Christian Association, and you will be hard pressed to find the *Christian* part anywhere on their properties. Vineyard started as a church-planting movement and then became a renewal movement. They were involved in so many organizations, causes, and groups that they didn't really plant churches anymore. In order to avoid "mission drift," tribal leaders should focus on God's primary calling for the tribe.

- *Moving too slowly:* It used to be that the big would eat the small. Things have changed. Today the fast eat the slow. Today it is not as much the size of a movement but its speed and ability to remain nimble and adaptable (so that momentum is not lost) that is the key. This is possible only when the tribal movement is broken into smaller working teams that remain nimble with delegated authority and power. Without this informal and efficient leadership, systems are birthed by virtue of necessity to get things done.

    The military has learned this. Instead of big battleships and big bomber planes, small units of highly trained specialists are often dropped into a hostile environment to take out a high-ranking target because they can get in, adjust, and get out fast. God so loved the world that he did not subject Jesus to a church committee. Otherwise they would still be debating whether he could turn water into wine, and it would be another two thousand years before they voted on whether he could die on the cross.

- *A lack of publishing:* Theodore Roosevelt once quipped that "every reform movement has a lunatic fringe." Christians call them heretics. Drunk on the new wine of change, they start rewriting Christian truth and causing a lot of controversy, confusion, and conflict. However, in the providence of God, heretics can be a real gift to a movement. They force tribal chiefs to go back to the Bible and start writing down their defenses of the true faith in the face of false teachers.

When movements fail to archive their thinking and development and to find ways to share their theological convictions en masse, they are nearing the end. There is a need to do much more publishing as a movement grows and new people with new questions join.

But here's what is scary: some would naively assume that all Christian publishers are Christian, but they are not. Many Christian publishers are mere subsidiaries of large, non-Christian media companies. Practically, this means that non-Christians now control the majority of book and Bible sales in the United States. Subsequently, I predict a slew of new evangelical publishers will come into existence as more false teachers get "Christian" publishing contracts from non-Christians. This is also why we started Resurgence Publishing—so we could control our message, because it's not about selling books; it's about telling the truth.

• *A failure to simultaneously honor the founder and the future:* One movement I have great respect for is Newfrontiers, founded by Terry Virgo and centered in Brighton, England. They have planted hundreds of churches around the world. I have learned a lot from their very godly and kind father figure of a founder, and I love a long list of their leaders, who are my friends. I had the honor of speaking at their international pastors' conference to some five thousand ministry leaders in Brighton. One sermon I preached I felt was a prophetic word for their movement about the vital matter of honoring their aging founder and their amazing future. They graciously received the word humbly, and I hope in God's grace I was able to begin a conversation that needs to be had but that everyone felt disrespectful initiating. Apparently a loud, rude American might be good for something after all.

Some tribal movements so honor the founder that they shipwreck the future. The leader or leaders stay in leadership long past their fruitful years. Or to honor the founder, the movement is handed to a close relative, with the hope that the juju will rub off, thanks to the juju fairy.

Some so honor the future that they shipwreck their founders. They rip the founders out of leadership abruptly and unkindly or destroy them through politicking, which divides the whole tribe.

This issue in many ways determines whether a tribal movement is a single-generational movement or a multigenerational movement. A healthy tribe will appropriately honor, support, and take care of its founder(s). Failure to do so shrinks the life span of a tribe because the God-given values of the founder get lost as the new movement leaders discount the worth of the "old-timers" of the tribe. Not honoring a founder hurts a movement.

But many movements fail to thrive for multiple generations because they fail to look to the future. Because they don't want to dishonor the founder(s), no one ever articulates the reality that the movement will need to be carried on beyond the lifetime of the founder(s). People tiptoe around the reality that at some point the founder(s) will die. No one wants to develop a succession plan because it feels like it undercuts the value of the founder(s).

The truth is this: What better way to support and honor the founder(s) of a tribal movement than by making sure the heritage is passed on to a next generation with great care? Successful, long-term tribal movements will simultaneously honor the founders and the future.

- *Friends and family take all the seats at the top:* As a tribal movement grows and becomes an institution, or even a museum, it has a lot of assets. So, as you would expect, old friends and family members find their way to the seats at the top. Rarely is it because they are the most gifted. Often it is because the founder is trying to share his or her wealth and power with those people most loved and appreciated. But that is not what is best for the mission of God.

When friends and family take all the seats at the top, there is no room for young, emerging leaders. As soon as that happens, the young leaders leave to start another movement. And the young guys of the past are in danger of becoming just like the old guys they never used to like in the first place.

Edmund Burke's statement rings true: "Those who don't know history are destined to repeat it." When your mission, your family's mission, your church's mission, your denomination's mission, your network's mission, or your tribe's mission becomes anything other than God's mission, it becomes Ichabod, as the glory of God departs when the Holy Spirit is ignored.

But there's even hope in that. Movements, like people, don't last forever. They undergo a life cycle and eventually die. By God's grace they can also resurrect into something alive, healthy, and vibrant if there is a return to Jesus Christ as revealed in the Bible, preached from the pulpit, and empowered by the Holy Spirit.

3. A WORD TO TRIBAL CHIEFS

Satan and his demons are real, and when the Bible speaks of a war raging between the Kingdom of God and the enemy, it is reality. Because tribal chiefs have such great influence within the church, Satan often focuses his most detailed and devastating attacks on them, much like any other war where the strategic advantage can be gained by taking out a high-ranking officer. Satan does this by setting three main traps for God's people in general but for tribal chiefs in particular—a moral trap, a financial trap, and a theological trap.

Moral Trap

The Bible speaks of elders and deacons with clear criteria by which people are to be tested if they hope to qualify as Christian leaders.* Since a tribal chief is a "pastor-plus," at the very minimum he has to meet the same sort of moral and spiritual qualifications that God demands of pastors and elders. It is a tragedy when a tribal chief is guilty of something serious—such as adultery—and little or nothing is done because he is "God's anointed" or some other gibberish that con men and charlatans throw around to keep people busy doing word studies on "anointed" while a scoundrel walks away laughing.

Financial Trap

Part of the apostolic ministry responsibility entrusted to a tribal chief is stewarding all that belongs to Jesus and has

---

* See 1 Timothy 3:1-13.

been given by him to manage. Sadly, many tribal chiefs have tended toward either prosperity theology or poverty theology.

Tribal chiefs guilty of prosperity theology are often known to be greedy, lavish, and lovers of money. In an overreaction, other tribal chiefs have become guilty of poverty theology, whereby their families are not well provided for because the tribal chiefs will not accept the generosity that would enable them in turn to be generous toward their families and ministries.

A tribal chief should be generous—first to his family and then to his church, as well as to the poor and individuals in need. This shows by example that God wants us to combat the errors of poverty and prosperity theology with generosity.

Theological Trap

Like all other sinners, a tribal chief needs to be not only *in* authority but also *under* authority. This is possible only when leaders in general, and tribal chiefs in particular, remain under the authority of God's Word, the Bible. Anytime one's pet author, personal experience, or preferred discipline (sociology, psychology, philosophy, for example) holds anywhere near scriptural authority—or, God forbid, equal to or above it—it's only a matter of time before everything blows up. This is true for all Christian leaders and doubly true for tribal leaders. Over the years, I have seen a parade of gifted tribal chiefs self-destruct, and every time it started when they lowered their commitment to the Bible as God's perfect, authoritative Word sent to us for obedience and not for editing.

It's easy for tribal chiefs to believe that God's favor is on them. But here's the reality: God's favor is always on his Word, and once we begin stepping away from Scripture, we are moving away from his blessing.

Believe it or not, this can actually be highly profitable for the leader. The secular media despise God's Word, and they love it when a compelling, fresh, former evangelical has become so "enlightened" that he or she now agrees with the unregenerate that at least parts of the Bible are untrue. People will line up to pay big money to read a book that encourages them to mock God rather than repent. When this happens, the tribal chief often stays in ministry for a while before the sheep realize that their shepherd is actually a wolf. Still collecting a paycheck, the chief continues to lead until eventually the church or ministry begins to die as the glory of the Lord departs. And then, not surprisingly, the chief suddenly feels called by God to do something else—usually something that does not keep the chief in community or under authority: being a consultant, conference speaker, or full-time author.

And I can tell you this dirty little secret: under nearly all opposition to Scripture is unrepentant sin—usually sexual in nature. When you are in sin and the Bible confronts you and the Spirit convicts you, you have only two choices: you change, or you change the Word of God. Most theological problems are simply moral problems in disguise, as people with zipper-related issues are prone to be good at syllogisms and Greek word studies and to know a really great agent and PR rep.

More than ever, it is important that godly tribal chiefs love one another, pray for one another, and labor together for the greater good of the Kingdom of God. This does not require watering down our convictions but rather adding to them the Bible's exhortations to love and unity. Sometimes the Holy Spirit even blesses these seasons with reformation and/or revival in the form of missional movements.

RECOMMENDED READING

Many great books deal expressly with theological concepts. However, the aim of this book is to examine the implications of various theological concepts as they work together. For the sake of brevity, I had to summarize some enormous theological concepts. For readers wanting to study those issues more deeply (particularly those in chapters 3 and 4), the following recommended reading list should be a helpful place to begin.

1. CALVINISM VS. ARMINIANISM

A. Multiperspectival

Hunt, Dave, and James White. *Debating Calvinism: Five Points, Two Views.* Sisters, OR: Multnomah, 2004. James White takes the Calvinist position, arguing against Dave Hunt, who takes the Arminian position. The two authors respond to and critique each other's arguments as they wrestle with scriptural interpretation and theological issues related to God's sovereignty.

B. *Calvinist*

Brown, Craig R. *The Five Dilemmas of Calvinism.* Lake Mary, FL: Ligonier, 2007. Brown examines the development of Calvinist and Arminian systems of thought and suggests that the problems Arminians see in Calvinist doctrine are unfortunate misunderstandings of the system.

Calvin, John. *Calvin: Institutes of Christian Religion,* 2 vols. Edited by John Turabian McNeill. Translated by Ford Lewis Battles. Library of Christian Classics XX–XXI. Philadelphia: Westminster Press, 1960. John Calvin's classic work provides a critical corrective to the view that Calvinism is nothing more than a system based on election and reprobation. Instead, Calvin's rich theology of the Holy Spirit, rooted in God's providence, provides a robust picture of God and his work in the world through Jesus Christ.

Horton, Michael S. *For Calvinism.* Grand Rapids, MI: Zondervan, 2011. Michael Horton offers a positive argument for Calvinism by refuting misunderstandings and showing its historical origins, its biblical grounding, and its resources for practical spirituality.

Peterson, Robert A., and Michael D. Williams. *Why I Am Not an Arminian.* Downers Grove, IL: InterVarsity, 2004. Peterson and Williams examine the biblical and theological problems commonly attributed to Arminianism, suggesting that the system has too high a view of human freedom and too low a view of God's sovereignty.

Steele, David N., Curtis C. Thomas, and S. Lance Quinn.
The Five Points of Calvinism: Defined, Defended, Documented,
2nd ed. Phillipsburg, NJ: P&R, 2004. Steele, Thomas, and
Quinn attempt to provide a biblical and theological statement
of the five main points of Calvinist thought.

C. *Arminian*

Olson, Roger E. *Against Calvinism*. Grand Rapids, MI:
Zondervan, 2011. Olson mounts an argument against
traditional and "new" Calvinist theology, suggesting that
the system has devastating consequences for one's doctrine
of God. Olson offers a positive argument for traditional
Arminian theology, which he sees ironing out the tensions
found in Calvinism and being more faithful to Scripture.

Olson, Roger E. *Arminian Theology: Myths and Realities*.
Downers Grove, IL: InterVarsity, 2006. Olson addresses ten
myths about Arminian theology and makes the case that the
system is every bit as evangelical as traditional Calvinism.

Stanglin, Keith D., and Thomas H. McCall. *Jacob Arminius:
Theologian of Grace*. New York: Oxford University Press,
2012. Stanglin and McCall offer a close examination of
Jacob Arminius's thoughts on God's relationship to creation,
providence and predestination, and sin and salvation. This
high-level academic work seeks to rehabilitate Arminius in a
time when his name is often derided.

Walls, Jerry L., and Joseph R. Dongell. *Why I Am Not a Calvinist*.
Downers Grove, IL: InterVarsity, 2004. Walls and Dongell
examine the tensions and weaknesses present in traditional
Calvinist doctrine. They suggest that it has both biblical and
theological problems and that Arminianism offers a coherent
and biblically faithful solution to Calvinism.

2. COMPLEMENTARIANISM VS. EGALITARIANISM

A. Multiperspectival

Belleville, Linda L., Craig L. Blomberg, Craig S. Keener, and
Thomas R. Schreiner. "Two Views on Women in Ministry,"
revised edition. *Counterpoints: Bible and Theology.* Grand
Rapids, MI: Zondervan, 2005. This edited volume is composed
of four essays, two in favor of complementarianism and two
in favor of egalitarianism. Belleville and Keener represent
egalitarianism, and Blomberg and Schreiner represent the
complementarian position.

B. Complementarian

Grudem, Wayne. *Evangelical Feminism & Biblical Truth.* Eugene,
OR: Multnomah, 2004. Grudem puts forth a detailed
argument for the complementarian position, arguing
specifically against egalitarian objections.

Grudem, Wayne. *Evangelical Feminism: A New Path to Liberalism?*
Wheaton, IL: Crossway, 2006. Grudem suggests that
underlying the shift to feminism in evangelicalism is the issue
of the authority of Scripture. He argues that the feminist
movement can lead people on a path to theological liberalism.

Kassian, Mary. *The Feminist Mistake: The Radical Impact of
Feminism on Church and Culture.* Wheaton, IL: Crossway, 2005.
Kassian takes a historical look at the origins of feminism and
mounts a critique of it from a complementarian perspective.

Köstenberger, Andreas, and Thomas Schreiner, eds. *Women in
the Church: An Analysis and Application of 1 Timothy 2:9-15,*
2nd ed. Grand Rapids, MI: Baker Academic, 2005. This
edited volume looks at the most hotly contested passage in
the gender debate: 1 Timothy 2:12. The essays argue that the
complementarian position best fits with the exegesis required
of the passage.

Köstenberger, Andreas. *God, Marriage, and Family: Rebuilding the Biblical Foundation*, 2nd ed. Wheaton, IL: Crossway, 2010. Köstenberger provides an extensive biblical-theological argument for a complementarian family structure. This highly exegetical work also devotes time to homosexuality, divorce, and women in church leadership.

Köstenberger, Margaret. *Jesus and the Feminists: Who Do They Say That He Is?* Wheaton, IL: Crossway, 2008. Köstenberger examines ways in which feminist theologians have portrayed Jesus, and she argues that these portrayals are flawed.

Piper, John, and Wayne Grudem, eds. *Recovering Biblical Manhood and Womanhood: A Response to Evangelical Feminism*. Wheaton, IL: Crossway, 1991. This volume, edited by Piper and Grudem, is considered a standard treatment of the issues related to the gender debate from a complementarian perspective. The authors of the essays in these volumes deal with a variety of biblical and theological topics and make the case for complementarianism.

Reaoch, Benjamin. *Women, Slaves, and the Gender Debate: A Complementarian Response to the Redemptive-Movement Hermeneutic*. Phillipsburg, NJ: P&R, 2012. Benjamin Reaoch offers a response to William Webb's redemptive-movement hermeneutic from a complementarian perspective, suggesting that Webb's view has undesirable consequences for the way Christians read Scripture.

Ware, Bruce A. *Father, Son, and Holy Spirit: Relationships, Roles, and Relevance*. Wheaton, IL: Crossway, 2005. Ware puts forth the complementarian understanding of the Trinity and how it relates to gender relationships between men and women.

C. Egalitarian

Bilezikian, Gilbert. *Beyond Sex Roles: What the Bible Says about a Woman's Place in Church and Family*, 3rd ed. Grand Rapids,

MI: Baker Academic, 2006. Bilezikian argues for the full equality of men and women from key biblical passages. This is a standard argument for the egalitarian position.

Brauch, Manfred T. *Abusing Scripture: The Consequences of Misreading the Bible.* Downers Grove, IL: InterVarsity, 2009. Brauch offers a crash course in hermeneutics. He argues that those who focus on issues of authority in the scriptural texts miss the point and cannot faithfully apply the Bible to real-life issues, such as gender roles.

Erickson, Millard. *Who's Tampering with the Trinity?: An Assessment of the Subordination Debate.* Grand Rapids, MI: Kregel, 2009. Millard Erickson evaluates the complementarian use of the Trinity as an argument for complementarity in male/female relationships. He says that one ought to be careful in drawing implications for familial relationships from the doctrine of God.

Giles, Kevin. *The Trinity and Subordinationism: The Doctrine of God and the Contemporary Gender Debate.* Downers Grove, IL: InterVarsity, 2002. Giles argues that, far from supporting the complementarian position, the historically orthodox view of the triune God actually supports egalitarianism. His view, opposite that of Bruce Ware, attends to history, Scripture, and theology.

Giles, Kevin. *Jesus and the Father: Modern Evangelicals Reinvent the Doctrine of the Trinity.* Grand Rapids, MI: Zondervan, 2006. Giles suggests that the Son is not eternally subordinate to the Father but instead is fully and eternally equal with the Father. The complementarian view, he says, leads to many problems associated with the early Trinitarian heresies.

Groothuis, Rebecca Merrill. *Good News for Women: A Biblical Picture of Gender Equality.* Grand Rapids, MI: Baker,

1996. Groothuis argues that too often the debates between complementarianism and egalitarianism focus on a few controversial texts. Because of this, she takes a step back to look at the "big picture" and says that biblical thought leans toward equality more than hierarchy.

Johnson, Alan F., ed. *How I Changed My Mind about Women in Leadership: Compelling Stories from Prominent Evangelicals.* Grand Rapids, MI: Zondervan, 2010. This volume offers the autobiographical accounts of a variety of different people from different denominations and ethnicities who have changed their mind about what the Bible says about women in Christian ministry. The work puts forth a positive vision for egalitarianism.

McKnight, Scot. *The Blue Parakeet: Rethinking How You Read the Bible.* Grand Rapids, MI: Zondervan, 2010. McKnight's book, while primarily a book about reading the Bible in today's culture, deals significantly with the issue of women in ministry. McKnight says that most of today's controversy over women in ministry is related to hermeneutics, and he thinks his view of Scripture allows Christians to read the Bible well while affirming women in all positions of church leadership.

Payne, Philip B. *Man and Woman, One in Christ: An Exegetical and Theological Study of Paul's Letters.* Grand Rapids, MI: Zondervan, 2009. In his study of the Pauline letters, Payne says that because men and women are viewed as one in Christ, there ought to be no restrictions on what positions of authority women can occupy in the church.

Pierce, Ronald W., and Rebecca Merrill Groothuis, eds. *Discovering Biblical Equality: Complementarity without Hierarchy,* 2nd ed. Downers Grove, IL: InterVarsity, 2005. This work is to egalitarianism what Piper and Grudem's *Recovering Biblical Manhood and Womanhood* is to complementarianism: the standard volume on the position. Twenty-six different authors take up the egalitarian position on numerous historical, biblical, theological, hermeneutical, and practical issues.

Stackhouse, John. *Finally Feminist: A Pragmatic Christian Understanding of Gender*. Grand Rapids, MI: Baker Academic, 2005. Stackhouse offers a nuanced trajectory hermeneutic for reading Scripture's view on relationships between men and women. Arguing for equality for women (Christian feminism), Stackhouse is careful to note that God allowed and regulated patriarchy in the Old Testament and New Testament to advance his Kingdom purposes.

Webb, William. *Slaves, Women, and Homosexuals: Exploring the Hermeneutics of Cultural Analysis*. Downers Grove, IL: InterVarsity, 2001. William Webb offers a redemptive-movement hermeneutic for reading Scripture, and he thinks his view provides a way for Christians to affirm the full equality of men and women without having also to affirm that homosexuality is a legitimate practice.

3. CONTINUATIONIST VS. CESSATIONIST

A. Multiperspectival

Gaffin, Richard B., Jr., Robert L. Saucy, C. Samuel Storms, and Douglas A. Oss. *Are Miraculous Gifts for Today? Four Views*. Edited by Wayne Grudem. Grand Rapids, MI: Zondervan, 1996. In this multiperspectival volume, four authors answer the question, "Are the miraculous gifts for today?" Represented in the work are the cessationist, open but cautious, third wave, and charismatic viewpoints.

B. Continuationist

Carson, D. A. *Showing the Spirit: A Theological Exposition of 1 Corinthians 12–14*. Grand Rapids, MI: Baker Academic, 1996. Carson offers a careful and balanced reading of 1 Corinthians 12–14 that undermines cessationist readings of the text. He says that while he acknowledges the gifts' abuse in some Pentecostal circles, there is no biblical basis for saying the miraculous gifts have ceased.

Deere, Jack S. *Surprised by the Power of the Spirit*. Grand Rapids, MI: Zondervan, 2006. Deere, formerly a cessationist, changed his mind about the miraculous gifts because of his reading of Scripture. He offers a defense of continuationism and provides advice for the use of spiritual gifts in the church.

Fee, Gordon D. *God's Empowering Presence: The Holy Spirit in the Letters of Paul*. Grand Rapids, MI: Baker Academic, 2009. Fee's exhaustive (almost thousand-page!) work on Paul's theology of the Holy Spirit is not specifically on spiritual gifts. However, Fee puts forth a compelling exegetical argument for the continuation of the miraculous gifts in the church today.

Grudem, Wayne. *The Gift of Prophecy in the New Testament and Today*, revised edition. Wheaton, IL: Crossway, 2000. Grudem argues that the Old Testament office of prophet is carried on in the New Testament through preaching. However, he is careful to note that such "prophecy" in the church today is not infallible, but rather God's way of bringing his word to the world.

C. Cessationist

Edgar, Thomas R. *Satisfied by the Promise of the Spirit: Affirming the Fullness of God's Provision for Spiritual Living*. Grand

Rapids, MI: Kregel Academic, 1996. Edgar claims that certain spiritual gifts have ceased today, and he critiques a number of prominent continuationist authors in a charitable manner.

Ferguson, Sinclair B. *The Holy Spirit*. Contours of Christian Theology. Downers Grove, IL: InterVarsity, 1997. While not a book specifically about spiritual gifts, Ferguson's work on the Holy Spirit offers a mild cessationism firmly rooted in Reformed theology and redemptive history.

Gaffin, Richard, Jr. *Perspectives on Pentecost*. Phillipsburg, NJ: P&R, 1993. Gaffin, like Ferguson, argues for a mild version of cessationism situated in the context of redemptive history and Reformed theology.

Thomas, Robert L. *Understanding Spiritual Gifts: A Verse-by-Verse Study of 1 Corinthians 12–14*. Grand Rapids, MI: Kregel Academic, 1998. In contrast to D. A. Carson's work on 1 Corinthians 12–14 that argues for continuationism, Thomas argues cessationism from the same chapters of Scripture.

4. MISSIONAL VS. FUNDAMENTAL

A. Missional

Beale, G. K. *The Temple and the Church's Mission: A Biblical Theology of the Dwelling Place of God*. New Studies in Biblical Theology. Downers Grove, IL: InterVarsity, 2004. Greg Beale examines the biblical-theological theme of the Temple and argues that the church's mission is one of eschatological "temple building." His study has numerous ramifications for missional theology today.

Bosch, David Jacobus. *Transforming Mission: Paradigm Shifts in Theology of Mission*. American Society of Missiology 16. Maryknoll, NY: Orbis, 2011. Bosch's work is one of the classic books on missional theology and a must-read for anyone interested in the topic. He lays out five historical paradigms in which Christians have thought about mission and offers characteristics of a contemporary reading of the immanence and transcendence of salvation, which has an impact on how the church ought to view its mission.

Chester, Tim. *Everyday Church: Gospel Communities on Mission.* Wheaton, IL: Crossway/Re:Lit Books, 2012. Chester's work is a manual for missional application. It shows how Christians can develop missional communities and be the church in their communities.

Guder, Darrell L., ed. *Missional Church: A Vision for the Sending of the Church in North America.* The Gospel and Our Culture. Grand Rapids, MI: Eerdmans, 1998. This classical work on missional theology situates the church in North America as a church that must be on mission in post-Christian, secular culture. Only by recovering certain insights about mission can the church properly exist in today's world.

Kaiser, Walter C., Jr. *Mission in the Old Testament: Israel as a Light to the Nations,* 2nd ed. Grand Rapids, MI: Baker Academic, 2012. Kaiser argues that Israel's mission was always to be a light for the nations as a missionary people, and that such a vocation was not a New Testament addition to the church.

Köstenberger, Andreas J., and Peter T. O'Brien. *Salvation to the Ends of the Earth: A Biblical Theology of Mission.* New Studies in Biblical Theology 11. Downers Grove, IL: InterVarsity, 2001. Köstenberger and O'Brien offer a biblical theology of mission and tease out the implications of their study for the church's existence in the world today.

Ott, Craig, Stephen J. Strauss, and Timothy C. Tennent. *Encountering Theology of Mission: Biblical Foundations,*

Historical Developments, and Contemporary Issues. Encountering Mission. Grand Rapids, MI: Baker Academic, 2010. This compendium of essays discusses a broad variety of topics related to mission. Its particular focus lies in the way it relates mission to evangelism, church planting, holistic mission, the Kingdom of God, and ecclesiology.

Wright, Christopher J. H. *The Mission of God: Unlocking the Bible's Grand Narrative*. Downers Grove, IL: IVP Academic, 2006. Wright claims that the central theme of Scripture is mission. When the Bible is read through this grand theme, God's mission to save the world and humanity's participation in this mission become clear.

Wright, Christopher J. H. *The Mission of God's People: A Biblical Theology of the Church's Mission*. Biblical Theology for Life. Grand Rapids, MI: Zondervan, 2010. Wright applies the findings of *The Mission of God* to the church in this work, addressing both ecclesiology and missiology.

B. Fundamental/Non-Missional

Dever, Mark. *Nine Marks of a Healthy Church*. Wheaton, IL: Crossway, 2004. Mark Dever's classic work argues for a specific conception of ecclesiology, which many see as incompatible with contemporary work on mission.

Dever, Mark. *The Church: The Gospel Made Visible*. Nashville: B&H, 2012. This book expands Dever's thoughts on the nature, purpose, and function of the church.

DeYoung, Kevin, and Greg Gilbert. *What Is the Mission of the Church?: Making Sense of Social Justice, Shalom, and the Great Commission*. Wheaton, IL: Crossway, 2011. DeYoung and Gilbert worry that the emphasis on mission can cause the church to forget its true purpose: evangelism and God's glory. By explaining the concepts of Kingdom, gospel, and social justice, the authors set forth a non-missional account of the nature of the church.

"The Church's Mission," *Nine Marks Journal* 3, no. 8 (October 2006), www.9marks.org/journal/churchs-mission. This issue of *Nine Marks Journal* offers extended critiques of the missional church by various authors and touches on a variety of issues central to mission.

5. CHURCH REVIVAL MOVEMENTS

A. Revival History

Johnston, E. A. *The Church in Revival.* Port Colborne, ON: Gospel Folio Press, 2008. In twenty different chapters on aspects of revival, Johnston sets forth the Old Testament pattern of revival, looks at hindrances to revival, and, among other things, shows what things must be present in a church for revival to occur.

Keller, Timothy J. *Center Church: Doing Balanced, Gospel-Centered Ministry in Your City.* Grand Rapids, MI: Zondervan, 2012. While not specifically about revival, Keller's work has a significant section on "gospel renewal" that is extremely relevant for a theology of revival.

Lloyd-Jones, Martyn. *Revival.* Wheaton, IL: Crossway, 1987. Lloyd-Jones's classic work on revival looks at what revival is, what characteristics accompany it, why it is needed, and what a church must do in order to experience it.

Murray, Iain H. *Revival and Revivalism.* Carlisle, PA: Banner of Truth, 1994. Through careful historical study, Murray argues that there is a difference between revival and revivalism, the latter being a man-centered, manipulative process and the former relying on an act of God's Spirit.

Ortlund, Raymond C., Jr. *When God Comes to Church: A Biblical Model for Revival Today.* Grand Rapids, MI: Baker, 2000. Ortlund looks at what happens in revival (God comes down, reinvigorates, heals, pours out his Spirit, raises us up, and restores us) and outlines what Christians must do in order to experience revival (return to God, seek God, and humble themselves).

B. *Revival Theology*

Bebbington, David. *Victorian Religious Revivals: Culture and Piety in Local and Global Contexts.* Oxford: Oxford University Press, 2012. In this historical study, Bebbington looks at numerous instances of revival and examines their differences and continuities. Through these continuities Bebbington argues that evangelicalism across the globe shares certain characteristics.

Bushman, Richard. *The Great Awakening: Documents on the Revival of Religion, 1740–1745.* Raleigh, NC: University of North Carolina Press/Institute of Early American History and Culture, 1989. This compendium of primary sources contains letters, correspondence, newspaper articles, and other documents of interest that are significant to the Great Awakening.

Hansen, Collin, and John Woodbridge. *A God-Sized Vision: Revival Stories that Stretch and Stir.* Grand Rapids, MI: Zondervan, 2010. This work is composed of spiritually enriching stories of revival from Scripture, the Reformation, the Great Awakenings, and China.

Kidd, Thomas S. *The Great Awakening: A Brief History with Documents.* Boston: Bedford/St. Martin's, 2007. Kidd's work provides a detailed history of the First Great Awakening and describes contemporary views on revivals.

Riss, Richard M. *A Survey of Twentieth Century Revival Movements in North America*. Peabody, MA: Hendrickson, 1988. This historical work sets out to recount the many oft-forgotten revivals of the twentieth century in North America. Riss also shows how these revivals shaped the contemporary church.

Tracy, Joseph. *The Great Awakening*. Port Colborne, ON: Banner of Truth, 1989. Tracy's classic history of the Great Awakening shows what true and false revival looked like in the days of Edwards and Whitefield.

6. MODERNISM AND POSTMODERNISM

A. Overviews of Modernism and Postmodernism

1. MODERNISM

Gillespie, Michael Allen. *The Theological Origins of Modernity*. Chicago, IL: University of Chicago Press, 2009. Rather than buy into the traditional secularization thesis, Gillespie argues that modernism originated out of important theological questions.

Green, Garrett. *Theology, Hermeneutics, and Imagination: The Crisis of Interpretation at the End of Modernity*. Cambridge: Cambridge University Press, 2007. Green's work examines the crisis of biblical hermeneutics in the modern and postmodern ages. He highlights the historical shift from modernity to postmodernity and proposes his own version of a postmodern hermeneutic for reading Scripture.

Taylor, Charles. *A Secular Age*. Cambridge, MA: Harvard University Press, 2007. Taylor's monumental work examines the secular aspects of modernity that developed in Western Christendom. Instead of the overthrow of the religious by the secular, Taylor narrates the story of modernity as the story of an increasing number of religious and antireligious options.

2. POSTMODERNISM

Grenz, Stanley. *A Primer on Postmodernism*, 2nd ed. Grand Rapids, MI: Eerdmans, 1996. Grenz seeks to give a popular-level introduction to the academic trends associated with postmodernism in order to ascertain how Christians can be faithful to the gospel in a new cultural climate.

Penner, Myron B. *Christianity and the Postmodern Turn: Six Views*. Grand Rapids, MI: Brazos, 2005. In this work, six different authors answer the question, "What perils and/or promises does the postmodern turn hold for the tasks of Christian thinkers?" and respond to one another with questions and objections.

Smith, James K. A., and Henry Isaac Venema. *The Hermeneutics of Charity: Interpretation, Selfhood, and Postmodern Faith*. Grand Rapids, MI: Brazos, 2004. This compendium of essays examines a number of ways in which postmodern thought and Christian theology intersect.

Vanhoozer, Kevin J., ed. *The Cambridge Companion to Postmodern Theology*. Cambridge Companions to Religion. Cambridge: Cambridge University Press, 2003. This volume situates different Christian doctrines and elements of Christian thought in dialogue with postmodernism. Postmodernism, in this volume, is not looked at as either good or bad; instead, it is viewed as a stream of thought with which theology must deal competently.

Ward, Graham. *The Blackwell Companion to Postmodern Theology*. Wiley-Blackwell Companions to Religion. Oxford: Blackwell, 2005. This volume offers numerous classic essays on postmodern theology. Specifically, it deals with the issues of aesthetics, ethics, gender, hermeneutics, phenomenology, Heidegger, and Derrida.

B. *Critical of Postmodernism*

Erickson, Millard J., Paul Kjoss Helseth, and Justin Taylor, eds. *Reclaiming the Center: Confronting Evangelical Accommodation in Postmodern Times.* Wheaton, IL: Crossway, 2004. This book represents an evangelical response to various aspects of postmodernism that relate to Christian doctrine. Specifically, the essays deal with truth, theological method, evangelical history, and post-postmodernism.

Piper, John, and Justin Taylor, eds. *The Supremacy of Christ in a Postmodern World.* Wheaton, IL: Crossway, 2007. In this work six authors ask how the gospel and Christ's supremacy shape how the church exists and ought to exist in a postmodern world.

Smith, Scott R., and J. P. Moreland. *Truth and the New Kind of Christian: The Emerging Effects of Postmodernism in the Church.* Wheaton, IL: Crossway, 2005. This book sets out to describe the postmodern climate, Christian postmodernism, and the emerging church, and it analyzes where postmodernism came from, critiques the emerging church, addresses the issue of relativism, and assesses the effect that postmodernism has had on Christian ministry.

Wells, David F. *The Courage to Be Protestant: Truth-Lovers, Marketers, and Emergents in the Postmodern World.* Grand Rapids, MI: Eerdmans, 2008. Wells offers a critique of postmodern Christianity and calls believers to return to a robust version of modern Reformed Protestantism.

Wells, David F. *Above All Earthly Pow'rs: Christ in a Postmodern World.* Grand Rapids, MI: Eerdmans, 2005. In this book Wells looks to describe what the postmodern ethos is and how it has impacted evangelicalism in a variety of ways. Wells critiques this new form of Christianity and urges his readers to the classic truths of the Christian church.

C. Receptive of Postmodernism

Caputo, John D. *What Would Jesus Deconstruct?: The Good News of Postmodernism for the Church*. The Church and Postmodern Culture. Grand Rapids, MI: Baker, 2007. Caputo takes the postmodern concept of deconstruction and argues that the church can use (and in fact needs) deconstruction to renew its life of liturgy, worship, preaching, and teaching for the future.

Grenz, Stanley J., and John R. Franke. *Beyond Foundationalism: Shaping Theology in a Postmodern Context*. Louisville, KY: Westminster John Knox, 2001. This book argues that the modern epistemology of foundationalism is inhospitable to Christian doctrine and that Christians would do well to appropriate elements of postmodern thought to move forward in doing Christian theology.

Leithart, Peter J. *Solomon among the Postmoderns*. Grand Rapids, MI: Brazos, 2008. In this book, Leithart reads the book of Ecclesiastes and says that Solomon connects in many significant ways to postmodernism. The author reflects on both the strengths and the weaknesses of the postmodern movement.

Smith, James K. A. *Who's Afraid of Postmodernism?: Taking Derrida, Lyotard, and Foucault to Church*. The Church and Postmodern Culture. Grand Rapids, MI: Baker, 2006. It is commonly held that the postmodern thinkers Derrida, Lyotard, and Foucault are antagonistic to Christianity; however, Smith argues that readers have misinterpreted these authors and that they actually have much to contribute to the Christian faith.

Westphal, Merold. *Whose Community? Which Interpretation?:
Philosophical Hermeneutics for the Church.* The Church
and Postmodern Culture. Grand Rapids, MI: Baker,
2009. Westphal argues that, contrary to popular thought,
postmodern hermeneutics do not entail relativism. Instead,
Westphal suggests, postmodern hermeneutics actually enable
Christians to read the Bible in a way that does justice to the
different interpretations of Scripture present in culture.

NOTES

CHAPTER 1. CHRISTENDOM IS DEAD: WELCOME TO THE UNITED STATES OF SEATTLE

1. Jesus tells us that he alone will judge people's eternal fate (see John 5:19-30), but he also tells us that we can tell a tree by its fruit (see Matthew 12:33-37). Paul says in 1 Corinthians 5:12, "What have I to do with judging outsiders? Is it not those inside the church whom you are to judge?" Regarding the spirituality of President Obama, in addition to Stephen Mansfield, *The Faith of Barack Obama* (Nashville: Thomas Nelson, 2011), the following insights are helpful:

   - Rick Warren appearance on *Hannity*: Rick Warren says, "As America is cut off from its moral and spiritual and ethical roots, we're now seeing the flower fade." Regarding Obama specifically, he says, "I think every leader disappoints. And there are certain things that President Obama's done I'm deeply disappointed in. I'll just leave it at that." ("Pastor Rick Warren Commemorates 10 Years of 'The Purpose Driven Life,'" *Hannity*, Fox News, November 28, 2012, www.foxnews.com/on-air/hannity/2012/11/29/pastor-rick -warren-commemorates-10-years-purpose-driven-life.)

   - Rick Warren interview after canceling Obama-Romney forum: "President Obama's policies clearly show what he values and I have told him that I adamantly disagree with those particular policies." (Erika I. Ritchie, "Rick Warren Cancels Obama-Romney Forum at Saddleback Church," *Orange County Register*, August 22, 2012, www.ocregister .com/articles/forum-369266-warren-civil.html.)

   - Rick Warren interview with CBN: "Our hope lies not in the man we put in the White House, but in the man we put on the Cross." Also,

"I clearly told the president I 100 percent disagree with him, and I actually said I would fight him on this issue of religious liberty, because he's dead wrong on it." ("Power Players Join the Brody File Show," *The Brody File*, CBN News, November 30, 2012, 3:20 p.m., http://blogs .cbn.com/thebrodyfile/archive/2012/11/30/power-players-join-the -brody-file-show.aspx; full interview starts at 22:30.)

- 2004 Obama interview: Obama says, "I am a Christian," but then goes on to explain, "I'm rooted in the Christian tradition. I believe that there are many paths to the same place." (Cathleen Falsani, "Obama on Faith: The Exclusive Interview Transcript," *The Dude Abides* [blog], http://cathleenfalsani.com/obama-on-faith-the-exclusive-interview/.)

- Obama, writing in *The Audacity of Hope: Thoughts on Reclaiming the American Dream*: "When I read the Bible, I do so with the belief that it is not a static text but the Living Word and that I must be continually open to new revelations—whether they come from a lesbian friend or a doctor opposed to abortion." (New York: Three Rivers Press, 2006, 350.)

- *Christianity Today* article titled "Why We Should Reexamine the Faith of Barack Obama": "Faith as construed by the President gives no offense and draws no boundaries. In the final analysis, what is missing from his theology is nothing other than the gospel." (Owen Strachan, June 21, 2012, www.christianitytoday.com/ct/2012/juneweb-only/why -we-should-reexamine-the-faith-of-barack-obama.html?start=2.)

2. "Remarks by the President at the Planned Parenthood Conference," *The White House*, April 26, 2013, www.whitehouse.gov/the-press-office/2013 /04/26/remarks-president-planned-parenthood-conference.

3. "President Obama's second inaugural address (Transcript)," *Washington Post*, January 21, 2013, http://articles.washingtonpost.com/2013-01-21 /politics/36473487_1_president-obama-vice-president-biden-free-market.

4. Elizabeth Tenety, "Louie Giglio Backs Out of Inaugural Benediction over Comments on Homosexuality," *Washington Post, Under God* (blog), January 10, 2013, www.washingtonpost.com/blogs/under-god/post/louie-giglio-backs-out -of-inaugural-benediction-over-comments-on-homosexuality/2013/01/10 /581a69de-5b29-11e2-9fa9-5fbdc9530eb9_blog.html.

5. Josh Israel, "Inaugural Benediction to Be Delivered by Pastor Who Gave Vehemently Anti-Gay Sermon," *ThinkProgress*, January 9, 2013, http://thinkprogress.org/lgbt/2013/01/09/1422021/inaugural -benediction-to-be-delivered-by-anti-gay-pastor/.

6. Tenety, "Louie Giglio Backs Out."

7. Jaweed Kaleem, "Luis Leon, Episcopal Priest, Will Deliver Obama's Inauguration Benediction, Replacing Louie Giglio," *Huffington Post*

Religion, January 15, 2013, www.huffingtonpost.com/2013/01/15/luis
-leon-benediction-obama-inauguration-louie-giglio_n_2468824.html.

8. Associated Press, "Tensions over the place of religion in America play out
in presidential inaugural," *Fox News*, January 19, 2013, www.foxnews.com
/us/2013/01/19/tensions-over-place-religion-in-america-play-out-in
-presidential-inaugural.

9. Ross Douthat, *Bad Religion: How We Became a Nation of Heretics* (New
York: Free Press, 2012), 3.

10. Robert Bellah, "Civil Religion in America," *Daedalus* 96, no. 1 (Winter):
1–21, www.robertbellah.com/articles_5.htm.

11. Ibid.

12. Patrick Henry, "'And I Don't Care What It Is': The Tradition-History of a
Civil Religion Proof-Text," *Journal of the American Academy of Religion* 49,
issue 1 (March 1981): 41.

13. www.evangelicalfellowship.ca/page.aspx?pid=775.

14. John S. Dickerson, *The Great Evangelical Recession: 6 Factors That Will
Crash the American Church . . . and How to Prepare* (Grand Rapids, MI:
Baker, 2013), 26.

15. Gary J. Gates and Frank Newport, "Special Report: 3.4% of U.S. Adults
Identify as LGBT," *Gallup Politics*, October 18, 2012, www.gallup.com
/poll/158066/special-report-adults-identify-lgbt.aspx.

16. Anugrah Kumar, "UK's Prince William 'Rarely' Attends Church He'll
Govern One Day," *Christian Post*, January 14, 2013, www.christianpost
.com/news/uks-prince-william-rarely-attends-church-hell-govern-one
-day-88206.

17. "'One in 10' Attends Church Weekly," *BBC News*, April 3, 2007,
http://news.bbc.co.uk/2/hi/uk_news/6520463.stm.

18. This data is available from *The Pew Forum on Religion and Public Life*,
http://religions.pewforum.org/portraits.

19. David Roach, "10 Reasons to Be Involved in a Church," *Bible Mesh blog*,
January 21, 2013, www.biblemesh.com/blog/2013/01/21/10-reasons
-to-be-involved-in-a-church.

20. Søren Kierkegaard, *Training in Christianity*, trans. Walter Lowrie (New
York: Random House, 2004), 31.

21. Yasmin Anwar, "Americans and Religion Increasingly Parting Ways,
New Survey Shows," *UC Berkeley News Center*, March 12, 2013,
http://newscenter.berkeley.edu/2013/03/12/non-believers.

22. "'Nones' on the Rise," *The Pew Forum on Religion and Public Life*, October 9,
2012, www.pewforum.org/Unaffiliated/nones-on-the-rise.aspx. "In U.S.,
Rise in Religious 'Nones' Slows in 2012," *Gallup Politics*, January 10, 2013,

www.gallup.com/poll/159785/rise-religious-nones-slows-2012.aspx. Diana Butler Bass, *Christianity After Religion: The End of Church and the Birth of a New Spiritual Awakening* (New York: HarperCollins, 2012).

23. Amy Sullivan, "The Rise of the Nones," *Time*, March 12, 2012, www.time .com/time/magazine/article/0,9171,2108027,00.html.

24. Karen Valby, "Jodie Foster: Unbreakable," *Entertainment Weekly*, August 31, 2007, www.ew.com/ew/article/0,,20054140_3,00.html.

25. Katherine Ozment, "Losing Our Religion," *Boston*, January 2013, www .bostonmagazine.com/2012/12/losing-our-religion-non-religious-parenting.

26. Ibid.

27. See Patricia O'Connell Killen and Mark Silk, eds., *Religion and Public Life in the Pacific Northwest: The None Zone* (Lanham, MD: AltaMira Press, 2004).

28. Dickerson, *The Great Evangelical Recession*, 117–120.

CHAPTER 2. STANDING KNOCKOUT: HOW WE GOT OUR BELL RUNG

1. Mark Noll, "Where We Are and How We Got Here," *Christianity Today*, September 29, 2006, www.christianitytoday.com/ct/2006/october/16.42 .html.

2. See Lesslie Newbigin, *The Gospel in a Pluralist Society* (Grand Rapids, MI: Eerdmans, 1989).

3. "Does Satan Exist? Part 6 of 10," www.youtube.com/watch?v =TiqUUB3VMrA.

4. Ibid.

5. See, for example, truthxchange.com or Peter Jones, *One or Two: Seeing a World of Difference* (Escondido, CA: Main Entry Editions, 2010).

6. Quoted in Henry F. Schaefer III, *Science and Christianity: Conflict or Coherence?* (Watkinsville, GA: The Apollos Trust, 2003), 82.

7. Larry Alex Taunton, "Listening to Young Atheists: Lessons for a Stronger Christianity," *The Atlantic*, June 6, 2013, www.theatlantic.com/national /archive/2013/06/listening-to-young-atheists-lessons-for-a-stronger -christianity/276584.

8. Heather Clark, "Episcopalian 'Bishop': Paul Bigoted for Not Embracing Diversity in Demon-Possessed Girl," *Christian News*, May 31, 2013, http://christiannews.net/2013/05/31/episcopalian-bishop-paul-bigoted -for-not-embracing-diversity-in-demon-possessed-girl/.

9. Neela Banerjee, "Use of Wiccan Symbol on Veterans' Headstones Is Approved," *New York Times*, April 24, 2007, www.nytimes.com/2007 /04/24/washington/24wiccan.html?_r=0.

10. See Christian Smith and Melinda Lundquist Denton, *Soul Searching: The Religious and Spiritual Lives of American Teenagers* (New York: Oxford University Press, 2005), 162ff, 166.

11. N. T. Wright, *Simply Christian: Why Christianity Makes Sense* (New York: HarperCollins, 2006), 61.

12. Among adults sixty-five and older, those numbers were 31 percent in favor of marriage and 51 percent for civil unions. "Asked about the perception that 'religious groups are alienating young people by being too judgmental about gay and lesbian issues,' 69 percent of the younger group agreed with the statement" (Associated Press, "Evangelical Churches Try to Find Right Balance on Gay Issues," *Yahoo! News*, February 1, 2013, http://news.yahoo.com/evangelical-churches-try-balance-gay-issues-155234219.html).

13. "Porn Sites Get More Visitors Each Month than Netflix, Amazon and Twitter Combined," *Huffington Post*, May 4, 2013, www.huffingtonpost.com/2013/05/03/internet-porn-stats_n_3187682.html.

14. http://internet-filter-review.toptenreviews.com/internet-pornography-statistics.html.

15. "Pornography Statistics: Annual Report 2013," *Covenant Eyes*, www.covenanteyes.com/pornstats/.

16. Jane D. Brown, Kelly Ladin L'Engle, Carol J. Pardun, Guang Guo, Kristin Kenneavy, and Christine Jackson, "Sexy Media Matter: Exposure to Sexual Content in Music, Movies, Television, and Magazines Predicts Black and White Adolescents' Sexual Behavior," *Pediatrics* 117, no. 4 (April 1, 2006): 1018–1027.

17. Elizabeth Terry-Humen, et al., "Trends and Recent Estimates: Sexual Activity Among U.S. Teens," *Child Trends Research Brief 2006–2008* (Washington, DC: Child Trends, 2006): 2.

18. Michael J. McFarland, Jeremy E. Uecker, and Mark D. Regnerus, "The Role of Religion in Shaping Sexual Frequency and Satisfaction: Evidence from Married and Unmarried Older Adults," *Journal of Sex Research* 47 (March 26, 2010): 1-12.

19. Mark Driscoll and Grace Driscoll, *Real Marriage: The Truth about Sex, Friendship, and Life Together* (Nashville: Thomas Nelson, 2012), 141.

20. See Naomi Schaefer Riley, "The Young and the Restless: Why Infidelity Is Rising Among 20-Somethings," *Wall Street Journal*, November 28, 2008, http://online.wsj.com/article/SB122782458360062499.html.

21. Mary P. Koss, C. Gedycz, and N. Wisniewski, "The Scope of Rape Incidence and Prevalence of Sexual Aggression and Victimization in a

National Sample of Higher Education Students," *Journal of Consulting and Clinical Psychology* 55 (1987): 162–70.

22. Callie Marie Rennison, "Rape and Sexual Assault: Reporting to Police and Medical Attention, 1992–2000," *Bureau of Justice Statistics*, August 1, 2002, www.bjs.gov/index.cfm?ty=pbdetail&iid=1133.

23. In their book *Rid of My Disgrace: Hope and Healing for Victims of Sexual Assault* (Wheaton, IL: Crossway, 2011), Dr. Justin Holcomb and his wife, Lindsey, who are leaders at Mars Hill Church, include the following definition of sexual assault:

> There are three parts to our definition of sexual assault: 1) any type of sexual behavior or contact 2) where consent is not freely given or obtained and 3) is accomplished through force, intimidation, violence, coercion, manipulation, threat, deception, or abuse of authority. . . . When defining sexual assault as any sexual act that is nonconsensual—forced against someone's will—it is important to understand that the "acts" can be physical, verbal, or psychological. . . . Sexual assault occurs along a continuum of power and control ranging from non-contact sexual assault to forced sexual intercourse. Sexual assault includes acts such as nonconsensual sexual intercourse (rape), nonconsensual sodomy (oral or anal sexual acts), child molestation, incest, fondling, exposure, voyeurism, or attempts to commit these acts.

24. Trevin Wax, "Mark Driscoll on Piers Morgan—Transcript," *The Gospel Coalition*, March 10, 2012, http://thegospelcoalition.org/blogs/trevinwax/2012/03/10/mark-driscoll-on-piers-morgan-transcript.

25. See D. A. Carson, *The Intolerance of Tolerance* (Grand Rapids, MI: Eerdmans, 2012), 3.

26. Douthat, *Bad Religion*, 12.

27. HarperOneVideo, "What We Talk About When We Talk About God by Rob Bell," *YouTube.com*, March 5, 2013, www.youtube.com/watch?v=rG1CDec4qkg.

28. David Blankenhorn, *Fatherless America* (New York: HarperCollins, 1996), 1.

29. Jason DeParle and Sabrina Tavernise, "For Women Under 30, Most Births Occur Outside Marriage," *New York Times*, February 17, 2012, www.nytimes.com/2012/02/18/us/for-women-under-30-most-births-occur-outside-marriage.html?ref=us.

30. W. Bradford Wilcox has conducted the most helpful research done on the difference active Christian faith makes in families. He is widely recognized as one of the most distinguished sociologists in America. Wilcox has undertaken the massive project of determining what effects religious belief

and participation have for men regarding their wives and children. The research confirms that "conservative Protestant married men with children are consistently the most active and expressive fathers and the most emotionally engaged husbands" (*Soft Patriarchs, New Men: How Christianity Shapes Fathers and Husbands*, Chicago: University of Chicago Press, 2004, 191).

31. Robin Marantz Henig, "What Is It about 20-Somethings?" *New York Times*, August 18, 2010, www.nytimes.com/2010/08/22/magazine /22Adulthood-t.html?_r=0.

32. For this and other statistics, see the "Knot Yet" report at twentysomething marriage.org.

33. Sabrina Tavernise, "Married Couples Are No Longer a Majority, Census Finds," *New York Times*, May 26, 2011, www.nytimes.com/2011/05/26/us /26marry.html.

34. David Popenoe and Barbara Dafoe Whitehead, "Should We Live Together? What Young Adults Need to Know about Cohabitation before Marriage—A Comprehensive Review of Recent Research," 2nd ed., *The National Marriage Project* (New Brunswick, NJ: The National Marriage Project, Rutgers University, 2002), 3.

35. Larry Bumpass and Hsien-Hen Lu, "Trends in Cohabitation and Implications for Children's Family Contexts in the U.S.," *Population Studies* 54 (2000): 29–41. Quoted in David Popenoe and Barbara Dafoe Whitehead, "Should We Live Together?", 3.

36. Ibid.

37. J. G. Bachman, L. D. Johnston, and P. M. O'Malley, *Monitoring the Future: Questionnaire Responses from the Nation's High School Seniors, 2000*. Quoted in David Popenoe and Barbara Dafoe Whitehead, "Should We Live Together?", 3.

38. Dickerson, *The Great Evangelical Recession*, 102.

39. Ibid., 98.

40. Ibid., 107.

41. *New York Times* columnist David Brooks writes, "In 1990, 65 percent of Americans said that children are very important to a successful marriage. Now, only 41 percent of Americans say they believe that. . . . This is not a phenomenon particular to the United States. . . . The number of marriages in Spain has declined from 270,000 in 1975 to 170,000 today, and the number of total Spanish births per year is now lower than it was in the 18th century. Thirty percent of German women say they do not intend to have children. In a 2011 survey, a majority of Taiwanese women under 50 said they did not want children. Fertility rates in Brazil have dropped from 4.3 babies per woman 35 years ago to 1.9 babies today." ("The Age

of Possibility," *New York Times*, November 15, 2012, www.nytimes.com /2012/11/16/opinion/brooks-the-age-of-possibility.html.)

42. Michael Smith, "U.S. Birth Rate Hit Historic Low," *MedPage Today*, February 11, 2013, www.medpagetoday.com/Pediatrics/GeneralPediatrics /37296.

43. Gene Balk, "In Seattle, it's cats, dogs and kids—in that order," *Seattle Times*, *FYI Guy* (blog), February 1, 2013, http://blogs.seattletimes.com /fyi-guy/2013/02/01/in-seattle-its-cats-dogs-and-kids-in-that-order.

44. Ibid.

45. Sharon Pian Chan, "Why I am not having kids," *Seattle Times*, January 30, 2013, http://seattletimes.com/html/opinion/2020250712_sharonpianchan columnkidsxml.html.

46. Ibid.

47. Dickerson, *The Great Evangelical Recession*, 82.

48. Ibid., 92.

CHAPTER 3. A NEW REALITY: FROM MODERNISM TO EVERYTHINGISM TO TRIBALISM

1. Seth Godin, *Tribes: We Need You to Lead Us* (New York: Portfolio, 2008), 1–2.

2. Ibid., 25.

3. David McCullough, "You're Not Special," June 1, 2012, transcript, www .myfoxboston.com/story/18720284/2012/06/06/full-transcript-youre-not -special-speech.

4. Pink Floyd, "Another Brick in the Wall (Part II)," *The Wall*, 1979.

5. Anthony C. Thiselton, *The First Epistle to the Corinthians: A Commentary on the Greek Text*, New International Greek Testament Commentary (Grand Rapids, MI: W. B. Eerdmans, 2000), 286.

6. Leon Morris, *The First Epistle of Paul to the Corinthians: An Introduction and Commentary*, 2nd ed., Tyndale New Testament Commentaries, vol. 7 (Downers Grove, IL: InterVarsity Press, 1985), 70.

CHAPTER 4. HOME SWEET HOME: UNDERSTANDING OUR BORDERS

1. The section titles in this chapter match the organization found in *Doctrine* (Wheaton, IL: Crossway, 2010), which I coauthored with Gerry Breshears.

2. This definition is adapted from Harold Best, *Unceasing Worship* (Downers Grove, IL: InterVarsity Press, 2003), 18.

3. Hilary of Poitiers, "On Matthew 24.7," *Commentarius in Evangelium Matthaei*, c.a. 356.
4. "Turkey," *Operation World*, 7th ed., www.operationworld.org/turk.
5. "State of the Bible in 2013," *American Bible Society*, www.americanbible.org/state-bible.

CHAPTER 5. THE HOLY SPIRIT: EMPOWERING THE CHURCH FOR MISSION

1. Cathy Lynn Grossman, "More U.S. Christians Mix in 'Eastern,' New Age Beliefs," *USA Today*, December 10, 2009, http://usatoday30.usatoday.com/news/religion/2009-12-10-1Amixingbeliefs10_CV_N.htm.
2. Tim Smith, "This Is What Mars Hill Believes about the Holy Spirit, Part 1," *Mars Hill Church*, October 28, 2010, http://marshill.com/2010/10/28/this-is-what-mars-hill-believes-about-the-holy-spirit-part-1.
3. Justin S. Holcomb, "Acts," in *Gospel Transformation Bible* (Wheaton, IL: Crossway, 2013); see notes on Acts 2:1-13.
4. Holcomb, "Acts," *Gospel Transformation Bible*.
5. See Ronald A. N. Kydd's book, *Charismatic Gifts in the Early Church: An Exploration into the Gifts of the Spirit During the First Three Centuries of the Christian Church* (Peabody, MA: Hendrickson Publishing, 1984).
6. D. A. Carson, *Showing the Spirit: A Theological Exposition of 1 Corinthians, 12-14* (Ada, MI: Baker Book, 1987), 166.
7. Holcomb, "Acts," *Gospel Transformation Bible*; see notes on Acts 19:1-7.
8. Justin S. Holcomb, "Acts," in *Acts: A 12-Week Study* (Wheaton, IL: Crossway, 2014); see "Week 11: The Gospel Goes to Rome (Acts 21:17–28:31)." Holcomb lists these passages to demonstrate "the triumphant march of the gospel mission in the book of Acts."
9. Christopher Wright, *The Mission of God: Unlocking the Bible's Grand Narrative* (Downers Grove, IL: InterVarsity, 2006), 455.

CHAPTER 6. REPENTANCE: A BIBLICAL RESPONSE

1. Charles Haddon Spurgeon, "The Lesson of the Almond Tree," *Metropolitican Tabernacle Pulpit*, no. 2678 (April 7, 1881): 4.
2. N. T. Wright, *Simply Christian: Why Christianity Makes Sense* (New York: HarperCollins, 2006), 65.
3. Nicola Menzie, "Rob Bell Supports Same-Sex Marriage, Says He Is for 'Fidelity and Love,'" *Christian Post*, March 18, 2013, www.christianpost.com/news/rob-bell-supports-same-sex-marriage-says-he-is-for-fidelity-and-love-92064/#yBA7hiSkxRfMpLJO.99.

4. Christine J. Gardner, "Tangled in the Worst of the Web," *Christianity Today*, March 5, 2001, www.christianitytoday.com/ct/2001/march5/1.42.html.

5. "Pornography Statistics: Annual Report 2013," www.covenanteyes.com /pornstats.

6. Luke Gilkerson, "Porn Stats: Most popular day to watch porn is Sunday," *Covenant Eyes, Breaking Free Blog*, June 16, 2010, www.covenanteyes.com /2010/06/16/porn-stats-most-popular-day-to-watch-porn-is-sunday.

7. See our book *Real Marriage* (Nashville: Thomas Nelson, 2012), chapter 7.

8. Binyamin Appelbaum, "Study of Men's Falling Income Cites Single Parents," *New York Times*, March 20, 2013, www.nytimes. com/2013/03/21/business/economy/as-men-lose-economic-ground-clues-in-the-family.html?_r=0.

9. See his books *Soul Searching: The Religious and Spiritual Lives of American Teenagers* (New York: Oxford University Press, 2005) and *Souls in Transition: The Religious and Spiritual Lives of Emerging Adults* (New York: Oxford University Press, 2009).

10. See Rob Moll, "Scrooge Lives!" *Christianity Today*, December 5, 2008, www.christianitytoday.com/ct/2008/december/10.24.html; Ron Sider, "A Lot of Lattés," *Books and Culture: A Christian Review*, October 30, 2008, www.christianitytoday.com/bc/2008/novdec/5.11.html.

11. Christian Smith and Michael O. Emerson, with Patricia Snell, *Passing the Plate: Why American Christians Don't Give Away More Money* (Oxford: Oxford University Press, 2008), 171.

12. Ibid., 43.

13. Ibid., 63.

14. Moll, "Scrooge Lives!", www.christianitytoday.com/ct/2008/ december/10.24.html.

15. Carson, *The Intolerance of Tolerance*, 103.

CHAPTER 7. MISSION: SEVEN PRINCIPLES FOR RESURGENCE

1. Ed Stetzer, "Calling for Contextualization: Part 2, The Need to Contend and Contextualize," *Christianity Today*, June 28, 2010, www. christianitytoday.com/edstetzer/2010/june/calling-for-contextualization-part-2-need-to-contend-and.html.

2. Carol Kuruvilla, "Seattle Church That Won't Accept Gay Members Moves into Gay Community," *New York Daily News*, January 15, 2013, www .nydailynews.com/news/national/pastor-draws-fire-blessing-closer-aids -patients-article-1.1240735.

3. Elizabeth Dias, "¡Evangélicos!" *Time*, April 15, 2013, 22–24.
4. Barna Group, *Hispanic America: Faith, Values & Priorities: 2012 Report* (Ventura, CA: Barna, 2012), 8.
5. Rodney Stark, *The Rise of Christianity: How the Obscure, Marginal Jesus Movement Became the Dominant Religious Force in the Western World in a Few Centuries* (New York: HarperCollins, 1996), 161.
6. Doug Wilson, "Counterfactuals, Convulsion, and Conquest," *Blog & Mablog* (blog), June 13, 2013, http://dougwils.com/s7-engaging-the-culture/counterfactuals-convulsion-and-conquest.html.

APPENDIX A: A WORD TO THE TRIBES

1. This material is adapted from the Resurgence website, http://theresurgence.com/2012/07/14/get-to-know-john-calvin.
2. Quoted in Frank A. James III, "Calvin the Evangelist," *Reformed Quarterly* 19, no. 2 (2001), http://rq.rts.edu/fall01/james.html.
3. Douglas A. Sweeney, *The American Evangelical Story: A History of the Movement* (Grand Rapids, MI: Baker Academic, 2005), 24.
4. For an example of this type of argument, see Iain H. Murray, *Revival and Revivalism: The Making and Marring of American Evangelicalism 1750–1858* (Edinburgh: Banner of Truth, 1994).
5. David W. Kling, "Second Great Awakening," in *Encyclopedia of Religious Revivals in America*, ed. Michael J. McClymond, 2 vols. (Westport, CT: Greenwood Press, 2006), 1:388.
6. Charles G. Finney, *Lectures on Revivals of Religion*, ed. William G. McLoughlin (Cambridge, MA: Harvard University Press, 1960), 12–13.
7. Quoted in David Bennett, *The Altar Call: Its Origins and Present Usage* (Lanham, MD: University Press of America, 2000), 108.
8. Quoted in Bruce J. Evensen, *God's Man for the Gilded Age: D. L. Moody and the Rise of Modern Mass Evangelism* (New York: Oxford University Press, 2003), 25.
9. Quoted in Michael J. McClymond, "Issues and Explanations in the Study of North American Revivalism," in *Embodying the Spirit: New Perspectives on North American Revivalism* (Baltimore: Johns Hopkins University Press, 2004), 19.
10. George M. Marsden, *Fundamentalism and American Culture: The Shaping of Twentieth-Century Evangelicalism, 1870–1925* (New York: Oxford University Press, 1980), 35.
11. Ibid., 35–38.
12. David W. Bebbington, *The Dominance of Evangelicalism: The Age of Spurgeon and Moody* (Downers Grove, IL: InterVarsity Press, 2005), 48–49.

13. Timothy George, *Mr. Moody and the Evangelical Tradition*, ed. Timothy George (New York: Continuum Books, 2005), 1.

14. Some details in this section are adapted from Michael Parker, "Mobilizing a Generation for Missions," *Christian History*, August 6, 2009, www.christianitytoday.com/ch/bytopic/missionsworldchristianity /mobilizinggenerations.html.

15. Dana L. Robert, *Occupy until I Come: A. T. Pierson and the Evangelization of the World* (Grand Rapids, MI: Eerdmans, 2003), 150.

16. Joel A. Carpenter, *Revive Us Again: The Reawakening of American Fundamentalism* (New York: Oxford University Press, 1997), 184.

17. For the definitions of Holiness, Pentecostal, and Charismatic movements, see Douglas A. Sweeney, *The American Evangelical Story: A History of the Movement* (Grand Rapids, MI: Baker Academic, 2005), 192.

18. Peter Althouse, *The Spirit of the Last Days: Pentecostal Eschatology in Conversation with Jürgen Moltmann* (London: T&T Clark, 2003), 13.

19. "The Alternative Jesus: Psychedelic Christ," *Time*, June 21, 1971.

20. Rosell, *The Surprising Work of God*, 13.

21. David Aikman, *Billy Graham: His Life and Influence* (Nashville, TN: Thomas Nelson, 2007), 66–67.

22. Garth M. Rosell, *The Surprising Work of God: Harold John Ockenga, Billy Graham, and the Rebirth of Evangelicalism* (Grand Rapids, MI: Baker Academic, 2008), 135.

23. Harold Lindsell, *Park Street Prophet: A Life of Harold John Ockenga* (Wheaton, IL: Van Kampen Press, 1951), 155–156.

24. Barry M. Horstmann, "Billy Graham: A Man with a Mission Impossible," *Cincinnati Post*, June 27, 2002.